T0136290

Profiling
COP-KILLERS

Profiling
COP-KILLERS

Ann R. Bumbak

CRC Press
Taylor & Francis Group
Boca Raton London New York

CRC Press is an imprint of the
Taylor & Francis Group, an **informa** business

Cover photo courtesy of Vaughn Gurganian, Oakland County, Michigan.

CRC Press
Taylor & Francis Group
6000 Broken Sound Parkway NW, Suite 300
Boca Raton, FL 33487-2742

© 2014 by Taylor & Francis Group, LLC
CRC Press is an imprint of Taylor & Francis Group, an Informa business

No claim to original U.S. Government works

Printed on acid-free paper
Version Date: 20130916

International Standard Book Number-13: 978-1-4822-1141-2 (Paperback)

This book contains information obtained from authentic and highly regarded sources. Reasonable efforts have been made to publish reliable data and information, but the author and publisher cannot assume responsibility for the validity of all materials or the consequences of their use. The authors and publishers have attempted to trace the copyright holders of all material reproduced in this publication and apologize to copyright holders if permission to publish in this form has not been obtained. If any copyright material has not been acknowledged please write and let us know so we may rectify in any future reprint.

Except as permitted under U.S. Copyright Law, no part of this book may be reprinted, reproduced, transmitted, or utilized in any form by any electronic, mechanical, or other means, now known or hereafter invented, including photocopying, microfilming, and recording, or in any information storage or retrieval system, without written permission from the publishers.

For permission to photocopy or use material electronically from this work, please access www.copyright.com (http://www.copyright.com/) or contact the Copyright Clearance Center, Inc. (CCC), 222 Rosewood Drive, Danvers, MA 01923, 978-750-8400. CCC is a not-for-profit organization that provides licenses and registration for a variety of users. For organizations that have been granted a photocopy license by the CCC, a separate system of payment has been arranged.

Trademark Notice: Product or corporate names may be trademarks or registered trademarks, and are used only for identification and explanation without intent to infringe.

Library of Congress Cataloging-in-Publication Data

Bumbak, Ann R.
  Profiling cop-killers / Ann R. Bumbak.
    pages cm
  Includes bibliographical references and index.
  ISBN 978-1-4822-1141-2 (alk. paper)
  1. Police murders--United States. I. Title.

HV8139.B8596 2014
364.152'308836320973--dc23   2013026228

Visit the Taylor & Francis Web site at
http://www.taylorandfrancis.com

and the CRC Press Web site at
http://www.crcpress.com

In memory of
Christine Dean
A generous woman whom I never met
May she rest in peace

Contents

Acknowledgments

Some journeys, both personal and professional, begin in ways we do not expect. We stumble into projects that grow to consume us, inspire us, and fuel our deeper understanding of the nature of life and death, pain, courage, sacrifice—indeed, even the very concepts of good and evil. I have taken a journey like this with the book you hold in your hands. I would like to thank those who have been my guides in this journey.

In November 2012, I traveled to Pennsylvania to make a final presentation of findings on my research into officer line-of-duty deaths based on my book, *Officer Down 2012*. This presentation focused on the very personal losses we police officers sustained the year before and what could be done to prevent similar incidents in the future. A fellow officer named Lt. John Christman had invited me to speak to a large group, and I was honored to accept. Just a few days before Thanksgiving, John offered me the gift of a lifetime: the opportunity to speak with a police officer who was the only witness to the murder of his friend, Officer Robert Lasso, in the line of duty.

Chief George Bruneio was a gray-haired, unassuming man with a friendly handshake and a straightforward manner. He shared his inspiring, personal, and tragic story of Robert's life, his final days, and his death. We laughed together about the small joys he and Robert had experienced over the years they had worked together. We also cried. Robert had been a good husband, a devoted father, and a careful police officer. He should not have died in service to his community. And, yet, he did.

At the end of our conversation, I asked George what he would like me to tell others about Robert Lasso. He said:

> I want you to tell them that Robert was fearless. He was a good cop and he did his job to the best of his ability every day. He wasn't afraid of anything.

For Robert and his family, I want you to know that he has not been forgotten.

For Chief Bruneio, thank you for sharing your story with me. Your courage keeps me from giving up on the work in which I believe so strongly, even when it becomes heart rending and difficult to continue. It is a labor of love, and I do this work for those who died, like Robert, and for those who survive, as you did.

For my family, thank you for your unending patience with my need to change the world, one book at a time. For my mother, who has worked tirelessly with the mentally ill for the past twenty years: I love you and respect you for the difficult work you do, every single day. Without your support, I could never have accomplished anything. Thank you for all that you do.

For my husband, Drew, who has given me the freedom to explore my full human potential as a writer, teacher, and mother: Despite everything we have been through over the past ten years, you still love the person I work hard to be. I do not deserve you. Thank you for loving me anyway.

For my son, Andrew: Your mere existence in this world is the greatest joy of my life. May all of your years be filled with sunshine as bright as the light that you bring into the world.

~ Ann

Introduction

On February 3, 2013, a shooter lay in wait in a condominium parking garage for Monica and Keith to arrive home from a dinner date. The shooter had previously conducted surveillance to determine the couple's habits. Then, he selected the date and time for his act and armed himself with a handgun. On foot, the shooter concealed himself in a darkened area of the garage. When the couple arrived, he took violent action to ambush and murder them both. He killed Keith first, because the shooter suspected that the man might be armed.

In truth, the shooter and Keith were not that different. The shooter was thirty-three, the victim, twenty-seven. They were both educated, aspiring black men who had shared a love of public service. One went to his death as a martyr, the other, as a villain. They had been given the same training and tactics because they were both police officers.

The shooter's name was Christopher Dorner. His victims, Monica Quan and Keith Lawrence, were killed in revenge against a fellow officer whom Dorner saw as instrumental in his firing from the Los Angeles Police Department (LAPD) in 2008. Monica Quan was the daughter of LAPD Lt. Randal Quan, who had represented Dorner in a disciplinary hearing. Keith Lawrence, a University of Southern California public safety officer, was her fiancé. He was collateral damage.

Perhaps most famously, Dorner foreshadowed his intent to commit murder with the following statement from his so-called "manifesto," addressed to his former colleagues and friends:

> I never had the opportunity to have a family of my own, I'm terminating yours.

The ensuing sordid tale of the subsequent attacks on police officers in the Los Angeles area was unprecedented in its scale and brutality. Police Officer Michael Crain was gunned down by Dorner just four days after Quan and Lawrence, while Crain and his partner were stopped at a red light. Dorner's last victim, Detective Jeremiah MacKay, was killed during the final firefight with the barricaded suspect at a remote mountain cabin. Facing apprehension for four murders, Dorner killed himself with a single gunshot to the head after the cabin became engulfed in flames. Like many cop-killers, he saw suicide as the only ending to his story.

Most people have heard all of the details of this case. But, as one of many cop-killers, was Christopher Dorner's story an unusual one? Sadly, the only unusual aspect of Dorner's story is that he was both widely successful in remaining at large to kill multiple police officers and that his crimes received major media attention. Unfortunately, police officers and ex-officers have committed murders before—not just of other police officers, but also of their own wives and families. They also commit suicide at a higher rate than the general population.

What is striking about Dorner's case is the public reaction to his vile, unprovoked acts on police officers who were engaged in standard patrol activities. His actions were reminiscent of the so-called "Beltway Snipers," John Muhammad and his protégé, seventeen-year-old Lee Malvo. In 2002, Muhammad and Malvo killed ten and wounded several others using a rifle in a shooting rampage in the Washington, DC, area. Muhammad, a Muslim extremist who reportedly targeted victims based on their race, was eventually sentenced to death. In exchange for testifying against his mentor, Malvo was given life in prison. Muhammad was executed by lethal injection in 2009.

There are important differences between these cases. Dorner targeted only other police officers, whereas Muhammad and Malvo targeted civilians. Even when given the opportunity to harm civilians, Dorner chose restraint rather than violence. Dorner's identity was discovered almost immediately after the murder of Quan and Mitchell; the identities of Muhammad and Malvo were not discovered for several weeks.

Some people reported that, during Dorner's rampage, they felt he was just an ordinary man who had rightfully risen up to challenge authority in a particularly violent and direct way. Some even took open, vicarious pleasure in hearing about his crimes of violence against his former colleagues under the umbrella of perceived injustice and racism. After he began shooting police officers, Dorner received 3,819 "likes" on Facebook. Sadly, Dorner is not the only cop-killer with a Facebook fan page. In 2011, Jamie Hood, who shot two police officers in the face during a high-risk traffic stop, was also the subject of thousands of Facebook "fans."

In truth, Dorner targeted cops for assassination and made no apologies for his acts. Yet, his motive was not to create terror and mayhem, as was the case with Muhammad and Malvo. Dorner's motive was revenge, pure and simple. Taking a page out of his military training book, he even referred to his chosen enemies—other police officers—as "high-value targets."

Despite his obvious criminal conduct and the commission of multiple murders, many people seem uncertain as to whether Chris Dorner was innately good or evil. As a figure of study, he may be the exception. His crimes are not.

Revenge is an all-too-common theme in many murders, including those of police officers. Other themes include drug use and trafficking, alcoholism, gang affiliation, mental illness, adrenaline-fueled terror, obsessive relationships, and the simple desire for self-annihilation.

Within the pages of this book, we will examine fifty more cop-killers. We will get to know them better as people, and as murderers. We will meet sixteen-year-old gang member Nicholas Lindsey, who shot a police officer to death because he was, in his own words, "afraid" of being arrested for possession of a handgun. We will meet Iraqi veteran Alan Sylte, who went to his ex-girlfriend's home with a gun to try to repair their relationship. Instead, he killed a police officer and then himself. We will also explore the case of Eli Myers, another former police officer who became a cop-killer in 2011.

Every day, people in the United States are murdered for causes as diverse as involvement in drug trafficking, preservation of gang turf, and perceptions of romantic infidelity and past wrongs—whether real or perceived—by another.

We kill others because we hate them, because they hurt us, or because they seek to control us when we do not wish to be controlled. Most murders are committed by someone close to the victim because murder is an inherently intimate act. The true "homicidal stranger" scenario is usually a dramatic device and pure Hollywood imagination. The reality of murder investigations is far less exciting.

One saying goes: *Women die in the house; men die in the street.*

When a woman is killed, detectives look to her lovers and, particularly, her ex-lovers. Most often, she has been murdered by someone who once knew her and loved her in an intimate and personal way. Indeed, murdered women die most often at the hands of a male family member, husband, or boyfriend.

The equation is somewhat more complicated when a man is killed. Although men do die as a result of intimate relationships, they are generally killed over issues of money, respect, influence, and power. And, they die most often at the hands of a man who looks like them. White men are killed by white men, and people of color are killed by those of their own race.

When a police officer is murdered, the reasons differ. Officers are usually killed to prevent an arrest from happening. They also die in the crossfire over drugs, money, and power. They are the casualties of disintegrating relationships, machinations of lust, property crimes, and gang violence, and they even become the targets of isolated mentally ill populations.

However, police officers arrest hardened criminals, murderers, and drug dealers every day and live to tell the tales of these arrests routinely. The question becomes: Why do certain people become cop-killers when so many others do not? What terrible moment of evil, rage, or despair drives the hand of those few offenders who pull the trigger and take the lives of our peacekeepers?

Herein is the journey of this book.

By innate design, human beings were not created to kill one another without cause. A latent opposition to taking the life of another is part of what it means to be human. In the study of other mammals, we can see countless examples of cunning, aggression, and violence in pursuit of aims involving sexuality, dominance, and, in the end, survival of the fittest. Yet, are human beings any more noble or civilized than other species?

The answer depends on the human being.

In a typical year, the number of American law enforcement officers killed by firearms is around fifty. We must understand that none of these terrible crimes can be called "typical." Each of them is a tragedy for society. The loss of any police officer diminishes the lives of ordinary people in extraordinarily painful ways. Wives and husbands lose their spouses, children lose their parents, and the ripples of these deaths continue to echo through the departments and the law enforcement profession itself for years to come. Monuments stand to honor those who are sacrificed but, in time, the memories of their sacrifices inevitably soften to sepia tones. This is not what heroes deserve.

Yet, police officers and their families are not alone in their losses. Families of cop-killers bear similar scars, though very often without the sympathy of others. Who casts the net of grief wide enough to understand the pain of the killers' parents and children, or even of the killers themselves? Not all cop-killers are the hard-core offenders or the sociopaths of society. This book attempts to paint a more recognizable picture of these human beings, without the accompanying stigma or judgment.

All of the cases in this book occurred in 2011. In that year, the number of officers who were killed by firearms was sixty. Several were killed in unintentional circumstances, such as that of mistaken identity, or they were killed in off-duty situations. This study examined only uniformed officers, detectives, and on-duty populations. Four shooters killed two officers in the same incident, leaving us with the fifty offenders discussed in this book.

As of 2010, about ninety percent of police officers in the United States were male. In most areas, white officers are the majority, although the numbers of African American and Hispanic officers are rising, especially in large police departments in culturally diverse areas like Baltimore; Washington, DC; and Los Angeles. Mirroring the larger trend of liberation of women in American culture, the number of female officers is also increasing.

Most of the officers in this study were white males. Most were killed by white male shooters. However, the entire story cannot be told in statistical analysis alone. Women and minorities also played a significant role in these slayings, both as victims involved in the incidents and as gun-wielding perpetrators.

The weapons used by these offenders vary, from small-caliber handguns to shotguns, rifles, and even fully automatic weapons, but the most common weapon was the handgun. Officers were ambushed, booby-trapped, and even summarily executed by their assailants. Yet, were the people who killed law enforcement officers one-dimensional, sociopathic, or less than human? The answer may surprise you.

This book will challenge you to think differently about the people who commit the murders of law enforcement officers. They are not necessarily the simple, unsympathetic killers that you might think. In fact, in treading in their shoes, you may recognize the signs of growing despair, defeat, and a gradually unraveling life in the study of their worlds, statements, behaviors, and levels of remorse. You may sense the impending doom that leads up to their final, violent acts.

Developing this understanding does not suggest that these killers deserve pity or special dispensation for their crimes. Those who murder a police officer and survive should be compelled to face the consequences of their actions. Many believe that the best form of justice for these killers is the judicious use of the death penalty. I leave it for the reader to decide the definition of justice for cop-killers.

I want my readers to know that this book does not seek to apologize for murderers, but to help others understand the warning signs that these offenders exhibit before they have a lethal confrontation with law enforcement. I never want to read again that an officer has been killed by someone whose family says: *We knew he was in trouble, but we didn't think he would kill anyone. We thought he would kill himself, but not anyone else*—or, perhaps an even worse comment that goes unreported to police, time and time again: *He told us he would kill the police before he went back to prison.*

This kind of incident should never happen again; yet it will, every year. This book aims to equip those who work with offenders, police officers, and the mentally ill to read the signs of future violence. I hope you will use the lessons of these incidents wisely to prevent unthinkable crimes.

In the killing of police officers—those ordinary heroes who dare to stand on the thin blue line between good and evil—cop-killers become infamous and evil personified. Many die immediately after committing the murders of police officers, either by swift retribution or their own hand. Those who survive will dwell in the custody of prisons with high walls and death sentences for the rest of their lives. Because of their crimes, they have entered a dark and terrible place from which they can never escape.

Walking with these offenders into the encounters that resulted in deaths of police officers is a dark and dangerous path to take.

However, there is always value in understanding another person's journey into darkness.

About the Author

Ann R. Bumbak has more than a decade of experience as a police officer and federal agent. She has served in a number of law enforcement roles, from patrol and field training officer with the Dallas Police Department to undercover antiterrorist operative after 9/11 and, finally, as an accomplished trainer of police officers, managers, and executives. A former train-the-trainer program manager with the state of Maryland, Ann has provided consulting expertise for agencies including the Federal Bureau of Investigation (FBI), the Department of Homeland Security (DHS), and the Drug Enforcement Administration (DEA), supporting the design of high-quality training solutions for law enforcement.

Ann is the author of four books, including *Dynamic Police Training, Survival Training for Law Enforcement, Officer Down 2012*, and *Officer Down 2013*.

She is also the founder of Dynamic Police Training, a consulting organization providing unique training solutions for law enforcement officers, mental health professionals, and others. Ann teaches hundreds of professionals each year at national conferences and seminars, delivering classroom and web-based instruction on issues of interest to the police profession.

Ann lives with her family in northern Virginia and welcomes all visitors to her website at www.dynamicpolicetraining.com.

There are people who are tormented and they don't know what they are doing. Other people sometimes have to pay the price for that.

—Veronika Posner, mother of 6-year-old Noah Posner, who was murdered in Newtown, Connecticut, on December 14, 2012

1

GANGSTER WALK: TEEN COP-KILLERS

Overview

In 2011, six uniformed law enforcement officers were feloniously murdered in the line of duty by teen offenders aged sixteen to nineteen. The six cases we will examine include:

- **Jahmell Crockam**, who murdered an officer who stopped to talk with him as he walked in a residential neighborhood
- **Nicholas Lindscy**, who killed an officer interviewing him near the scene of a car burglary
- **Kion Dail**, who fired at police through a locked door when they came to serve a warrant for his arrest, killing one officer
- **Jonathan Bun**, who murdered an officer during a traffic stop
- **Kyle Williams**, who killed an officer who was patting down him and his friends during the investigation of a disturbance in a neighborhood park
- **Stephon Carter**, who killed an officer who was investigating an attempted drive-by shooting in which Carter was involved

In addition to their ages, what other traits did these youthful offenders have in common? This chapter explores the nature and character of these youthful offenders through a comparative analysis of these incidents, with a focus on age, race, gang affiliation, criminal history, motive, and circumstances of these murders. Unlike many other cop-killers, each of the teen offenders survived.

Case 1: Jahmell "Savage" Crockam, Nineteen

On January 14, 2011, Officer Christopher Matlosz was murdered as he sat behind the wheel of his squad car conducting a field interview with a pedestrian in the middle of a residential street. After the officer waved down a young man whom he seemed to recognize, the suspect pulled a handgun from his waistband and fired three times, killing the officer, before fleeing into the woods. The suspect was apprehended when a tipster reported his location four days later.

Jahmell "Savage" Crockam, nineteen, was affiliated with the Bloods, a violent street gang. Crockam's family had a long history in the area as a respectable and conservative family that attended church together on a weekly basis. Unlike some other troubled youths, Crockam had successfully graduated from high school and applied to attend a local vocational and technical school. However, despite his upbringing and history, Crockam was not a model citizen.

About three months before he shot and killed Officer Matlosz, Crockam and an accomplice known as "Money" killed a third man in a gang-related incident. Crockam's brother was also shot in a gang-related incident in December 2010.

Crockam's motive in this case was relatively clear: to avoid apprehension on a warrant that had been issued for his arrest. Crockam was wanted by police for possession of an illegal rifle and hollow-point ammunition. When he was confronted by a police officer, he simply decided that committing another murder was preferable to arrest.

Crockam's case can be summarized as follows:

Name	Crockam, J.
Age	19
Race	B
Gang affiliation or criminal HX	Yes—Bloods
	Weapons, murder
Social factors	Gangster lifestyle
Mental factors	Imminent arrest for warrant
	Bloodlust—committed recent murder of civilian
Motive	Avoid arrest on warrant
Circumstances	Pedestrian stop
	Shot and killed officer in front of witnesses
Outcome	Fled on foot
	Captured

Case 2: Nicholas Lindsey, Sixteen

On February 21, 2011, Officer David Crawford was gunned down as he spoke to a pedestrian in the roadway while investigating a suspicious-person call. Wearing a black hooded sweatshirt, his assailant returned to the family home and went to bed. Nicholas Lindsey, sixteen years old, was arrested the following day and confessed to the crime by stating:

> I was really scared...I knew I had the gun on me...I didn't want to go to jail.

Nicholas Lindsey was born into a difficult set of circumstances. In the year before his son's birth, Lindsey's biological father pled guilty to charges that he operated a "crack house." At the age of fourteen, Lindsey was arrested twice for stealing cars, but he had no history of violence. One of his relatives reported that Lindsey was involved in a poorly organized, informal street gang known as "Bethel Heights," named after the apartment complex where he and other disenfranchised youths lived.

At the time he was confronted by Officer Crawford, Lindsey had just walked away from a Dodge Neon that he had unsuccessfully attempted to steal. Using a brick to gain entry to the locked vehicle, he had been unable to disable the ignition lock with a screwdriver and had decided to leave the area. As he walked away from the scene of his crime, Officer Crawford approached in a patrol car, abruptly parked blocking the roadway, and alighted from the patrol car to speak with Lindsey, who had his back to the officer. A witness to the incident reported that, as the officer motioned to him, Lindsey drew a handgun and fired five shots, fatally striking the officer four times.

As the officer returned fire, Lindsey fled on foot and returned home. The next morning, Lindsey awoke and had breakfast with his family as the television broadcasted coverage of the officer's overnight murder. Lindsey's mother immediately recognized the image of her son in the surveillance video footage that was shown on the news and confronted Lindsey:

> I knew it was him. I told him to man up.

Lindsey did not immediately turn himself in to police. Instead, he took his four-year-old brother to a neighborhood playground, as hundreds of officers searched his community for the unidentified cop-killer who had vanished into the night. However, that evening, Lindsey was arrested and taken to the police station for questioning. During the video, Lindsey transforms from a hardened youthful offender with nothing to say into a helpless, crying child who tearfully admits to killing the officer out of fear of arrest for possession of a handgun.

Lindsey admitted during the video that he shot Officer Crawford because he was afraid of going to jail. He added that the shooting was accidental; he admitted that he had his finger on the trigger when he pulled out the handgun. Lindsey's parents were in the interrogation room with him at the time of his confession. His parents, who were patient and supportive of their son during the interview, were instrumental in the successful outcome of the interview.

Lindsey's case can be summarized as follows:

Name	Lindsey, N.
Age	16
Race	B
Gang affiliation or criminal HX	Yes—Bethel Heights for Life
	Theft of vehicle
Social factors	Impoverished family
Mental factors	Crime in progress
	Alone with officer
Motive	Avoid arrest for breaking into vehicle and handgun possession
Circumstances	Pedestrian stop
	Fled on foot
Outcome	Captured by police

Case 3: Kion Dail, Sixteen

On June 9, 2011, Investigator Warren "Sneak" Lewis was seeking several suspects who were wanted on an arrest warrant for first-degree murder. Investigator Lewis and his team met outside the target residence and spoke with the father of one of the suspects, who insisted that the suspect was not inside. Investigator Lewis and three other officers made entry to search the building, which was a single-family home that had been converted into several apartments. During the search, Investigator Lewis was shot and killed by sixteen-year-old Kion Dail, who fired from behind a locked inner door of a residence.

Despite his apparent precocity to commit violent crimes, Kion Dail had no prior arrest history. Little is known about the suspect beyond the fact that Dail had been kicked out of school and reportedly lived with a single mother. However, despite his lack of previous contact with law enforcement, Investigator Lewis was not the first man Dail had shot and killed. Dail had bragged to a girlfriend about killing a man in a street robbery over a bicycle just one week before. He was wanted for first-degree murder at the time he shot and killed Investigator Lewis.

Following the shooting, Dail remained barricaded inside a residence with four other suspects. Along with a twenty-six-year-old with a lengthy criminal history, sixteen-year-old Dail was arrested with an eighteen-, a seventeen-, and a fifteen-year-old. Several of the suspects—including Dail—were affiliated with the Crips, a violent street gang.

Dail's motive in this incident was clear: He did not want to be arrested. Dail was wanted for first-degree murder and did not want to be taken into custody.

Dail's case can be summarized as follows:

Name	Dail, K.
Age	16
Race	B
Gang affiliation or criminal HX	Yes—Crips
	Murder
Social factors	Impoverished family
	High school dropout
	Other suspects present
	Gangster lifestyle
Mental factors	Bloodlust—committed recent murder of civilian
	Imminent arrest for warrant served at his home
Motive	Avoid arrest for murder
Circumstances	Warrant service
Outcome	Captured by police

Case 4: Jonathan Bun, Seventeen

On July 20, 2011, Deputy Rick Daly was killed during a traffic stop by a man who exited the passenger side of a vehicle and fired on him without warning. Deputy Daly had been called to assist undercover officers who were conducting surveillance on a subject, Jonathan Bun, who was wanted for armed robbery. After shooting Deputy Daly, Bun ran into the woods, where he stripped down to his underwear and called his mother on his wireless phone and told her he had "shot a cop" and was scared.

Bun had a history of criminal conduct from the age of ten, including drugs, violence, and property crime. His first offense involved bringing a large knife to class in his elementary school. Bun became a member of a street gang at the age of thirteen, when he was "jumped in" to the Bloods during a stay in a juvenile detention center. He also self-reported an ongoing substance abuse problem with marijuana and methamphetamine during one of his contacts with law enforcement.

Bun began running away from home around the time he got involved in gang activity, at the age of thirteen. He was arrested for burglarizing a middle school and marijuana possession that same year. The judge in Bun's criminal case made an unusual assessment of this unusually defiant offender:

> I don't get these kinds of cases in my courtroom at thirteen years old. He had no signs of remorse. And that's scary.

Bun was placed in comprehensive community supervision usually reserved for older offenders, in which probation officers picked him up from school; brought him to the juvenile detention center, where he was given dinner and homework assistance; and returned him to his home around 9 p.m. After his release, Bun continued his violent and unpredictable behavior both at home and in school. In 2009, Bun was arrested for trashing the family home. In 2010, he was charged with disrupting school.

In January 2011, Bun walked into a gift shop and asked for a drink of water. When the employee took him to the office area to give him a cup, Bun placed a gun to her head and robbed the store of two hundred dollars. His image was captured on surveillance cameras, leading to his identification. Soon afterward, a warrant was issued for his arrest, leading to the surveillance operation that led him to murder Deputy Daly.

Bun's motive in this incident is increasingly common among the offenders in this study: to avoid arrest on a warrant for a felony offense. Rather than surrender to police and face the consequences of his actions, Bun chose to kill a police officer and flee the scene.

Bun's case can be summarized as follows:

Name	Bun, J.
Age	17
Race	A
Gang affiliation or criminal HX	Yes—Bloods
	Armed robbery, drugs, and violence
Social factors	Troubled childhood
	Marijuana and methamphetamine use
	Gangster lifestyle
Mental factors	Imminent arrest for warrant
	High on drugs (suspected)
Motive	Avoid arrest for armed robbery
Circumstances	Warrant service
	Traffic stop—passenger
Outcome	Fled on foot; captured by police

Case 5: Kyle Williams, Nineteen

On December 18, 2011, Officer Arnulfo Crispin was assassinated during a street encounter with five "suspicious subjects" in a neighborhood park. Officer Crispin radioed in to mark out at the location to speak with the group of men, including nineteen-year-old Kyle Williams. According to witnesses, Williams was about to be patted down for weapons and drugs when he placed a gun to the back of the officer's head and pulled the trigger. Williams surrendered to police the following day, after his mother reported his involvement in the offense.

Kyle Williams's early history is not known. He had recently moved into the area with his family and lived in an apartment near the park where the shooting occurred. Prior to this incident, Williams had been charged with burglary, resisting a law enforcement officer, and disorderly conduct. One source reported Williams had been involved in local gang activity.

On the night of the murder, Williams showed the handgun to one of the men who was with him during the encounter and would become a witness to the offense. Williams was identified within hours of the shooting and surrendered to police. After his arrest, he told police where they could find the handgun; it had been stashed in an outdoor crawl space of a stranger's apartment near his residence.

Why did Williams choose to commit a cold-blooded execution-style murder of a law enforcement officer? The motive in this case is not as clear as some of the others in this study. However, circumstantial evidence suggests one of two possibilities. Williams was most likely attempting to avoid his certain arrest for weapons charges by Officer Crispin. However, given the circumstances, Williams could have attempted to flee on foot but did not do so. A more remote possibility is that Williams sought to commit a violent act against a police officer to further his reputation as a gang member.

Williams's case can be summarized as follows:

Name	Williams, K.
Age	19
Race	B
Gang affiliation or criminal HX	Yes—unknown (local)
	Burglary and violence
Social factors	Other suspects present
	Gangster lifestyle
Mental factors	Imminent arrest for handgun possession
Motive	Avoid arrest for handgun possession
Circumstances	Disturbance involving males in a park
	Pat down
	Execution of officer
Outcome	Fled on foot
	Captured by police

Case 6: Stephon Carter, Nineteen

On December 20, 2011, Officer Scotty Richardson responded to back up another officer who conducted a traffic stop on a vehicle matching the description of a Chevrolet Impala that had been involved in a "shots fired" call minutes before. The original call involved a known male firing at two teen boys who were visiting the area from a nearby city for the Christmas holidays. Stephon Carter was named as the suspect and was soon stopped by police.

When Officer Richardson arrived, Carter was outside his vehicle being questioned. When one of the officers asked Carter to remove his hands from his pockets, Carter brought out a handgun and fired, shooting one officer and then killing Officer Richardson. Carter was then shot by other police officers. He survived and was immediately taken into custody.

Stephon Carter was born into tragic circumstances. When Carter was three months old, his estranged father kidnapped his mother from her workplace and murdered her. After being shot four times, Carter's mother was left to die inside a parked car on a dirt road. Carter's father began serving a life sentence for this crime in 1993. Orphaned, Carter was raised by his grandparents. However, when he was nine years old, Carter's grandfather died of natural causes. He was the only father figure that Carter had ever known. At seventeen, Carter was arrested for armed robbery.

In July 2010, Carter reported he had been shot. Subsequent investigation revealed that Carter had accidentally shot himself. He was charged with filing a false report. In March 2011, Carter was present at a "shots fired" call and fled from police. He was apprehended and searched, but was found to be unarmed. When asked why he fled, Carter stated he was afraid of the police. In July 2011, Carter was charged with possession of a firearm with an obliterated serial number. He was released on ten thousand dollars' bond. Just three weeks before he killed Officer Richardson, Carter was indicted by a grand jury on this charge. He was out on bond at the time of his encounter with police.

Carter's motive in the shooting of Officer Richardson is unequivocal: He did not want to be arrested for possession of a handgun for a second time. His alternative: shoot and kill the police officers who interviewed him on the side of the road.

Carter's case can be summarized as follows:

Name	Carter, S.
Age	19
Race	B
Gang affiliation or criminal HX	Unknown—likely Armed robbery and weapons
Social factors	Troubled childhood

	Gangster lifestyle
Mental factors	Imminent arrest for attempted murder, handgun possession
Motive	Avoid arrest for attempted murder, handgun possession
Circumstances	Traffic stop
	Shots-fired call
Outcome	Shot by police
	Captured

Discussion: Age

Offenders aged sixteen to nineteen were responsible for six line-of-duty law enforcement murders involving the use of firearms in 2011. Approximately eleven percent of officers killed by firearms in 2011 faced this group of youthful offenders. In general, the younger offenders in this study demonstrated less planning and overt brutality than the older offenders. Most of their actions could be characterized as fear based.

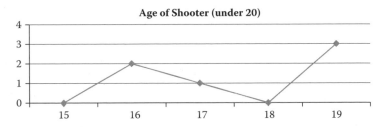

Youthful age is also positively correlated with lack of injury to the shooter during the incident, fleeing on foot from the scene, quick apprehension, involvement of the family in the arrest, and motivation to shoot police officers to avoid arrest.

Discussion: Race

Of the six teen shooters who killed police officers in 2011, five were black (eighty-three percent) and one was Asian. Despite this controversial-sounding statistic, it is unlikely that race played a factor in the decisions of these offenders to use lethal resistance in their encounters with police.

Race of Offender (16–19)

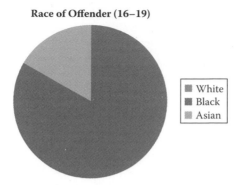

White
Black
Asian

Representing only 12.6% of the US population according to the 2010 US Census, blacks are disproportionately represented as shooters involved in the murder of police officers in 2011. However, they are not the only ethnic group with this pattern. American Indians are also over-represented. Counted as 0.9% of the US population, American Indian shooters were responsible for 5.3% of the murders in this study.* Examining the larger pool of all cop-killers who used firearms against police in 2011, the statistics will tell a slightly different story.

We should also reference the races of the officers involved in these murders. Of the six officers who were killed by this age group of offenders, five were white (eighty-three percent) and one was Hispanic. However, we cannot simply assume a racial prejudice is involved in these statistics.†

---

* It should be noted that one of the two American Indian shooters in the study was responsible for the deaths of two police officers in a single incident.

† Of the officers who were included in the study, fifty were white (87%), four were Hispanic (7.0%), two were black (3.5%), and one was an American Indian (1.7%). Nearly half of the cop-killers in the study are white (45.6%), nearly matched by the number of black shooters (43.8%). Thus, the most common incident in 2011 involved the killing of a white law enforcement officer by a white offender (45.6%). The second most common incident involved the killing of a white law enforcement officer by a black offender (43.8%).

Race of Officer Killed by
Offenders (16–19)

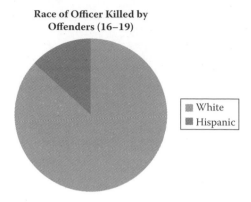

White
Hispanic

Extrapolation of race data alone to predict violence against law enforcement is spurious at best. Minority groups in the United States are over-represented in arrest statistics, as victims, and in number of contacts with police. Within the cases in this study, all of the offenders responded to their imminent arrest with poor judgment and split-second violence, not well-considered decisions involving some aspect of racial bias against the officer. It is highly doubtful that these offenders, whatever their race, would have chosen a different path if the officer had been of the same race as the offender. These offenders reacted to the officer's badge and arrest authority and what that authority represented to their immediate freedom, not to the color of the officer's skin.

Discussion: Gang Affiliation

All of the shooters in this age group were members of gangs, including well-organized and national-level criminal gangs or more informally organized street gangs active in their neighborhoods. Three of the shooters were confirmed gang members of the Bloods or the Crips.

Affiliation with a gang has a high correlation with willingness to commit violence against police, firearms possession, and the acquisition of a criminal history early in life.

Discussion: Criminal History

All of the shooters in this age group had acquired a criminal history before their fatal encounter with police. Some of the shooters, such as

Jonathan Bun, could be classified as an unusually hardcore offender. With a history of disturbing criminal conduct that dated to his years in elementary school, Bun may have been a sociopathic personality with no feeling of remorse and little possibility of rehabilitation.

Like Bun, Carter had a history of armed robbery, which is a crime of violence, intimidation, and extraordinary aggression. Dail surpasses all other offenders in this study in his level of violent criminal behavior, having become a murderer of a civilian during a street robbery in the week prior to his encounter with law enforcement. These three offenders "fit the mold" in their acts against law enforcement as an expression of their deviancy, delinquency, and criminological potential. All were violence oriented and vicious.

From the perspective of offender history, the two other offenders—Crockam and Lindsey—are less archetypal cop-killers. Nineteen-year-old Crockam was the product of a stable home and a high school graduate who had made some efforts toward achieving independence by applying to technical school. However, like Dail, Crockam had also committed a gang-related murder. At age sixteen, Lindsey was more child than man, slight in build, living with his parents and four-year-old brother and, like Crockam, a member of a traditional, loving family.

Less is known about Williams, but clearly he had taken up with a group of young men in his neighborhood who may have been involved in criminal activity. His execution-style murder could not have been predicted by his criminal history alone. It is interesting to note that, among the cases in this study, Williams is the only teen shooter with a criminal history of violence against police.

Discussion: Social Factors

The social factors impacting this group of offenders include lifestyle, family history, and environmental factors at the time of the incident.

Let us examine the cases side by side:

Crockam	Gangster lifestyle
Lindsey	Impoverished family
Dail	Impoverished family
	High school dropout
	Other suspects present
	Gangster lifestyle

Bun	Troubled childhood
	Marijuana and methamphetamine use
	Gangster lifestyle
Williams	Other suspects present
	Gangster lifestyle
Carter	Troubled childhood
	Gangster lifestyle

Four of the six shooters (sixty-six percent) had a troubled childhood or an impoverished family background. The majority of shooters in this age group were living a "gangster" lifestyle, characterized by criminal conduct, lack of respect for authority, and violence.

One offender reported drug use, but others may have been involved in such conduct.

Discussion: Mental Factors

The mental factors of the offenders in this age group are varied. Let us examine the cases side by side:

Crockam	Bloodlust—committed recent murder of civilian
Lindsey	Crime in progress
	Alone with officer
Dail	Bloodlust—committed recent murder of civilian
	Imminent arrest for warrant served at his home
Bun	High on drugs (suspected)
Williams	None
Carter	Imminent arrest for attempted murder, handgun possession

We see two offenders in this group who were affected by what we will call "bloodlust." These offenders had already killed a civilian when they were confronted by law enforcement. Others were influenced by drugs or escaping from the scene of a crime.

As we move forward to examining other age groups, we will see that the mental factors that influence shooters' decisions will expand to include relationships, perceptions, mental illness, and other categories.

Discussion: Motives

All of the shooters in this age group had the same motivation: to avoid imminent arrest. Williams and Crockam, both nineteen years of age, acted most precipitously of all of the shooters in the study. After being stopped for field interviews, both men chose to execute the officer who confronted them in front of several witnesses. These egregious acts of violence suggest the high likelihood that these shooters were routinely involved in violent acts against other victims, likely as a part of criminal gang lifestyle involving drugs, robbery, and other street crimes, prior to their confrontation with police. Most jurisdictions would not count these men as juvenile suspects, but would automatically handle them as adult offenders.

Lindsey, sixteen, and Bun, seventeen, both acted with little forethought in their encounters with police. Both were stopped by an officer in a patrol car. Lindsey was afraid of being caught breaking into cars. Bun was wanted for robbery and did not want to return to custody; he may have also been involved in significant substance abuse that impaired his judgment. Fearing apprehension, both of these shooters acted with little concern about the consequences of their actions. In true teen fashion, they made an important decision that would affect the rest of their lives in the space of less than ten seconds.

Dail, sixteen, fired a handgun at police who were searching a residence for him. Shooting through the interior door while in the company of four other young men, Dail may have had the lowest level of malice of all shooters in this study. His intent in firing the handgun through the door may have been to show off to his friends, frighten the police, or simply see what would happen. It is highly unlikely that Dail intended to kill the police officer who was struck by the rounds he fired. However, this does not diminish the principle of his actions and the need for appropriate punishment in this case.

Finally, nineteen-year-old Carter acted with exceptional violence when he shot two police officers who were questioning him about his involvement in a drive-by shooting attempt minutes before. One officer was saved by his bullet-resistant vest; the other was struck fatally in the head. Carter's motive was simple: He did not want to be arrested and acted with violence of action before the police could take him into custody. His actions were unpredictable, at best. Given his actions, he was truly lucky to survive this incident with a single gunshot wound.

Discussion: Circumstances

Half of the shooters in this age group were stopped by police as pedestrians in a public place. Crockam was summoned to speak with an officer as he walked in a neighborhood. Lindsey was walking away from a late-night attempt to steal a car. Williams was stopped with a group of other young men in a park by an officer who reported them as "suspicious."

Half of the shooters—Crockam, Dail, and Bun—were facing arrest as subjects with active felony warrants. Crockam, discussed earlier, was wanted for weapons violations. Dail was wanted for murder. Bun was wanted for armed robbery. Two of the shooters—Bun and Carter—were traveling in vehicles at the time of the encounter. Bun was a passenger in his friend's car; Carter was a driver.

All of the shooters shared one unfortunate trait: the willingness to act with violence first and reflect on that act and its consequences later.

Discussion: Outcomes

All of the shooters in this age group were captured by police. More than half of the shooters (sixty-six percent) fled on foot after the shooting. One was shot by police during his apprehension.

Crockam	Fled on foot; captured by police
Lindsey	Fled on foot; captured by police
Dail	Captured by police
Bun	Fled on foot; captured by police
Williams	Fled on foot; captured by police
Carter	Shot by police; captured by police

In contrast to other age groups, the majority of the shooters aged sixteen to nineteen were uninjured. This suggests that police officers did not view these suspects as dangerous during their initial encounters with them.

Conclusion

In 2011, youthful offenders proved that they are as effective at killing police officers as their adult counterparts. We can draw the following conclusions from the study of these six offenders:

- Police should use extra caution when involved in warrant service or pedestrian stops of teen suspects. Teen offenders carry weapons and use them against police. They often do not have the maturity to anticipate the consequences of their actions.
- All of the shooters in this age group were members of formal or informal gangs. Teens who are gang members are riskier suspects than non-gang-member counterparts.
- When police encounter a teen while investigating evolving crimes that have just occurred, they should use the same degree of caution as they would with an adult suspect. Male suspects between the ages of sixteen and nineteen can be unpredictable in their behavior when confronted and are easily underestimated as threats by law enforcement.
- Without the benefit of emotional maturity and the ability to predict consequences that adults possess, youthful suspects can act rashly and violently, using lethal resistance to prevent their own apprehension.
- Teen cop-killers often shoot first and then flee on foot, seeking escape from capture and the help of their families in evading the price for their crimes. However, families can be key in the successful surrender and interview of teen suspects once they are in custody.

Bibliography

Altman, H. "'I Knew It Was Him,' Suspect's Mom Says," *Tampa Tribune*, February 24, 2011, p. 1.

Anderson, D. "Probable Cause Hearing in Homicide Cases Today," *Free Press*, June 30, 2011, Kinston, NC: McClatchey-Tribune Business News.

APP video. "Jahmell Crockam Initial Appearance" [video], January 19, 2011. *YouTube*. Retrieved November 23, 2011, from http://www.youtube.com/watch?v=vk6Mfb7jNmE

Associated Press. "17-Year-Old Arrested in Killing of Georgia Deputy," July 21, 2011, Jonesboro, GA: APO.

———. "17-Year-Old Faces Murder Charges in Deputy's Death," July 21, 2011, Jonesboro, GA: APO.

———. "Possible Weapon Found in Lakeland Cop Shooting," December 20, 2011, Lakeland, FL: APO.

————. "Teen Charged with Murder in Aiken Officer's Death," December 23, 2011, Aiken, SC: APO.

Auer, D., and Hamilton, B. "Bloods Put Bounty on NJ Cops: Report," *New York Post,* January 16, 2011. Retrieved November 23, 2011 from http://www.nypost.com/p/bloods_put_bounty_on_nj_cops_report_rxf7PH1fwgovxkx4uGNokI

Boone, C., and Garner, M. "Clayton Shooting; Teen Faces Two Murder Counts in Deputy's Death," *Atlanta Journal-Constitution,* July 22, 2011, p. 1B.

Brantley, A. "'It Was Shocking,'" *Wilson Daily Times,* June 11, 2011, Nashville, TN: McClatchey-Tribune Business News.

Brown, W. "Death Penalty Eyed in Homicide," *Free Press,* June 11, 2011, Kinston, NC: McClatchey-Tribune Business News.

————. "Resident Complaint Led Lawmen to Murder Suspects and to Another Shooting," *Free Press,* June 14, 2011, Kinston, NC: McClatchey-Tribune Business News.

————. "Investigators Learned Murder Suspects Planned Shootout with Police Hours before Officer Shot," *Free Press,* July 6, 2011, Kinston, NC: McClatchey-Tribune Business News.

————. "Autopsy: U.S. Marshal Shot Multiple Times in Kinston Homicide," *Free Press,* September 21, 2011, Kinston, NC: McClatchey-Tribune Business News.

COMTEX News. "St. Petersburg Officer Killed in Line of Duty," COMTEX News Network, February 23, 2011, St. Petersburg, FL: Benzinga.com

Considine, B. "Cop-Killing Suspect Has Been Wanted for a Month; Lakewood Man Was Already Wanted on Weapons Charge," *Times of Trenton,* January 16, 2011, p. A09.

Considine, B., and Calefati, J. "Massive Manhunt in Cop Killing; Lakewood Suspect Already Wanted on Weapons Charge," *Star-Ledger,* January 16, 2011, p. 001.

Crawford, S. "Man, 19, Charged in Officer's Death," *Augusta Chronicle,* December 23, 2011, p. A1.

"Crawford Was Holding a Notepad When Shot," *Tampa Tribune,* February 24, 2011, p. 6.

Creech, S. "Letters Seized in Marshal's Death," *Wilson Daily Times,* July 22, 2011, Nashville, TN: McClatchey-Tribune Business News.

Daily, K. "Suspect in Police Shootings Gets Lawyer," *Aiken Standard,* December 29, 2011, Aiken, SC: McClatchy-Tribune Business News.

Dolianitis, A. "Man Accused of Killing Officer in Jail," *Aiken Standard,* January 3, 2011, Aiken, SC: McClatchy-Tribune Business News.

Ernst, E. "Investigation Continues in Fatal Shooting of Lakewood Police Officer," *Asbury Park Press,* January 15, 2011, Asbury Park, NJ: APP.

Ernst, E., and McGrath, M. "Significant Development to Be Announced in Slaying of Lakewood Police Officer," *Asbury Park Press,* January 15, 2011, Asbury Park, NJ: APP.

Gibbons, M. "Carter Suspect in Earlier Call for Shots Fired, Report Shows," *Aiken Standard,* December 24, 2011, Aiken, SC: McClatchy-Tribune Business News.

Girona, J. "Chief: No Hope for Officer," *Tampa Tribune,* December 21, 2011, p. 3.

Joyner, T. "Youth Has Grim Past with Crime," *Atlanta Journal-Constitution,* August 7, 2011, p. 1B.

"Judge Refused to Release Dashcam Video in Aiken Cop's Death," March 1, 2012. Retrieved May 6, 2012, from http://www.midlandsconnect.com/news/story.aspx?id=725707

Kyriakakis, G. "Trial Date Set for Alleged Killer of Officer Matlosz," *Manalapan Patch,* July 30, 2011. Retrieved November 23, 2011, from http://manalapan.patch.com/articles/trial-date-set-for-alleged-killer-of-officer-matlosz

"Lakeland Police Officer Won't Survive Shooting." *St. Petersburg Times,* December 21, 2011, p. 1B.

Lush, T. "Fla. Police-Killing Suspect Known as Quiet Teen," Associated Press, February 23, 2011, St. Petersburg, FL: AP.

McConville, J., and McGrath, M. "Lakewood Shooting Suspect Arrested, Faces Murder Charges in Officer Christopher Matlosz Death," *Asbury Park Press,* January 16, 2011, Asbury Park, NJ: APP.

McGrath, M. "Lakewood Police Officer Reported to Have Died after Shooting," *Asbury Park Press,* January 14, 2011, Asbury Park, NJ: APP.

———. "Family of Jahmell Crockam, Accused of Fatally Shooting Officer Christopher Matlosz, Say Case Built on Hearsay, Rumors," *Daily Record,* January 21, 2011, Morristown, NJ: DR.

Megerian, C., and Queally, J. "Christopher Matlosz 'Was the Best of Us'; Authorities Launch Manhunt for Gunman with 'No Soul,'" *Star-Ledger,* January 15, 2011, p. 001.

Moon, J. "5 Held in Fatal Shooting of Lawman Identified; Four Have First Appearance," *Free Press,* June 10, 2011, Kinston, NC: McClatchey-Tribune Business News.

Moore, S. Murder suspect's mother arrested. Eyewitness News 9, December 13, 2011. Retrieved February 17, 2012, from http://www2.wnct.com/news/2011/dec/13/murder-suspects-mother-arrested-ar-1710108/

Morelli, K. "Site Where Officer Shot: A Drug Haven," *Tampa Tribune,* December 20, 2011, p. 1.

Morelli, K., Shaw, R., Altman, H., and Thompson, S. "Teenager Jailed in Officer Slaying," *Tampa Tribune,* February 23, 2011, p. 1.

Morris, M. "Clayton Teen Appears in Court," *Atlanta Journal-Constitution,* August 3, 2011, p. 3B.

Nipps, E. "Driver Found, Tried to Help Wounded Officer," *St. Petersburg Times,* February 23, 2011, p. 4A.

O'Connor, A., and Schweber, N. "New Jersey Police Officer Is Shot Dead during Encounter with Pedestrian," *New York Times,* January 15, 2011, p. 18.

O'Connor, J. "Officer Lived and Died for the Badge He Cherished; From an Early Age, He Set Out to Be a Cop," *Star-Ledger,* January 16, 2011, p. 008.

Parry, W. Emotional hunt under way in NJ town. Associated Press Online, January 15, 2011, Lakewood, NJ: AP.

Stacy, M. "1 Suspect in Custody after Florida Officer Shot," Associated Press, December 19, 2011, Lakeland, FL: APO.

———. "Florida Police Officer Dies Days after Being Shot," Associated Press, December 21, 2011, Lakeland, FL: APO.

Stix, N. Accused cop/serial killer Jahmell Crockam is an innocent, church-going fall guy and victim of police brutality and racism, says family [blog post], March 23, 2011. Retrieved November 23, 2011, from http://www.nicholasstixuncensored.blogspot.com/accused-cop-serial-killer-jahmell.html

Strunsky, S. "Manhunt Concludes; Police Find Suspect at an Apartment in Camden," *Times of Trenton,* January 17, 2011, p. A01.

———. "As Community Grieves, Alleged Lakewood Cop Killer Due in Court," *Times of Trenton,* January 18, 2011, p. A07.

Thalji, J., Krueger, C., Nipps, E., and Stanley, K. "The Hunt Ends," *St. Petersburg Times,* February 23, 2011, p. 1A.

Thalji, J., and Nohlgren, S. "'Tell Us What Happened,'" *St. Petersburg Times,* April 12, 2011, p. 1A.

United Press International. "Florida Police Officer Dies from Gunshot," December 21, 2011, Lakeland, FL: UPI.

Van Sickler, M., Valentine, D., and Krueger, C. "How a Good Cop Died," *St. Petersburg Times,* February 24, 2011, p. 1A.

2

WILD BOYS: COP-KILLERS IN THEIR EARLY TWENTIES

Overview

In 2011, nine law enforcement officers were murdered in the line of duty by offenders aged twenty to twenty-four. These cases include:

- **Daniel Butts,** who killed an officer during the attempted theft of a vintage car
- **Johnny Simms,** who killed two detectives who came to his home to serve a murder warrant
- **Alexander Haydel,** who murdered an officer he encountered in a stairwell after killing his wife's ex-husband
- **Daniel Tiger,** who killed two officers interviewing him about a disturbance involving alcohol
- **Dejon White,** who murdered a police officer he flagged down after shooting a stranger in the face with a shotgun
- **Ryan Heisler,** who murdered the officer who responded to assist his probation officer at a home check
- **Ross Ashley,** who killed an officer who was seated in his patrol car writing a traffic ticket to another motorist

When compared with the teen offenders already examined in Chapter 1, we will begin to see many commonalities in the characteristics and motives of these shooters. However, the outcomes for these offenders were markedly different.

Case 7: Daniel Butts, Twenty-One

On January 5, 2011, Chief Ralph Painter responded to a report of a burglary in progress at a stereo installation store located in a strip mall. Going inside, he located Daniel Butts behind the wheel of a late 1960s red Chevrolet Chevelle that was inside the garage area of the business awaiting service. Butts was attempting to steal the vehicle. Painter approached and then sprayed Butts with oleoresin capsicum (OC) spray. When Chief Painter pointed his handgun at Butts, he was disarmed and killed by Butts. Butts was immediately confronted by arriving police who surrounded the business. Still armed with the officer's gun, Butts was shot once in the back by police and taken into custody.

Butts had a somewhat troubling family history. His mother had previously been married to his uncle. When that relationship failed, Butts's mother moved in with her brother-in-law and had two children with him. Butts was the older child. After the birth of his sister, Butts's mother left the relationship, abandoning the children. Despite his childhood, Butts was seen as a gifted student who tested high on an IQ test at the age of ten. In high school, he played two sports with some ability before dropping out. Butts reportedly used marijuana and alcohol from time to time and had become demotivated to accomplish much after high school. He stayed in the family home, waiting for his sister to graduate from high school and spoke of earning an auto mechanic certification in trade school. He also developed an interest in vintage cars.

During this period in his life, Butts was able to purchase a 1969 Chevrolet Malibu and worked to restore it. About a week before the shooting, Butts and his sister were shopping inside the tire store located next to the stereo installation business where the red Chevelle was parked. Butts entered the garage to admire the vehicle up close. The owner of the store felt that something was wrong with Butts when he confronted him. When he asked Butts to leave, Butts simply answered:

I ain't stealing nothing.

It was an ominous, self-incriminating prediction. Days later, Butts killed the officer who tried to stop him from stealing the car.

Butts's motive in this incident was to avoid arrest. Yet, there may have been something less obvious motivating him. His family described the emergence of a pattern of maladjustment in the months leading up to the shooting. His sister said:

> He'd be sad and then he'd be happy. It started out that he would be around and do a bunch of work. And then, the next day, he'd say "I don't want to do anything today."

In particular, the diagnosis in this case may have been onset of bipolar disorder. Butts's real motivation to steal the car and kill the police officer in this incident may have been triggered by an unpredictable combination of onset of mental illness in young adulthood and past or present drug and alcohol use.

Butts is one of only a few offenders in this study who disarmed the officer involved in the incident, either before or after the shooting. Most offenders bring their own firearm to the encounter.

Butts's case can be summarized as follows:

Name	Butts, D.
Age	21
Race	W
Gang affiliation or criminal HX	No
Social factors	Troubled childhood
	High school dropout
	Alcohol and marijuana use
Mental factors	Bipolar (suspected)
	Crime in progress
	Alone with officer
Motive	Avoid arrest for stealing vehicle
Circumstances	Burglary in progress
	Shooter disarmed officer when confronted
Outcome	Shot by police; captured

Case 8: Johnny Simms, Twenty-Two

On January 20, 2011, four members of a career criminal apprehension unit of the Miami-Dade Police Department arrived at Johnny Simms's mother's home in an impoverished housing project. Simms was wanted on a first-degree murder warrant for the killing of another man during a street argument four months earlier. When police knocked and announced their presence, Simms's mother answered the door and stepped aside to allow the officers to enter. As they made entry, Simms emerged from another room of the house and opened fire, killing Detectives Roger Castillo and Amanda Haworth before he was fatally wounded by a third officer.

Simms was born into a family affected by poverty. His mother was a single mother who had moved from Washington, DC, to Miami, Florida, to attempt to provide a better environment for her children. By the time Simms was in middle school, he had already begun "running the streets." At age fourteen, Simms was arrested for burglarizing a neighbor's home. Eleven more arrests as a juvenile followed. At one point, Simms became so out of control that his mother kicked him out of the family home.

As a young adult, Simms was sent to prison and, when released, refused to comply with his parole requirements. Exactly four years before he killed two officers who came to his home to serve a warrant, one of the victim officers (Detective Roger Castillo) arrested Simms for a probation violation. As a result of this arrest, Simms was returned to prison.

Just three weeks after he was released again, Simms got into an argument with Larry Cornelious, a twenty-seven-year-old man, who was cursing in the street and showing disrespect to Simms's younger sister. Simms rode over to the location on a bicycle and confronted Cornelious. When Cornelious refused to back down from the fight, Simms shot and killed him in front of several witnesses. Simms then left the location. A warrant was soon issued for his arrest, leading to the officers' arrival at his home to serve the warrant.

Simms's motivation during this incident was to avoid a certain return to prison for the offense of murder. He had told his mother that he was not going back to prison. She later said that she was shocked that her son used lethal force against police. Like any mother, she did not want to believe that her son was a violent criminal. Yet, Simms was merely a product of the streets where he chose to spend the majority of his adolescent and adult life, beginning around age twelve.

Street credibility is a concept that some will die for. The idea of having "juice" or "respect" is more important to these populations than most observers realize. Allowing another man or the authorities to "disrespect" a subject who values his street credibility above all other traits can cause an offender to react violently to the intervention of law enforcement. These encounters can become more aggravated by the presence of family or friends; the location of the encounter, such as the offender's home or neighborhood; and underlying racial tensions.

Simms is not the first example of this kind of offender in the study.[*] Some offenders simply will not comply with law enforcement under any circumstances, especially when the likely outcome of the encounter will lead to a return to prison.

Simms's case can be summarized as follows:

Name	Simms, J.
Age	22
Race	B
Gang affiliation or criminal HX	Yes—burglary, theft, armed robbery, cocaine distribution
Social factors	Impoverished family
	Teen offender
	Hard-core criminal
	Drug dealer
	Family members present
	Gangster lifestyle
Mental factors	Bloodlust—committed recent murder of civilian
	Imminent arrest for warrant served at his home
	Prior contact with victim officer
Motive	Avoid arrest on warrant
Circumstances	Warrant service
	Shot and killed multiple police officers
Outcome	Killed by police

Case 9: Alexander Haydel, Twenty-Two

On July 3, 2011, Alexander Haydel shot and killed his wife's ex-husband at a family reunion inside a downtown Memphis hotel. Police arrived at the hotel and began ascending the stairs of the ten-story building, searching for the gunman. Officer Timothy Warren's team exited the stairway on the eighth floor. Officer Warren continued up to the ninth floor alone and encountered Haydel fleeing down the

---

[*] Recall Jahmell Crockam's (Case 1) behavior when he was innocuously confronted by a police officer. Crockam and Simms were both involved in gang activity and previous murders.

stairs. Haydel shot Officer Warren in the head and then disarmed him. He then set up a crude booby trap to target first responders. He was quickly apprehended by other officers and was not injured during his capture.

Little is known about Alexander Haydel's early life, but he had no reported criminal history. He had at least one sibling, a twin brother. After finishing high school, both men enlisted in the Army National Guard in 2007. Haydel had long desired a military career. However, in 2010, Haydel was honorably discharged prematurely for an unknown medical reason, just before he was scheduled to deploy to Iraq.*

After his discharge, he returned home to his parents' house, where he exhibited a lot of anger and a desire to party and drink an excess of alcohol. His father said:

> For years, he's had this anger thing, and it got out of control.

Haydel's parents did not approve of his behavior and, after repeatedly breaking the house rules, he moved out. Haydel then went to work for a tractor supply company. Once he left home, Haydel had little contact with his parents. Just months before the shooting, Haydel married Bobbie Warren.† Bobbie was an older woman who had two adult daughters with her ex-husband, Arthur Warren. Although Bobbie had been separated from Arthur for some time, their divorce had just been finalized, allowing Bobbie to marry Haydel quickly.

For the July 4 weekend, Haydel and around a dozen of his wife's relatives drove to Memphis from the Cleveland area to celebrate together. As members of the same extended family group, the traveling group included Bobbie, her two daughters, ex-husband Arthur, and new husband Haydel in multiple cars. After a verbal confrontation between Arthur and Haydel, Haydel retrieved a handgun from his car and went to Arthur's hotel room, where he shot and killed his rival.

Did Haydel demonstrate evidence of underlying mental illness? He was suddenly discharged from the military under unexplained

---

* Haydel's parents believed that Haydel's medical issue was related to an ear problem. A spokesman for the Army National Guard disputed this report in the media.

† Bobbie Warren, Arthur Warren, and Officer Timothy Warren all share the same surname. Interestingly, Officer Warren and Arthur Warren were reportedly distant relatives who had never met. The civilians are referred to by first name to distinguish them from the officer in this incident.

circumstances, demonstrated an excess of anger, and sought out the opportunity to be involved in myriad types of substance abuse, including use of excessive alcohol. He quickly married a newly divorced near-stranger who was at least fifteen years older. Just months later, the relationship became unstable. Haydel then got into a heated confrontation with a man almost thirty years his senior and made the decision to kill him over a minor argument. He later told police that he thought he could escape the consequences for his actions, booby-trap the officer's body, and kill many more officers in the ensuing mayhem. In truth, Haydel's reality had become fairly delusional.

Clearly, Haydel was in a downward spiral that looks a lot like the pattern of other mentally ill offenders. Haydel seemed to be exhibiting signs of manic behavior that may have signaled the onset of bipolar disorder.* The court agreed and ordered a full mental evaluation for Haydel after his arrest. The results were not released to the public. Whatever his diagnosis, Haydel was found competent to stand trial.

Besides the onset of mental illness, what else could explain Haydel's conduct in the months after his discharge from the military? Illicit drug use is another possibility. His violent behavior could be consistent with the abuse of cocaine, opiates, or methamphetamine.

Haydel is not the first offender to kill a police officer in the immediate aftermath of another killing, a condition we will call "bloodlust." Along with Crockam, Dail, and Simms, the shooter in this case had just committed a murder before being confronted by police. Like Butts, Haydel is the second offender to disarm an officer during the incident. Haydel is also the first shooter with three critical traits or behaviors of cop-killers, which we will see again in this study:

- The suspect was a military veteran.
- He booby-trapped the officer's body.
- He was involved in an obsessive romantic relationship.

Haydel's case can be summarized as follows:

Name	Haydel, A.
Age	22
Race	W

---

* The typical age of onset for bipolar is the late teen to early adulthood period. Haydel was twenty-two years old at the time of the shooting.

Gang affiliation or criminal HX	No
Social factors	Military training
	Family members present
	Obsessive relationship
Mental factors	Bloodlust—committed recent murder of civilian
	Involved in escape from crime scene
	Alone with officer
Motive	Avoid arrest for murder
Circumstances	Shots-fired call
	Confronted in hotel stairwell
	Disarmed officer after death
	Booby-trapped officer's body
Outcome	Captured by police

Case 10: Daniel Tiger, Twenty-Two

On August 2, 2012, three officers went to investigate a report of a disturbance involving alcohol. Three men and a woman were located on a street corner. Two of the men were carrying bottles of alcohol. A neighbor later reported that the conversation between the officers and suspects appeared cordial and nonconfrontational, stating that one of the officers exchanged a "fist bump" with one of the subjects during the interview. When one of the subjects provided a false name and date of birth, the officers became suspicious.

After about ten minutes, the officers told the three subjects who had been identified—two men and the woman—that they were free to leave. They then turned their attention to the unidentified suspect, Daniel Tiger. The discussion turned violent when Tiger pulled a .357 caliber handgun from his waistband and fired a single shot at Officer Nick Armstrong. As he collapsed, Officer Armstrong drew his duty weapon but, fatally wounded, he was unable to fire.

Tiger immediately turned toward Officer Tim Doyle and fired a second shot, striking Doyle in the face. Officer Doyle fell to the ground, but was able to draw his weapon and fire a single shot at Tiger. Tiger then fired the remaining four rounds in his weapon in the direction of Officer Ryan McCandless, who was about thirty feet away. However, Officer McCandless had already begun firing at the suspect when he was struck once in the chest through his armpit. After firing fourteen rounds at the suspect, Officer McCandless collapsed and died at the scene, probably due to blood loss.

Tiger was shot twice by Officer McCandless, in the pelvic area and the right arm, shattering one of his arm bones. While Tiger was being treated at the scene, he expressed responsibility and remorse for the shooting. At the hospital, his blood alcohol panel revealed a level of 0.098, well over the legal limit for intoxication. He also tested positive for marijuana use. Tiger did not survive the incident and died the following day.

Both Officer Armstrong and Officer McCandless were killed by Tiger during this incident. Officer Tim Doyle survived being shot in the face and returned to full duty just weeks after the shooting.

The early history of Daniel Tiger is not known. Tiger was quite well known to law enforcement as he had been involved in a dozen criminal incidents since turning eighteen. Charges to which he pled guilty included assault, assault on a law enforcement officer, alcohol violations, disorderly conduct, and petty theft. Strangely, Tiger had multiple offenses involving the charge of intentionally contacting a person with bodily fluids.

A former high school classmate of Tiger said:

> He was always with the wrong crowd of kids, wanting to be a thug gangster. He always picked on kids smaller than him.

In 2007, eighteen-year old Tiger went to prison for assaulting a police officer. After doing five months in prison, he was released on parole. Several weeks later, he violated his parole, and was sent back for eleven months.

Two weeks before the shooting, an unknown suspect burglarized a local middle school and robbed a Circle S convenience store. Tiger was under investigation as the main suspect in both offenses. On July 12, he was arrested for approaching two other police officers with a concealed knife. At the time of the shooting, he was serving a thirty-day suspended sentence as a result of this incident.

A few days before the shooting, Tiger told a close female friend that he wanted to die because he had no job, no home, and nothing to live for. He confessed he was facing prison time if he was arrested again and did not want to go back to prison. Tiger also stated he wanted to go out with a "bang" and asked his friend if she had ever heard of the term "suicide by cop," claiming this was the method he would choose for his own death. Four days later, he made this plan a reality.

In 2011, one in five cop-killers was twenty-five years of age or younger, including five shooters who were the same age as Tiger: twenty-two years old. Daniel Tiger represents a classic example of a wayward, violent, youthful criminal offender with one foot in adolescence and one in adulthood, but who was fully capable of deadly violence against law enforcement. He also had a previous history of animosity toward police.

Tiger's case can be summarized as follows:

Name	Tiger, D.
Age	22
Race	I (American Indian)
Gang affiliation or criminal HX	Theft, disorderly conduct, alcohol violations, assault, and history of violence against police
Social factors	Made suicide-by-cop statement
	Alcohol and marijuana use
Mental factors	Gave false identity
	High on alcohol and marijuana
Motive	Avoid arrest for handgun possession by felon
	Suicide by cop
Circumstances	Pedestrian stop
	Shot three officers total, killing two officers
Outcome	Killed by police

Case 11: Dejon White, Twenty-Two

On August 6, 2011, Dejon White visited his family, washed his car, and left his mother's home. Returning to his apartment, he penned a suicide note. White then drove his black Audi to a local restaurant, walked up to a parked car, and shot stranger Martin Hanna in the face with a shotgun. White then drove onto the freeway, where he was pursued by police. They discontinued the chase when White's highway speed exceeded one hundred miles per hour. A short time later, while driving on a residential street, White flashed his headlights at a police car in front of him.

White then pulled up next to Officer Jeremy Henwood and fired a single shotgun blast through the window of the car, killing the officer. White drove away. After a caller reported Officer Henwood had been shot, the police dispatcher sent all available units and a medic unit to the location. As ground units searched for the gunman, others set up a perimeter and a police helicopter arrived. Minutes later, a 911 caller reported that the gunman was parked at his home less than a block away. The caller stated that the gunman had identified himself to her as the shooter. The helicopter immediately spotted the Audi and, then, the shooter.

As White returned to the scene of Officer Henwood's shooting at the end of his street, he reached for the shotgun and was shot by other officers. He did not survive. A two-page suicide note was found at White's apartment. The note focused on White's belief in reincarnation and outlined his rambling apology for violating The Earth Center's teachings and commandments. White had recently become involved with the group, which his family characterized as a "cult."

The original shooting victim, Martin Hanna, was transported to the hospital where he underwent several reconstructive surgeries on his face. Although he was significantly disfigured, Hanna miraculously survived the incident. No motive or link between White and Hanna was ever determined. * Hanna denied that any confrontation had occurred between him and White prior to the shooting. The incident might have been racially motivated, a case of mistaken identity, or simply random homicidal action.

White grew up in San Diego as part of a large, extended family. He played football in high school until he had a knee injury that required surgery. He graduated high school and, at eighteen, went to work at a local Sears department store. Later that year, he was arrested for attempting to steal a $2,700 television from his employer. He pleaded guilty and was placed on three years of probation. A string of minor charges followed: resisting an officer, reckless driving, jaywalking, and theft.

In December 2010, White lived and worked at a local homeless shelter, where he was recruited by a spiritual group called The Earth Center. The group subscribed to a vision of restoring the original faith of ancient Egypt through beliefs in meditation, reincarnation, yoga,

---

* White's religious beliefs included the idea that the original Egyptian culture had been usurped by other groups, including Muslims. Martin Hanna was an Iraqi man who may have appeared to White to be one of the enemies responsible for the suffering of his ancestors.

and afrocentric ideas. During this period, White radically changed his diet in accordance with his new beliefs and adopted lifestyle changes that concerned his family.

In January 2011, White was given an opportunity to enroll in a job training program through the Urban Corps. White did well in the program designed for underprivileged youth and, in April, he moved into his own apartment close to his family. He continued to be involved in The Earth Center religious group and began setting up job interviews. One week before the shooting, White stopped going to work and missed a forklift driving course. He ignored calls from his employer checking on him and did not tell his family. On the morning of the shooting, White went to his mother's home, a mile away, washed his car, and watered his mother's lawn. He then waved goodbye, telling his mother he would be back. They would never again see him alive.

Like Tiger, White had a prior history of animosity toward police. Along with Crockam, Dail, Simms, and Haydel, the shooter in this case had just committed another murder before being confronted by police. Unlike those offenders, White invited the confrontation by flagging down the officer.

White's case can be summarized as follows:

Name	White, D.
Age	22
Race	B
Gang affiliation or criminal HX	Theft, reckless driving, history of violence against police
Social factors	Impoverished family
	Involvement in religious cult
Mental factors	Bloodlust—committed recent attempted murder of civilian
	Suicidal (wrote note)
Motive	Suicide by cop (suspected)
Circumstances	Initiated encounter with officer
	Returned to scene with shotgun
Outcome	Killed by police

Case 12: Ryan Heisler, Twenty

On October 28, 2011, a police officer responded to assist a probation officer at the apartment home of a supervised felon, Ryan Heisler. The officer soon called for assistance on the radio, indicating that he and the suspect were in the parking lot of the location. In the few minutes that elapsed between his call and the arrival of backup officers, Heisler drew a handgun and shot Officer Brad Jones multiple times, killing him. Heisler then stole the officer's handgun, wallet, and key to his patrol car. After crashing the patrol car several blocks away, Heisler fled on foot and was shot by police. Heisler survived multiple gunshot wounds, including a head shot, with critical injuries.

Heisler grew up in Arizona, where he was raised by a single mother and never knew his father. At the age of ten, he became associated with a hip-hop-inspired street gang called the "Juggalos." He was expelled from high school for threatening, fighting, and skipping school. By the time he was eighteen in 2009, he was engaging in petty crime, using drugs, and homeless. Heisler was sent to prison after he and a group of fellow gang members broke into a home where they stole a laptop, cameras, jewelry, and other items that were pawned for drug money.

On the day he was released, in July 2010, Heisler attacked a woman in an alleyway after midnight. Grabbing her from behind and clamping his hand over her mouth, Heisler tried to drag the woman to another location, presumably to commit a sexual assault. The victim in this case was able to claw his face and escaped. Heisler's DNA was found underneath the woman's fingernails. Heisler was not arrested until October 2010 for this offense. He claimed the incident was not as the victim described, but a personal matter that had gotten out of hand. However, he pled guilty to a lesser charge of unlawful imprisonment, hoping to avoid prison time.

He was sentenced to another six months in jail. As he was preparing to finish his prison term, his probation officer made a passionate argument to retain Heisler in custody for an additional six months, given the severity of the offender's potential crime, sexual assault. He wrote:

> The defendant's progress is overshadowed by the escalation in severity of his criminal behavior, lack of deterrent value of probation for this individual and the lasting negative emotional impact suffered by the victim.

The system disagreed, releasing Heisler to community supervision on April 27, 2011. Six months later, he became a cop-killer. An eyewitness account described the actions of the suspect as he shot Officer Jones:

> You could see his face. He [Heisler] was just walking up towards him [Officer Jones], no remorse, just kept shooting. [He] got over on top of him and unloaded the whole gun . . . [then] he grabbed the cop's gun and shot him one more time, with his own gun.

Heisler survived the incident and was apprehended, but it is unlikely that he will recover to stand trial for his crimes. Because of the seriousness of his injuries, he will likely remain in a vegetative state for the rest of his life.

One of the aspects of this case that makes it more disturbing is the use of overkill against the victim officer. Overkill refers to the excessive use of lethal force against a victim. In some cases, overkill means multiple fatal shots were fired *even after the officer was no longer able to resist or fire on the suspect.* Cases that could be classified as overkill include nearly forty percent of officers killed in 2011.

What can lead a suspect to engage in overkill acts? One answer might be mental illness. In some of the cases in this study, the shooters were medically delusional. Another answer might be drug use. Substance abuse of methamphetamine, cocaine, and heroin can lead subjects to perceive reality differently than a normal offender would. Fitting this profile, Heisler was a serious drug abuser who was probably high at the time of the incident. There is one final answer: simple, abject hatred of law enforcement officers. Offenders who can fall into this category are often the hard-core offenders and gang members—often one and the same—like the suspect in this case.

From the mile-high view, the suspect in this case was clearly a convicted felon who had no remorse about his lifestyle of victimization, street crime, and, in the end, murder of a law enforcement officer. However, Heisler's family was shocked to hear of his involvement in the shooting. It appeared that Heisler's family was completely unaware of his ongoing criminal activities. They reported he had been attending substance abuse classes and was looking for work. Shockingly, though, Heisler had been identified by law enforcement as a gang member at the age of ten.

Heisler's age suggests his crime might be better classified with the youngest offenders in this study. A wayward, violent young man, he is most similar to the teen offenders. He is one of only two offenders who were gang members in this age group.

Heisler's case can be summarized as follows:

Name	Heisler, R.
Age	20
Race	W
Gang affiliation or criminal HX	Yes—Juggalos
	Theft, burglary, attempted sex assault
	On probation/parole
	Hardcore criminal
Social factors	Drug use (unknown type)
Mental factors	Facing probation revocation
	High on drugs (suspected)
	Alone with officer
Motive	Avoid arrest for handgun possession
Circumstances	Confronted at home
	Disarmed officer after death
	Led police on high-speed chase in stolen police car
Outcome	Shot by police; in vegetative state

Case 13: Ross Ashley, Twenty-Two

On December 8, 2011, Ross Ashley walked up to the driver's side door of a police officer's car with a gun in his hand. The officer was busy conducting a traffic stop. With no apparent motive, Ashley shot Officer Deriek Crouse in the head and then ran away. About thirty minutes after the shooting, as police converged on him, he committed suicide.

Ashley seemed to be an unlikely murderer, as he was apparently a bright and gifted young man. He graduated from a rural high school in 2007, where he was a running back on the football team. He won numerous academic awards, as well as being a talented athlete. Ashley was offered several scholarships to college when he graduated. He initially selected a University of Virginia (UVA) campus, but later transferred to Radford University, about fifteen miles from the Virginia Tech campus where he would eventually kill a police officer.

A fellow student from the UVA campus later recalled Ashley as prone to depression and angry outbursts. Ashley studied business and was on target to graduate in 2012. Like many undergraduates, he lived in the dorms initially. His resident advisor reported that Ashley got in trouble for routine infractions: breaking a dorm room chair, smoking, and skating in the hallways. In January 2011, Ashley legally purchased the handgun he would use in the shooting from a licensed handgun dealer. In October 2011, Ashley received a speeding ticket for driving thirty-eight miles per hour in a twenty-five miles-per-hour zone. A hearing was set for February 2012. This is the only known contact Ashley had with law enforcement.

A few days before the shooting, Ashley shaved his head. At the time of the shooting, Ashley lived in a second-floor apartment near Radford University. His apartment was managed by a property management service called Gilbert Real Estate. The day before the shooting, Ashley calmly walked into the Gilbert Real Estate office and asked to see the office manager. The receptionist who spoke with Ashley described him as a handsome, clean-cut young man just like hundreds of other college students who leased apartments through the agency. She promptly took Ashley to the woman's office.

Ashley then asked the woman for the keys to her car. At first, she laughed at his request, thinking he was joking. Ashley then pulled out a .40 caliber black handgun and pointed it at her. She produced the keys to her 2011 Mercedes and handed them to Ashley. Ashley then told the women not to do anything stupid and left the location in the stolen car. The women called police and reported the incident. She could not identify the suspect by name, but gave a description to police.

At some point between the time he took the vehicle and the time of the shooting, Ashley drove the stolen Mercedes to the Virginia Tech Transportation Institute and abandoned it on a gravel driveway. It was reported to police as an abandoned vehicle at around 9:30 a.m., approximately three hours before the shooting occurred. After killing Officer Crouse, Ashley fled on foot. As the suspect fled on Washington Street, multiple witnesses called police to report the shooting and a description of the suspect.

At around 1:00 p.m., an officer spotted a suspicious man making furtive movements inside a fenced-in parking lot known as "the cage" about half a mile from the shooting location. As an officer circled back around in his patrol car to investigate, the man—suspect Ashley—committed suicide by shooting himself in the head.

Ashley is the first subject in this study to commit suicide. Although this pattern will become very common among cop-killers in this study, he is the only shooter to do so in the under-age-twenty-five group. Given his strange pattern of behavior in the days before the shooting, including shaving his head and committing an armed robbery and carjacking of his landlord's office manager, Ashley seems to be an offender who, like Butts, underwent a mental change that may point to the onset of bipolar disorder. Unlike Butts, Ashley had no reported history of drug or alcohol use. He may have just simply "snapped" and vented his rage on law enforcement.

Ashley's case can be summarized as follows:

Name	Ashley, R.
Age	22
Race	W
Gang affiliation or criminal HX	No
Social factors	None
Mental factors	Bipolar (suspected)
Motive	None identified
Circumstances	Initiated encounter with officer
	Ambush and execution of officer
	Fled on foot
Outcome	Committed suicide

Discussion: Age

Despite our society's embrace of the fixed age of maturity, we see offenders in this group who might be better classified as adolescent in their actions, because of their inability to plan or anticipate consequences. There is a very specific age pattern to offenders in this group, but is also seen in the teen offenders. Perhaps this is because the transition from adolescence to adulthood is not truly complete by age eighteen.

In the following chart, we can see clusters of these young offenders of certain ages, with peaks every three years—at sixteen, nineteen, and twenty-two:

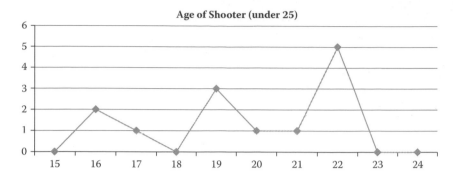

It appears that offenders who are twenty-two years of age encompass the largest number of cop-killers in our study so far. This is also the threshold age of onset for a number of mental illnesses that may affect offenders in their transition to full adulthood. Is this a coincidence or a trend? The answer is not entirely clear.

We will examine this area more closely as we continue in this study.

Discussion: Race

The first case in this group marked the initial appearance of white male shooters in our study. In fact, within the age group of twenty to twenty-four, we see emergence of remarkable diversity when compared with the teen shooters in the previous section. In this age group, white shooters accounted for more than half of the cop-killers, as compared with none of the cop-killers in the teen group.

However, when examined on a larger scale of all cop-killers under age twenty-five, blacks are still seen as outnumbering other offenders by a more than a two-to-one margin, with one American Indian and one Asian shooter.

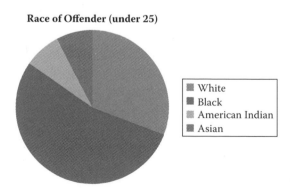

As we move into the examination of older cop-killers, we will see this trend begin to change.

For comparison with offenders, we should also briefly examine the role of the officers' races in this group:

**Race of Officer Killed by
Offenders (under 25)**

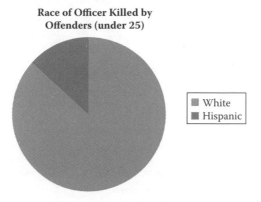

White
Hispanic

Of the fifteen officers in the study killed by offenders under age twenty-five, thirteen (eighty-six percent) were white; two officers were Hispanic.

Discussion: Gang Affiliation

Only one of the cop-killers in this group was affiliated with a gang. This is a significant decrease from the teen offender category, where every offender was involved in gang activity.

It may be that by the time an offender reaches age twenty, he is less likely to engage in a deadly assault incident on law enforcement because of his maturity level. An alternative explanation might be that many gang members who are hard-core offenders are incarcerated by the age of twenty-one, only to be released several years later. Perhaps, as with studies on initiating drug use, initiation into gang activity for young men who have "aged out" of the vulnerable adolescent period by age twenty is rare.

Gang membership by age of offender is shown in the following chart:

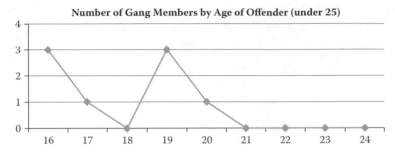

We may see the gang membership trend go up with other age groups later in the study.

Discussion: Criminal History

The offenders in this group include some unexpected murderers. Several of the offenders had no criminal history, including three of the four white cop-killers. Of those offenders who have a criminal history, many demonstrate the same kinds of criminal history. The top five offenses are shown in the following chart:

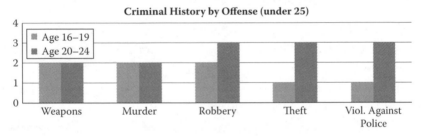

Most often, cop-killers under age twenty-five have prior arrests or convictions for armed robbery (thirty-eight percent), followed by weapons (thirty percent), episodes of violence against law enforcement, theft, and murder (thirty percent). Although it is not shown in the diagram, burglary and drugs were also seen as a common criminal history for cop-killers under twenty-five years of age in this study.

Discussion: Social Factors

The social factors affecting this group of offenders are sundry and diverse. Let us look at the comparisons of offenders in this group across the cases:

Butts	Troubled childhood
	High school dropout
	Alcohol and marijuana use
Simms	Impoverished family background
	Family members present
	Gangster lifestyle
Haydel	Military training
	Family members present
	Obsessive relationship
Tiger	Made suicide-by-cop statement
	Alcohol and marijuana use
White	Impoverished family background
	Involvement in religious cult
Heisler	Drug use (unknown type)
Ashley	None

Mental illness, which was not apparent in the teen group, makes its first appearance with this group. Butts is our first cop-killer who could be labeled as bipolar (suspected). His law-abiding behavior suddenly turned deadly after one contact with police.

The same is true of Ashley. He had led a stable life and was preparing to graduate from college when he suddenly executed a police officer on the campus of Virginia Tech. White may also fall into this category. His family claimed he had been "brainwashed" by a religious cult. However, the so-called cult seemed to be fairly benign in its teachings, emphasizing nonviolence and peace, albeit through emphasizing the belief in a superior race. White's suicide note did reference his self-professed inability to follow the cult's rules as a reason for his final acts.

Simms and Heisler have the more typical hard-core criminal profile seen with many older offenders. Each was a convicted felon involved with drugs and/or gangs, and each was apparently remorseless about his criminal behavior. Interestingly, these types of offenders survive deadly encounters more often than other types of offenders in this study.

Given his criminal history, Tiger could be characterized as an offender who was simply angry and hostile to police. Just weeks before the shooting, he had approached other officers while armed with a knife. He also stated he wanted to die in a suicide-by-cop encounter.

Tiger may have been mentally ill, but he was also overtly criminal in his behavior and history.

At least three of the offenders—Butts, Simms, and White—came from a disadvantaged or troubled family background. This pattern is similar to that of several of the teen offenders, including Lindsey, Dail, and Carter. A history of drug and alcohol use is also prevalent in this age group.

Discussion: Mental Factors

Examining the mental factors, we can see some definite trends in the behaviors and functioning states of these offenders.

Let us examine them side by side:

Butts	Bipolar (suspected)
	Crime in progress
	Alone with officer
Simms	Bloodlust—committed recent murder of civilian
	Imminent arrest for warrant served at his home
	Family members present
	Prior contact with victim officer
Haydel	Bloodlust—committed recent murder of civilian
	Involved in escape from crime scene
	Alone with officer
Tiger	Gave false identity
	High on alcohol and marijuana
White	Bloodlust—attempted recent murder of civilian
	Suicidal (wrote note)
Heisler	Facing probation revocation
	High on drugs (suspected)
	Alone with officer
Ashley	Bipolar (suspected)

Two offenders initiated the deadly encounter with police. However, several of the offenders in this age group can be classified in the following states: high on drugs/alcohol, mentally ill (suspected), bloodlust, and/or alone with a single officer. As with the teen group, we continue to see offenders in this age group who are recent murderers in a state of "bloodlust," engaged in a homicidal series of actions against civilians that ends with the killing of a police officer.

Compared with the teen offenders, we also begin to see some new trends:

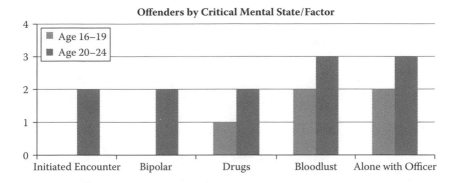

Offenders by Critical Mental State/Factor

Nearly half of the offenders in this group were alone with the officer they killed, which may have led them to believe that they could escape apprehension for the offense. However, this was a wrong assumption. Every cop-killer in this study was apprehended or killed by law enforcement.

Discussion: Motives

Like the teen offenders, most of the offenders in this group were facing imminent arrest for a warrant or active crime in progress.

Let us examine the motives of the subjects in this group in side-by-side comparison:

Butts	Avoid arrest for stealing vehicle
Simms	Avoid arrest on warrant
Haydel	Avoid arrest for murder
Tiger	Avoid arrest for handgun possession by felon
	Suicide by cop
White	Suicide by cop (suspected)
Heisler	Avoid arrest for handgun possession
Ashley	None identified

Clearly, there is a trend. The most common motive by far in this age group and the teen group is to avoid imminent arrest for a crime. These offenders are wanted by police as a result of an arrest warrant, extant illegal conduct (e.g., felon carrying a handgun), or during a crime in progress.*

Motive of Offender (under 25)

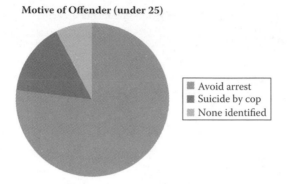

Legend:
- Avoid arrest
- Suicide by cop
- None identified

None of the teen offenders demonstrated a desire to be killed by law enforcement in a suicide-by-cop encounter. The initial appearance of this motive in the age group twenty to twenty-four may predict a shift in older populations toward a different set of motivations to kill law enforcement officers, including the desire for self-annihilation.

Discussion: Circumstances

What were the circumstances of the encounters with police that led to the deadly outcomes in this group? Let us examine these events side by side:

Butts	Burglary in progress
	Shooter disarmed officer when confronted
Simms	Warrant service
	Shot and killed multiple police officers
Haydel	Confronted in hotel stairwell
	Disarmed officer after death
	Booby-trapped officer's body
Tiger	Pedestrian stop
	Shot three officers, killing two
White	Initiated encounter with officer
	Returned to scene with shotgun
Heisler	Confronted at home
	Disarmed officer after death
	Led police on high-speed chase in stolen police car

---

* Recall that all six teen offenders had the same motive: to avoid imminent arrest.

Ashley	Initiated encounter with officer
	Ambush and execution of officer
	Fled on foot

Interestingly, we have two shooters—White and Ashley—who initiated contact with police. Most of the offenders in this age group were either the subjects of warrants or calls to police:

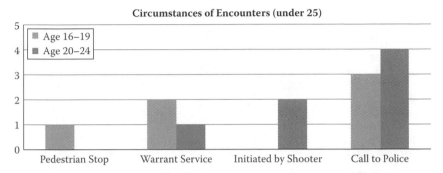

Circumstances of Encounters (under 25)

The most common circumstance for this age group leading to contact with law enforcement was a call to police.* Unlike the teen offenders, only one offender in this group was the subject of a warrant service operation.

Discussion: Outcomes

Although every officer in this study was killed, an examination of the outcome of the incident for offenders provides some interesting data. Let us examine the cases side by side:

Butts	Shot by police; captured
Simms	Killed by police
Haydel	Captured by police
Tiger	Killed by police
White	Killed by police
Heisler	Shot by police; vegetative state
Ashley	Committed suicide

---

* The shooters who were subjects of calls to police included teen shooters Lindsey (burglary in progress), Williams (disturbance in park), and Carter (shots fired). Shooters from this age group included Butts (burglary in progress), Haydel (shots fired), Tiger (disturbance involving alcohol), and Heisler (assist probation officer). As we continue in the study, we will differentiate the types of calls.

In significant contrast to the teen shooters, only one offender in this age group survived without injury. One committed suicide. The rest of the offenders were shot and/or killed by police.

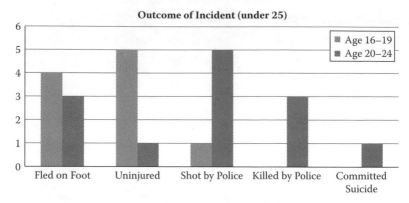

Outcome of Incident (under 25)

Thus, the most common outcome for deadly encounters with this age group involved the death of the shooter at the hands of police who returned fire. This provides an interesting contrast to the teen offenders, who were more likely to flee on foot and much more likely to survive the deadly confrontation uninjured.

Conclusion

Among shooters in the twenty to twenty-four age group:

- Most of the cop-killers in this age group were black or white males who were twenty-two years of age.
- All except one shooter used a handgun in the incident.
- Most cop-killers in this age group had a criminal history, including theft, robbery, murder, and/or violence against police.
- Only one shooter was a gang member.
- Most were the subject of a call to police and were seeking to avoid arrest at the time of the incident.
- Nearly half had committed another murder prior to killing a police officer.
- Nearly half were alone with the officer at the time of the shooting.
- Most were shot by police, including nearly half who were killed by police. One shooter committed suicide.

Bibliography

Adams, D., and Retting, A. "Details Trickle Out in Shooting of Tech Officer," *Roanoke Times,* December 11, 2011, p. A1.

Anderson, C. "Miami Shootout Suspect Considered Career Criminal," Associated Press, January 22, 2011, Miami, FL: APO.

Associated Press. "Police Identify 2 Officers Killed during Shootout," Associated Press Online, January 20, 2011, Miami, FL: APO.

———. "Records Show SD Shooting Suspect Had Criminal Past," August 4, 2011, Rapid City, SD: APO.

———. "2nd Rapid City Police Officer Dies from Shootout," August 8, 2011, Rapid City, SD: APO.

———. "Autopsy Results in Memphis Officer's Death," October 15, 2011, Memphis, TN: APO.

———. "Glendale Officer Dies after Late-Night Shooting," October 29, 2011, Glendale, AZ: APO.

Bailey, C. "Parents of Man Charged in 2 Hotel Shooting Deaths: 'We Know He Did It,'" *Commercial Appeal,* July 5, 2011. Retrieved February 23, 2012 from http://www.commercialappeal.com/news/2011/jul/05/parents-man-charged-2-hotel-shooting-deaths-say-th/html

Bailey, C., and Callahan, J. "Gunfire and a Premonition; Details Still Hazy, with No Charges Yet and Possible Family Tie Adding Irony," *Commercial Appeal,* July 5, 2011, p. A1.

Beasley, A., Ovalle, D., and Burnett, J. "The Killer: Career Criminal with 'Savage' Tattoo," *Miami Herald,* January 20, 2011, Miami, FL: TMH.

Blumenstock, K. "Ross T. Ashley's Motive Sought in Virginia Tech Murder of Deriek Crouse," December 13, 2011. Retrieved April 27, 2012 from http://www.wusa9.com/cleanprint/?unique=1335451715253

Brokaw, C. "Chief: Suspect in SD Police Shootout Dies," Associated Press, August 3, 2011, Pierre, SD: APO.

Brown, J. "New Details Emerge on Fatal Shooting of Two Miami-Dade Officers," *Miami Herald,* January 23, 2011, Miami, FL: TMH.

Burks, M. "Slain Officer's Gesture to Boy in McDonald's Captures Mourners," *Speak City Heights,* August 15, 2011 [website]. Retrieved March 15, 2012, from Burnett, J. "Johnny Simms' Mother Struggles to Explain Son's Demise," *Miami Herald,* January 22, 2011, p. 20.

Burton, L. 2011. Investigative narrative: Dejon Marquee White [autopsy report]. San Diego (CA) medical examiner.

Callahan, J., and Goetz, K. "Deadly Dispute; MPD Officer Slain after Responding to Call Downtown," *Commercial Appeal,* July 4, 2011, p. A1.

CNN. "Video from Slain Virginia Tech Officer's Car Shows Man with Gun," December 9, 2011, Blacksburg, VA: CNN Wire.

———. "Police Try to Uncover What Led to Virginia Tech Shooting," December 9, 2011, Blacksburg, VA: CNN Wire.

CNN/Reuters. "Shootout Kills 2 Miami Police," *Chicago Tribune,* January 21, 2011, p. 19.

Davis, K. "Video Shows Officer's Final Moments," *San Diego Union-Tribune,* August 17, 2011, p. B1.

Davis, K., and Baker, D. "Suspect's Family Stunned," *San Diego Union-Tribune,* August 9, 2011, p. A1.

Davis, K., Baker, D., and Shroder, S. "City Mourns Officer," *San Diego Union-Tribune,* August 8, 2011, p. A1.

Dodson, A. "Midland Native, Slain Officer Mourned," *Bay City Times,* August 12, 2011, p. 3.

Duara, N. "Oregon Police Chief Killed in Struggle with Suspect," Associated Press Online, January 6, 2011, Rainier, OR: AP.

———. "Witnesses Recount Oregon Shootout That Killed Officer," Associated Press Online, January 6, 2011, Rainier, OR: AP.

Dumond, C. "Same Gun Used in Both Fatal Shootings at Virginia Tech," *News and Advance,* December 9, 2011, Lynchburg, VA: TN&A.

Gabbatt, A. "Virginia Tech Shooting Captured on Slain Police Officer's Dash Camera," *Guardian Unlimited,* December 9, 2011, London: GU.

Gangloff, M. "Campus Seeks Answers after Virginia Tech Officer Killed," *Roanoke Times,* December 9, 2011, Roanoke, VA: TRT.

———. "Police Identify Virginia Tech Shooter as Radford University Student," *Roanoke Times,* December 9, 2011, Roanoke, VA: TRT.

Gangloff, M., and Valencia, J. "Motive Still a Mystery," *Roanoke Times,* December 10, 2011, p. A1.

Goetz, K. "Head Wounds Killed Officer Warren," *Commercial Appeal,* October 15, 2011, p. B1.

Gotfredson, D. "Family Claims Gunman Who Killed SDPD Officer Was Brainwashed," CBS 8 [website] October 1, 2011. Retrieved March 16, 2012, from http://www.cbs8.com/story/15592688

Graham, L. "Radford University Thought SUV Theft Was Isolated Event," *Roanoke Times,* December 13, 2011, Blacksburg, VA: McClatchy-Tribune Business News.

Halverstadt, L. "Slain Glendale Officer 'Loved to Help People,'" *Arizona Republic,* November 2, 2011, p. 4.

IBTimes. "Killed South Dakota Officer Was Michigan Native," August 3, 2011, Rapid City, SD: Newstex, LLC.

———. "Virginia Tech Gunman Ross Ashley a Two-Sided Figure, Motive Still Unknown," December 13, 2011. Retrieved April 27, 2012, from http://www.ibtimes.com/art/services/print.php?article id = 266410

KSWB-TV. "Officer Shot to Death Was Marine Reservist," McClatchey-Tribune Business News, August 7, 2011, San Diego, CA: KSWB.

Laboy, S. "2 Officers, Suspect Killed during Miami Shootout," Associated Press, January 21, 2011, Miami, FL: APO.

Lammers, D. "Investigators: Officers' Use of Force Justified," Associated Press, August 23, 2011, Sioux Falls, SD: APO.

Lewis, B. "Virginia Tech Shooter ID'd: Ross Truett Ashley, 22, Had No Ties to Officer or the University," *Lewiston Morning Tribune,* December 10, 2011, Blackburg, VA: TPS.

Major, J. "Father Recalls Fallen Officer as a Generous, Giving Person," WLBT, July 6, 2011. Retrieved February 23, 2012, from http://www.wlbt.com/story/15036083

McClatchey Newspapers. "2 Miami Officers Killed by Suspect; Police Were Trying to Serve a Warrant," *Buffalo News,* January 21, 2011, p. A5.

McKenzie, K. "Suspect's Family: 'We Know He Did It'; Accused Killer Charged in Double Homicide at Hotel Tells Police of Using Military Tactics," *Commercial Appeal,* July 6, 2011, p. A1.

Montgomery, D. "Shooting Suspect Had Long History of Trouble," *Rapid City Journal,* January 21, 2011. Retrieved March 14, 2012 from http://bit.ly/n8CHfe

Ovalle, D. and Weaver, J. "Miami-Dade's Top Cop: Fallen Officers Did All They Could," *Miami Herald,* January 22, 2011, p. 1.

Perry, T. "Killer Signaled Officer before He Opened Fire; San Diego Cop Shot in His Patrol Car Had Just Returned from Tour of Duty in Afghanistan," *Los Angeles Times,* August 8, 2011, p. 1.

———. "Suspect in San Diego Officer Slaying Left Rambling Suicide Note," *L.A. Now,* August 8, 2011, San Diego, CA: Newstex.

———. "'There's an Officer Shot,'" *Los Angeles Times,* August 21, 2011, p. 1.

"Police Radio Transmissions Tell Story of Officer's Shooting," *San Diego Union-Tribune,* August 9, 2011, p. A7.

Pollock, J. 2011. A private investigator's analysis of the Virginia Tech murder [blog post]. Retrieved May 15, 2012, from http://www.bulldogpi.com/2011/12/17/a-private-investigators-analysis-of-the-virginia-tech-murder

Roberts, L. "Suspect's Family Trying to Understand," *Arizona Republic,* November 1, 2011, p. B1.

Sainz, A. "Mississippi Man Charged in Shooting of Memphis Officer," Associated Press, July 6, 2011, Memphis, TN: APO.

Sampson, Z. "Virginia Tech Gunman Changed Clothes after Shooting Cop," Associated Press, December 9, 2011, Blacksburg, VA: APO.

———. "Virginia Tech Has Another Violent Day," *Lewiston Morning Tribune,* December 9, 2011, Blacksburg, VA: Tribune Publishing Company.

Santana, S. "Broward Neighbors Recall Slain Officers," *Sun-Sentinel,* January 21, 2011, p. 1A.

Shan, J. "San Diego Police Officer Shot in Head in Critical Condition, Suspect Later Killed by Other Officers," *Hinterland Gazette,* August 7, 2011, San Diego, CA: Newstex.

South Dakota Division of Criminal Investigation. Rapid City police department shooting summary, August 23, 2011.

Spagat, E. "San Diego Officer Dies; Suspect Left Suicide Note," Associated Press, August 8, 2011, San Diego, CA: APO.

———. "San Diego Police Killing Suspect Seemed Untroubled," Associated Press, August 8, 2011, San Diego, CA: APO.

State News Service. "Officer Who Died in Shooting Was High-Ranking CAP Cadet," August 9, 2011, Rapid City, SD: SNS.

Targeted News Service. "Rapid City Police Department Officer Involved Shooting Summary Released," August 23, 2011, Pierre, SD: TNS, LLC.

Terry, L., and Tomlinson, S. "Man Erratic before Killing of Police Chief," *Oregonian,* January 7, 2011, Portland, OR: TOSE.

Tomlinson, S., and Bernstein, M. "Rainer Mourns Fallen Police Chief," *Oregonian—Sunrise Ed.,* January 6, 2011, Portland, OR: TOSE.

Toppo, G. "State Police: Virginia Tech Gunman Acted Alone," *USA Today,* December 9, 2011, Blacksburg, VA: Gannett News Service.

"Tracking Gunman's Steps," *Virginian-Pilot,* December 10, 2011, p. A1.

Vela, H. "Officer Shot and Killed" [video], ABC15 News, November 1, 2011. Retrieved April 21, 2012, from http://www.fugitive.com/2011/11/04/glendale-police-officer

Wang, A. "Wounded Glendale Officer Dies," *Arizona Republic,* October 30, 2011, p. A1.

3

DETERIORATION: COP-KILLERS IN THEIR LATE TWENTIES

Overview

In this chapter, we will examine ten cases involving shooters aged twenty-five to twenty-nine. This age group is the largest group of shooters in our study. The ten cases include:

- **Lee Welch**, who killed an officer after killing his wife and taking his young daughter as a hostage
- **Jesse Mathews**, who killed an officer during the robbery of a pawn shop
- **Cesar Leon**, who killed an officer during a traffic stop
- **Jayson Eggenberg**, who killed an officer who intervened in a roadside argument between him and his estranged wife
- **Matthew Connor**, who killed an officer who came to his home to serve a warrant for his arrest
- **Joshua Russell**, who killed an officer during a foot pursuit
- **Christopher Hodges**, who killed an officer who stopped to investigate during a roadside argument between him and his girlfriend
- **Skyler Barbee**, who executed an officer who was leaving a call at his neighbor's home
- **Lamont Pride**, who murdered an officer while fleeing a robbery
- **Alan Sylte**, who killed an officer who responded to a call of domestic violence at his girlfriend's home

In this group, we will begin to see a change in the circumstances in which these offenders encounter law enforcement and the outcomes of the incidents. Obsessive relationships, deteriorating marriages, and involvement in crimes in progress compose the bulk of the backstory of these cases.

Of these shooters, seventy percent were killed during the incident. Surprisingly, they were not killed by police. The vast majority committed suicide.

Case 14: Lee Welch, Twenty-Seven

On February 18, 2011, Poughkeepsie, New York, police received a call reporting shots fired in a parking lot near the city's train station. Upon arrival, Officer John Falcone and other officers saw the suspect, Lee Welch, holding a toddler in his arms and waving a .380 handgun. Welch had been shot once in the chest and was trying to leave the scene on foot. Officer Falcone got close to Welch and wrenched the three-year-old girl out of Welch's grasp, handing her off to a bystander. Welch began to run, then fired twice at police, striking Officer Falcone once in the head, killing him. As he was taken to the ground, Welch was able to fire a final shot into his own head, fatally wounding himself.

After Welch committed suicide, police located his wife, Jessica, inside a parked car. She had been shot twice in the head and did not survive. The toddler involved in the incident was Forever Welch, the couple's daughter. She was unharmed.

Welch had spent the last ten years of his life in a volatile relationship with his wife. After more than eight years together and two children of their own, he finally married her. They had been married just eighteen months when his wife left him for the last time.

Before the Welches were even married, the violence between them had already begun. Two years before he killed a police officer, Welch threw a large rock through the window of a vehicle where his wife and two children were sitting during a domestic dispute. Jessica filed charges and Lee turned himself in two days later. He was charged with two misdemeanors—damaging a vehicle and endangering a child. However, the Welches stayed together and married later that same year.

Three weeks before the shooting, Welch was arrested for family violence assault on his wife. He posted one thousand dollars' bail and, three days later, was arrested for violating a protective order. This time, he posted a twenty thousand dollar bond. He was out on bond at the time he shot and killed his wife, Officer Falcone, and himself.

Two weeks before she was killed, Jessica left her husband. A few days later, Jessica got a text from Welch. He wanted to meet her to give back her car, a Chevrolet Blazer. Jessica's mother insisted that she forget about the car, that Welch could not be trusted. However, Jessica told her mother that he had said he knew she was not going to come back. She agreed to meet him in a Poughkeepsie parking lot near the train station. Jessica caught a train, bringing their three-year-old daughter, Forever, with her.

After the shooting, the media interviewed the suspect's mother. She said:

> I feel so sorry for the officer . . . [Welch] loved her . . . [but] my son was a sick-minded individual. There are a lot of sick-minded individuals and there is no help for them.

Jessica's mother added:

> He was very controlling. He had to control every aspect of her life.

Welch was driven to murder his wife rather than lose her, even though his daughter was in the car with them to witness the event. He could envision no life after Jessica, so he shot her and then himself. However, he chose not to shoot himself in the head—as he had done to his wife—and shot himself in the chest instead. He quickly discovered that he did not die right away. His plan may have been to die slowly alongside his wife, but when faced with the intervention of arriving police, he suddenly changed his mind. Grabbing his small daughter, he tried to flee with her as a hostage. The question is: What was Welch planning to do?

It is no coincidence that Welch shot the same officer who took his child from his arms. Reverting to a very primitive state, bleeding profusely from his self-inflicted wound to the chest, the suspect certainly felt rage and helplessness as his child was snatched away. Welch felt himself losing control, trapped and bested by police—as he had been more than once in the confines of his relationship with Jessica. He channeled all of his emotion and rage into the most convenient target available: the officer who had just taken his child by force. Welch fired his gun intentionally at the officer, killing the man he felt was most responsible for his deteriorating situation.

Welch's case can be summarized as follows:

Name	Welch, L.
Age	27
Race	B
Gang affiliation or criminal HX	Domestic violence (×2)
Social factors	Separated from wife
	Obsessive relationship
Mental factors	Bloodlust—committed recent murder of civilian
	Had shot self in chest (suicide attempt)
Motive	Suicide by cop
Circumstances	Shots-fired call
	Had shot self in chest (suicide attempt)
	Hostage (child)
Outcome	Committed suicide

Case 15: Jesse Mathews, Twenty-Five

On April 2, 2011, a silent alarm was triggered at the US Money Shops, a pawnbroker located in a strip mall shopping center. Sgt. Tim Chapin and three other officers responded to the call. Once police arrived at the location, a masked robber—suspect Jesse Mathews—began firing an automatic rifle through the glass front of the business at police. One of the suspect's rounds struck a police officer nonfatally in the back.

Mathews then fled out a side door. Along with officers on foot, Sgt. Chapin pursued Mathews in his patrol car. After approximately 200 yards, Mathews turned and fired at Sgt. Chapin, striking the vehicle's windshield. Sgt. Chapin then struck Mathews with the patrol car, knocking him to the ground. As he fell, Mathews dropped his gun. Sgt. Chapin exited the patrol car, took out his Taser, and ordered Mathews to stay on the ground. When Mathews tried to get up, Sgt. Chapin fired the ECW (electronic control weapon), but it had no effect on Mathews. With his back to the officer, Mathews reached inside his jacket with his left hand and drew a second pistol.

Mathews slowly walked toward Sgt. Chapin, firing a handgun at him. As Mathews neared, Sgt. Chapin fired repeatedly, striking Mathews multiple times in the chest and legs. However, Mathews continued to close the distance and shot Sgt. Chapin once in the face, killing him instantly. As he tried to flee, Mathews was taken into custody by a citizen armed with a handgun who witnessed the murder.

Mathews was a convicted felon who had escaped from a halfway house after serving almost eight years in prison for armed robbery. Mathews had numerous tattoos of handguns and other weapons on his chest and arms, along with the personal slogan "tools of the trade."

Mathews was born into a family with a history of legal troubles. About a year before Mathews's birth, his mother completed a prison term in Florida for manslaughter. In the late 1990s, the family moved to Colorado where, at age thirteen, Mathews was arrested for stealing a car and burglary. He soon dropped out of high school and went to work as a grocery store bagger.

In 2002, the seventeen-year-old went on a crime spree, robbing eight different locations and individuals, including a church, at gunpoint. He was charged as an adult with thirty-one counts, including armed robbery, kidnapping, and handgun possession. Four months later, he entered a guilty plea to a single count of armed robbery and received a twenty-year prison sentence.

Mathews obtained his GED in prison and attended a variety of seminars in anger resolution, Biblical studies, and a vocational janitorial program. As soon as he was eligible, Mathews applied for parole; after being rejected the first time, he was successful in his application and was released to a halfway house in Colorado Springs in late 2010, after being incarcerated almost eight years. Within months, Mathews returned to his violent, criminal ways.

In January, Mathews signed the halfway house log to indicate he was going shopping at Kmart; instead, he robbed a Carl's Jr. fast-food restaurant. In February, Mathews signed out to go to work; instead, he borrowed his girlfriend's car and robbed a Cash American pawn shop at gunpoint, acquiring sixteen handguns, jewelry, and fifteen thousand dollars in cash. Mathews and his girlfriend spent some of the money at a local hotel before Mathews returned to the halfway house with five guns taped to his body.

On February 12, Mathews signed out to go to work. Instead, he wired money to his sister, Rachel, who then bought a plane ticket to Colorado. Over the next several days, Mathews stayed in different hotel rooms in the Colorado Springs area rented by his girlfriend and sister. When he did not return to the halfway house, a warrant was issued for his arrest.

On February 14, Mathews robbed a local Walgreens, adding to his cash supply. Mathews and his sister then traveled together by bus from Colorado to Nashville, Tennessee, using fake names. Rachel's boyfriend agreed to drive them from Nashville to the family home in Asheville, North Carolina, for a thousand dollars in cash.

On March 6, Mathews moved himself and his parents into the Microtel Inn in Chattanooga, Tennessee, using a fake name. Ten days later, Mathews set his parents up in a rental house nearby. Mathews paid two months' rent in cash, telling the landlord he earned the money while serving in the military. Mathews then moved in with his new girlfriend, an employee who worked at the Microtel Inn where he had recently been staying.

On March 27, Mathews and his new girlfriend attended a gun show in Chattanooga. After speaking with a dealer at the show, Mathews telephoned his father and said:

Bring the family collection.

Within an hour, the elder Mathews brought twelve handguns to his son, who traded three of them for an M-4 assault rifle. The M-4 was one of two firearms that he would use to rob the US Money Shops. Mathews reportedly carried the M-4 around in a guitar case after purchasing it.

Six days later, Mathews walked into the US Money Shops armed with a rifle, wearing a vest and a mask. He pointed a gun at two employees, forced them to lie on the ground, and ordered one of them to open the safe. One of the men triggered a silent alarm, leading to the police response that took the life of Sgt. Chapin. Mathews survived the incident and awaits a death penalty trial.

Mathews' case can be summarized as follows:

Name	Mathews, J.
Age	25
Race	W
Gang affiliation or criminal HX	Armed robbery, kidnapping, handgun possession
Social factors	High school dropout
	Teen offender
	On parole

Mental factors	Crime in progress
	Affinity for guns
Motive	Avoid arrest for armed robbery; felon in possession of firearm
Circumstances	Armed robbery of pawn shop
Outcome	Shot by police; captured

Case 16: Cesar Leon, Twenty-Seven

On May 2, 2011, Officer Rolando Tirado and his partner were working an off-duty job providing security for a mixed-use, private entertainment establishment called El Gran Mercado. The location catered to Hispanics and had been the venue for a 2009 Maricopa County raid in which fifty-three people were arrested. Half of the arrestees were illegal aliens.

The location was hosting a dance for around a hundred people that had ended around midnight. The gates of the business had been closed and the officers were preparing to end their tour when they spotted a Chevrolet Tahoe driving erratically in the parking lot. Officer Tirado stopped the vehicle and contacted the driver. Two other men were inside the vehicle, including the suspect, Cesar Leon. During the encounter, Leon exited and circled around the back of the vehicle. Leon then shot the officer twice in the back and turned the gun on the officer's partner.

Leon shot Officer Tirado's partner at least three times, striking him in the shoulder, neck, and lower body. Officer Paz returned fire, killing the suspect. Both officers were wearing full police uniforms and vests. Although he survived, it is not clear if Officer Paz will make a full recovery.

The shooter Leon was a permanent legal resident with an extensive and violent criminal history. He had spent several years in a California prison before moving to Arizona. He was born in Mexico and became a permanent legal US resident before his criminal history began. In 2004, he pled guilty to a charge of being involved in a street gang. The following year, in 2005, he was convicted of vehicle theft and possession of a firearm by a felon. At the age of twenty-one, Leon received a nine-year sentence in a California prison.

After serving at least five years, Leon was paroled and moved to Arizona. His activities before the night of the incident are unknown. Until he shot Officer Tirado in the back, he was just another convicted felon out on parole. He did not survive to face trial in this case.

Traffic stops, especially those conducted in the darkness of night, can be very dangerous activities for police officers. Having little or no information about the driver and passengers, the lone officer must initiate contact and request identification, often with only a radio or dispatcher to back him up. Having a backup officer can reduce but not eliminate the possibility of a violent encounter. Leon took advantage of the circumstances to attempt to prevent his rearrest for possession of a firearm by using lethal force. He was not successful.

Leon's case can be summarized as follows:

Name	Leon, C.
Age	27
Race	H
Gang affiliation or criminal HX	Yes—unknown gang
	Vehicle theft, possession of firearm by felon
Social factors	On parole
Mental factors	None
Motive	Avoid arrest for possession of firearm by felon
Circumstances	Traffic stop—passenger
Outcome	Killed by police

Case 17: Jayson Eggenberg, Twenty-Seven

On June 6, 2011, Deputy Keith Bellar drove up on an accident that had just occurred involving a red pickup and a gray car. Suspect Jayson Eggenberg and his wife were present at the scene. As Deputy Bellar placed his vehicle in park, Eggenberg walked up to the patrol car on the driver's side. Before the officer could react, the man shot him once in the forehead. After shooting Deputy Bellar, the suspect walked behind his wrecked truck to stand in front of his wife's car window. He then shot himself once in the head (Greenberg 2011).

Eggenberg had spent his life in Dickson County, Tennessee, where he graduated from high school in 2002; ironically, he and the victim officer were the same age and graduated the same year. Eggenberg married his wife, Kimberly, in 2007. He worked as a cable television installer and a volunteer fireman, serving on the county rescue squad in the local community for several years. He had no reported criminal history. At some point before the shooting, Eggenberg and his wife separated.

On the day before the shooting, the suspect spent the day fishing with his brother. Afterward, they returned to the brother's home and grilled hot dogs. That night, Eggenberg expressed his concern about his relationship with his wife to another family member, but generally seemed in good spirits. Kimberly Eggenberg was a deep-nights 911 dispatcher for the Dickson Police Department. The morning of the shooting, Eggenberg lay in wait for his wife near her workplace. As she drove past him, Eggenberg followed her and then crashed into her car, forcing her off the road in a residential area. As Eggenberg approached his wife's car, Deputy Bellar pulled up to the scene in his patrol car and became the sole focus of Eggenberg's wrath. Neither man survived the incident. Kimberly Eggenberg was not injured during the incident.

Eggenberg had reportedly been diagnosed with bipolar disorder. Along with offenders who are on alcohol and drugs at the time of the shootings, bipolar offenders are also unpredictable and violent under the right circumstances. Shooter Daniel Butts (Case 1) already illustrated the risks to police who confront the bipolar offender in the throes of a manic or depressive episode. Eggenberg is not the last bipolar subject in this study.

In addition to his diagnosis, Jayson Eggenberg also demonstrates parallels with the shooter Lee Welch (Case 14), who murdered his wife and tried to commit suicide in front of the couple's young daughter. Both men were faced with the dissolution of a marriage and unable to cope with the consequences of their actions and failures in a love relationship.

Clearly, Eggenberg was in crisis. It is very likely that Eggenberg's plan was to kill his wife and then himself. Had Deputy Bellar arrived five minutes later, Eggenberg's plan would have succeeded; the police would have arrived at the roadside scene of a murder–suicide. In truth, like the other women who are romantically involved with the unstable, high-risk offenders in these incidents, Kimberly Eggenberg is very lucky to be alive. Her emotional trauma in witnessing two violent deaths must be horrific.

Eggenberg's case can be summarized as follows:

Name	Eggenberg, J.
Age	27
Race	W
Gang affiliation or criminal HX	No
Social factors	Separated from wife
	Obsessive relationship
Mental factors	Bipolar
Motive	Unknown
Circumstances	Minor traffic accident
	Crime in progress (murder–suicide)
Outcome	Committed suicide

Case 18: Matthew Connor, Twenty-Five

Two days before he killed a police officer, suspect Matthew Connor was experiencing a delusional and violent episode at his father's home. Connor got into an argument with his father, sister, girlfriend, and a family friend over an unknown matter. During the argument, Connor pulled out a handgun and fired several times into the ground, threatening to kill them all. Afterward, he penned a suicide note and told his family he would commit "suicide by cop." The family contacted the police and turned over Connor's suicide note to the authorities.

After securing a warrant, a task force of local and state police and the US Marshals went to Connor's home, in a rural setting sixty miles northwest of Philadelphia. When police arrived at around 6:30 p.m., they spoke with Connor's girlfriend. Suddenly, Connor appeared, dressed in full camouflage including a mask and gloves, and fled into the woods behind the home.

The officers pursued Connor, with Officer Kyle Pagerly in the lead. As they topped a small ridge, Officer Pagerly's K-9, Jynx, alerted his handler to the presence of Connor, who was concealed inside a sniper's nest on the hillside. Moments later, Connor stood up holding an assault rifle. When officers ordered him to drop the weapon, he refused and then fired on Officer Pagerly, killing him. He was then killed by police who returned fire.

Matthew Connor was a convicted felon with a history of significant mental illness. When he was seventeen, Connor was convicted of burglary and adjudicated as a delinquent juvenile. Connor dropped out of high school in the eleventh grade and was unable to keep a job because of his deviant behavior. In 2004, when he was eighteen, Connor was diagnosed with schizophrenia and oppositional defiant disorder. He spent nine months as an inpatient in a psychiatric hospital, but the medications were not effective and caused harsh side effects. Connor went off his medications and had difficulty complying with any further treatment. He also began abusing alcohol and street drugs.

Connor was prohibited from purchasing firearms because of his felony conviction, but arranged for his father to purchase an AK-47 for him from a local sporting goods store. The same year, his father retired from a local police department after serving twenty years as a law enforcement officer. Connor also convinced a family friend to purchase three additional handguns for him in 2004 and 2005.

In July 2009, Connor's mother died in a tractor accident on the family property. The suspect was heartbroken, as his mother had been his tireless advocate and caregiver for many years. In October 2010, Connor's father remortgaged the family home to pay for his son's move to Hawaii, where he planned to open a restaurant with his girlfriend. Connor planted banana and coconut trees, which he lovingly tended for months. In May 2011, his partner committed suicide, ending his dream.

On June 2, Connor returned to the family home, feeling that he was a failure. He was too disruptive to live in the house, so Connor routinely slept in a van and a tent he set up on the 12½ acre property. Spending most of his time outdoors, Connor returned to the family home to cook his meals.

Two days before the shooting, on June 27, Connor threatened his family with a handgun before firing several shots into the ground. Connor then placed the handgun in his mouth. Later that day, he penned a suicide note, which he left for his family. Alarmed, his father contacted police and requested their assistance.

However, from his family's perspective, Connor's behavior was not that unusual. Connor's seventy-year-old father later said:

> I wish I had a dollar for every time he had a gun in his mouth.

On the day of the shooting, Connor's father left the home on an errand, but received a call from the suspect around midday. In the call, Connor told his father that he wanted to leave the state. His father later said:

> I don't know what transpired after that to change his mind . . . I [always] did everything I knew how to do to help him.

Connor's seventeen-year-old sister, Claire, returned home just as officers arrived to serve the warrant. She quickly left, afraid of what might happen with her brother. Later, she told investigators she was not surprised at the outcome:

> I knew they were coming for him, and it probably wasn't good. It was just a matter of time.

Connor's father also noted that his son's troubles had multiplied in the weeks before the shooting leading up to the second anniversary of the mother's death on July 5, 2009.

After shooting Officer Pagerly, Connor was killed by officers who returned fire. A search of Connor's body revealed that he was carrying two large knives, two handguns, and a number of high-capacity magazines for the AK-47. Connor's father defended his failed attempts to help his son over the past seven years since his diagnosis, including inpatient treatment, medication, and therapy. He cited the mental health system in the United States as "not very effective."

Taking subjects into custody who have pervasive, serious mental illness can be a deadly business for police officers. Along with bipolar disorder, schizophrenia presents an especially high risk to law enforcement because of the likelihood that a subject with this diagnosis can experience realistic delusions and may see visions or hear voices. Very high levels of paranoia can cause these suspects to take violent, unpredictable action against police.

Connor is the first schizophrenic suspect in our study. He is also the first suspect to fire from a sniper's nest in the woods of a rural area. Both circumstances will be seen again later in the study.

Connor's case can be summarized as the following:

Name	Connor, M.
Age	25
Race	W
Gang affiliation or criminal HX	Burglary

Social factors	High school dropout
	Teen offender
Mental factors	Schizophrenia
	Drug user (unknown type)
	Family members present
	Anniversary marker (death of mother)
	Affinity for guns
Motive	Avoid imminent arrest for warrant
	Suicide by cop
Circumstances	Warrant service
Outcome	Killed by police

Case 19: Joshua Russell, Twenty-Five

On August 24, 2011, Officer Justin Sollohub was patrolling the streets of Anniston, Alabama, in a residential neighborhood on the north side of the city. The officer exited his patrol car to speak with the suspect, Joshua Russell, who was on foot. Russell fled and Officer Sollohub chased him, radioing for assistance. As Officer Sollohub ran around the corner of a house, Russell fired once, striking the officer in the head.

Russell was a convicted felon who was wanted on a warrant for assaulting police at the time of the incident. In 2009, Russell was convicted on drug distribution and obstruction of justice charges. He was sentenced to four concurrent five-year sentences; however, he was released after serving just over a year in prison under the state's "Good Time Law," which promotes early release for cooperative inmates.

After Russell's release, just three months before the shooting, two detectives investigating a theft encountered Russell and another man in a convenience store parking lot. When questioned, Russell stated he did not have any identification on his person and gave police a false name. After a pat-down revealed his identification, the detectives tried to take Russell into custody. Russell punched one of the detectives in the face and fled on foot, escaping capture. Several weeks later, a warrant was issued for his arrest.

Two months later, Russell left his fingerprints at the scene of a residential burglary. It is not clear what Russell may have done to draw the attention of the officer at the time of this incident. However, he had an active warrant at the time he was confronted.

After shooting Officer Sollohub fatally in the head, Russell fled on foot. The suspect was later apprehended about two hundred yards from the scene after an intensive manhunt revealed his identity. Charged with capital murder, Russell may face the death penalty for his crime. In January 2012, the suspect pled not guilty by reason of mental defect. No additional information is available about his claims of diminished responsibility in this offense.

Russell's case can be summarized as follows:

Name	Russell, J.
Age	25
Race	B
Gang affiliation or criminal HX	Drug dealing, assault on police, theft, burglary
Social factors	None
Mental factors	Alone with officer
Motive	Avoid imminent arrest for warrant
Circumstances	Pedestrian stop
	Fled on foot
Outcome	Captured by police

Case 20: Christopher Hodges, Twenty-Six

At around 1:15 a.m. on October 23, 2011, Deputy James Paugh was driving his police motorcycle home from an evening shift at the state fair. Although he was off-duty, he was still in uniform. Spotting a Cadillac on the grassy shoulder, Deputy Paugh passed by and took a close look at the car. Seeing something suspicious, the officer doubled back to the scene and pulled his motorcycle behind the parked vehicle. The driver, Christopher Hodges, opened fire on Deputy Paugh with an M-4 rifle, striking him nine times.

Hodges's early history is not known, but he had no criminal history. He was an active duty member of the Tennessee National Guard and had served with the Third Infantry Division in Iraq in 2007. In May 2011, Hodges was sent from his home in Tennessee for military training in Georgia. Although Hodges was reportedly married and lived with his wife near Memphis, another woman, Raven Harper, reported to police that she had been dating the suspect during his time in Tennessee. Hodges's wife was described by neighbors as also serving in the military.

Hodges had no record of trouble during his years of military service and no history of mental illness or drug use. He was just over two weeks away from successfully completing his training and returning home.

On the night of the incident, Hodges was apparently intoxicated when he got into an argument with Harper while they were at a friend's house. Hodges and his girlfriend left the party, but Hodges became physically violent while in the car. Harper asked Hodges to stop the car, which he did. Enraged, Hodges then got out of the car and went to the trunk to retrieve an M-4 assault rifle. As Harper watched in terror, Hodges began firing the weapon at passing vehicles. Hodges emptied one magazine and loaded another, firing nearly forty rounds before he was confronted by police.

After being shot nine times, the officer was able to return fire, firing three rounds, before the suspect's rounds disabled his handgun. One of the officer's rounds struck the suspect in the left forearm. Officer Paugh collapsed to the ground on the shoulder of the highway beside his toppled motorcycle and died from his wounds. Hodges then hoisted the M-4 to his head and fired once, killing himself.

Christopher Hodges is yet another suspect who was heavily under the influence of alcohol at the time of the shooting. In fact, this study reveals that alcohol use is one of the top characteristics of cop-killers. More often than gang membership, the presence of mental illness, or the use of harder drugs like cocaine, heroin, or marijuana, it is alcohol use that is the most common thread among cop-killers in this study. Although American society often minimizes the role alcohol plays in violence, criminal activity, and other negative behaviors, alcohol use presents a significant risk factor involved in the deaths of police officers.

According to the Centers for Disease Control (CDC), fifty-two percent of Americans aged twelve and older describe themselves as regular alcohol users. Criminal populations report roughly the same degree of alcohol use as the general population, around fifty-one percent. Around six percent are heavy drinkers and fifteen percent are binge drinkers, meaning they consume five or more drinks at a time. This equates to a large group of people who are very impaired due to alcohol use on any given day. Some of these people will inevitably come into contact with law enforcement. Yet, what is the relationship between alcohol or drug use and violent behavior? The answer is not totally clear.

Based on the work of Paul Goldstein, Gilgun (2000) describes three models relating the interaction of substance abuse and violence in a study of convicted felons:

- Economically compulsive
- Systemic
- Psychopharmacological

In the economically compulsive model, offenders commit crimes in order to get money for drugs or, less often, alcohol. This model is well known. Offenders with this kind of relationship with substance abuse will come to law enforcement's attention while trying to flee from a scene or via involvement in stolen goods transactions.

The systemic model refers to the use of violent crime as a means to support illegal drug trafficking activity. In this model, murders are committed to protect turf or to send a message to rival gangs or cartels—often while under the influence of substances, both illicit (street drugs) and licit (alcohol). Law enforcement can be caught up in this kind of incident as officers intervene to protect citizens or investigate these crimes. An example of this kind of incident can be found in the case of Lamont Pride (Case 22), in the latter part of this study.

Finally, in the psychopharmacological model, offenders use drugs and alcohol to increase or decrease certain feelings, such as irritability, irrationality, or anger. Some offenders report using drugs, including alcohol, to get "hyped up," creating a temporary period in which they will act out, commit crimes, and, sometimes, encounter law enforcement. The majority of the offenders in this study are engaged in this kind of substance abuse. An example of this kind of incident can be found in Christopher Hodges's behavior.

Whether the offenders are motivated by the sensation, the cash, or the drug-dealing enterprise itself, the risks to law enforcement officers are high when they must take action in circumstances where offenders are impaired by drugs or alcohol. Police officers and mental health professionals need to understand the role that substance abuse can play in the precipitation of violence toward law enforcement.

Hodges's case can be summarized as follows:

Name	Hodges, C.
Age	26

Race	B
Gang affiliation or criminal HX	None
Social factors	Military training
Mental factors	Girlfriend present
	High on alcohol
Motive	Unknown
Circumstances	Disabled motorist
	Domestic violence
Outcome	Committed suicide

Case 21: Skyler Barbee, Twenty-Five

On December 9, 2011, Sgt. David Enzbrenner was assisting other officers who were serving a nuisance order at a residence. The site of the order was a home that had become littered with scrap metal and junk, in violation of city codes. Suspect Skyler Barbee had occasionally lived across the street from the location with his grandparents.

As the officers returned to their vehicles to clear the scene, Barbee, who was not involved in the call, walked up to Sgt. Enzbrenner in front of numerous witnesses. Without saying a word, Barbee then shot the officer once in the back of the head. He then committed suicide by shooting himself in the head.

Skyler Barbee had a difficult childhood that is shrouded in some mystery. The oldest of four children, Barbee was remembered as a youth who took care of his siblings regularly. In both grade school and high school, Barbee lived with his grandparents in the home across the street from the location where he would eventually kill a police officer.

The reasons for Barbee's absence from his parents' home are not entirely clear, but may have been due to instability or criminal activity in the home. Barbee's father was sentenced to life in prison without parole in Louisiana for armed robbery when Barbee was fifteen. His grandparents stepped in to provide a home for all of the children until the family could stabilize. At the time of the shooting, Barbee lived with his mother and stepfather in Atchison, Kansas.

Barbee had only one known contact with police prior to the murder of Sgt. Enzbrenner. On August 2, 2011—four months before the shooting—Barbee became involved in a disagreement with police officers who were investigating a vehicle burglary. The argument escalated into violence, resulting in the arrest of Barbee for the car burglary, obstruction, and battery of two police officers. Barbee was sentenced to forty-five days in jail. He was released from custody on October 24, 2011. The victim officer in this case was not involved in the August incident.

Barbee seemed to have carried a grudge against police after his arrest in August 2011. After his release, he grew increasingly angry toward law enforcement and the court system. After the shooting, Barbee's grandfather, who was a local reverend, said:

> Skyler was upset at the justice system. It bothered him . . . In the last year or so, he started having emotional problems. The anger consumed him.

So many desperate offenders in this study have reasons to commit murder. They are three-time felons, drug users, fleeing from crimes in progress, or mentally ill. They face the loss of their relationships, families, property, or dignity. Barbee displayed none of these factors. There were no reports of odd behavior, no drug use, no gang activity, and no errant mental breakdown. Barbee was not stopped while driving at high speed, dealing drugs, running from the police, or holding someone hostage. He was an ordinary man on an ordinary day. Why did he choose to kill a police officer on such a day?

Disturbingly, this incident is almost identical to the execution-style shooting of Officer Deriek Crouse by Ross Ashley (Case 13) on the campus of Virginia Tech just one day earlier. Both incidents involved a youthful shooter who approached an officer on foot while the officer was engaged in another enforcement action. Both men chose the shooting victim randomly. Both shooters also committed suicide. Did Skyler Barbee see the news coverage about the Virginia Tech shooting and decide he would become a copycat killer? The answer may never be known. His real motive may have been revenge.

Let us take a closer look at Skyler Barbee and what motivated him. No doubt, Barbee had a troubling childhood. However, despite his challenges, he remained out of law enforcement's view until he was involved in a disturbance over the summer when he was arrested and charged with assaulting police. Was Barbee really guilty of burglarizing a vehicle during this incident or was his crime something more personal in nature?

Four months before the shooting, Barbee argued with officers, resisted arrest, and was charged with three serious offenses. He spent the next several weeks in jail. However, is it possible that Barbee did not commit a vehicle burglary at all, but merely chose that location and time to give police a hard time? Could it be that he was an innocent but belligerent young man who was arrested for "pissing off the police"? Is it possible that Barbee felt he had been mistreated because of his race? If the answers to these questions are yes, it seems to characterize and even explain Barbee's violent episode.

The price of his actions was steep. Motor vehicle burglary can be classified as a felony in Kansas. When he accepted a plea deal and served forty-five days in jail, Barbee may have become a convicted felon as a result of a single consequential encounter with police. What if he was innocent of the burglary charge? What would that kind of experience do to a normal person? Would it make him homicidal? Suicidal?

We cannot know for certain what was in Barbee's mind, but we can examine his means, opportunity, and motivation: his means—a loaded handgun; his opportunity—three police officers across the street from his grandparents' home, aggravating his neighbors with a junk removal order; his motivation—revenge. Barbee wanted revenge in the most classical sense, in order to execute his wrath on the object of his anger and to self-annihilate. And, Barbee was committed to death for himself before he even approached the victim officer.

Barbee's case can be summarized as follows:

Name	Barbee, S.
Age	25
Race	B
Gang affiliation or criminal HX	Vehicle burglary, assault on police
Social factors	Troubled childhood
Mental factors	None
Motive	Unknown
Circumstances	Initiated encounter with officer
	Ambush and execution of officer
Outcome	Committed suicide

Case 22: Lamont Pride, Twenty-Seven

At around 2:20 a.m. on December 12, 2011, a building owner called police to report a burglary in progress at a basement apartment. The first officers to arrive found the tenant of the apartment lying on the floor with a head injury. Two other men were present near the victim when the officers arrived. They explained that they were "good Samaritans" who had come to the apartment after hearing a commotion to see if they could help the victim.

The victim, a Hispanic male, was semiconscious and incoherent; police called an ambulance to transport him to the hospital. As the officers tried to speak with the victim further, they were not aware that two suspects were hiding in another room of the apartment, unable to escape. One of the suspects was Lamont Pride.

Officer Figoski and his partner, Officer Glen Estrada, responded to provide backup. They stationed themselves outside at the foot of the stairs to the basement. As the officers inside the apartment focused on the victim, the two concealed suspects seized the opportunity to flee, running out of the apartment directly into Officers Figoski and Estrada.

Both officers seized the men and began to struggle with them. Officer Figoski fought to restrain Pride while Estrada grappled with the other male. Pride, armed with a 9mm handgun, then fired once at Officer Figoski, striking him in the left cheek. As Officer Figoski fell to the ground, mortally wounded, Pride ran away, leaving his fellow suspect behind. On seeing his partner down, Officer Estrada released the suspect in his grasp and began chasing Pride. After a foot chase over more than four blocks, Pride threw his gun under a parked car and flung his ski mask into the gutter. He was taken into custody at gunpoint.

Officers took the two so-called "good Samaritans," in for further questioning. Within hours, they broke down and admitted they had participated in the robbery and had pretended to be bystanders in an attempt to fool police. The final investigation revealed that four men, including Pride, committed the robbery while a fifth man acted as the getaway car driver. All were described as Latin Kings gang members.

The 9mm Ruger that Pride had used in the shooting had been purchased in a Virginia pawn shop, but was reported as stolen. When recovered, the weapon was "stove-piped," or jammed, with a spent shell casing lodged in the ejection port. Ten live rounds remained in the magazine of the weapon. A search of the basement apartment where Officer Figoski was shot revealed a second handgun, a .38-caliber Smith & Wesson, inside a microwave. The suspects had taken $770 and a cheap watch from the victim.

Pride was also interviewed at length by detectives after his arrest. After waiving his Miranda rights, he claimed that he had gone to the location to purchase marijuana from the victim, saw a gunman, and tried to help the police officers. He then revised his story to describe how he was holding the gun when it went off accidentally. Excerpts of Pride's videotaped interview were released, detailing his far-fetched and changing story.

Pride had a long history of criminal conduct. He had been arrested ten times for crimes ranging from drug possession and sales to grand larceny and criminal trespassing. He also was wanted on a warrant for aggravated assault at the time of the incident.

In January 2006, Pride was arrested for marijuana possession. He was sentenced to jail time. Pride may have become affiliated with the Latin Kings while incarcerated. In 2009, Pride was arrested three separate times in two months. One of the arrests was for robbery with a deadly weapon. He soon progressed to kidnapping and aggravated assault. Pride was finally sentenced to sixteen months in jail. He was released in October 2010.

On August 5, 2011, Pride was involved in a gang fight in Greensboro, North Carolina. The victim in this incident was shot in the leg while running away from the fight. Pride was named as the shooter and an arrest warrant was issued for him.

On November 3, 2011, just a month before the shooting, Pride was inside an apartment in Brooklyn when police came to serve a warrant. Inside the home, police found ten bags of crack cocaine and marijuana. They also found two children living in filthy conditions. Pride was charged with possession of drugs and child endangerment. Police also discovered the active North Carolina warrant on Pride. However, the warrant specified in-state extradition only. After repeated unsuccessful requests by NYPD to have the warrant amended to allow Pride to be extradited, he was arraigned on the New York charges and released.

At the time of the shooting, Pride was living in a Coney Island housing project. His neighbors described the location as a high-crime area:

On weekends, there are shoot-outs, robbery, and drug-dealing.

On the night of the shooting, Pride went to a meeting in a Queens apartment. The suspects believed a man was selling marijuana out of a basement apartment. Targeting a fellow drug dealer would reduce the opportunity that the crime would be reported. By 1 a.m., Pride and his four accomplices had planned the haphazard robbery. They would steal any cash or jewelry they could find and teach the dealer a lesson he would not forget. Instead, Pride became a cop-killer.

Pride's case can be summarized as follows:

Name	Pride, L.
Age	27
Race	B
Gang affiliation or criminal HX	Yes, Latin Kings
	Drug dealing, theft, trespass, child endangerment, gang violence
Social factors	Hard-core criminal
Mental factors	Other suspects present
	Involved in escape from crime scene
Motive	Avoid arrest for crime in progress
Circumstances	Crime in progress—robbery
Outcome	Fled on foot
	Captured by police

Case 23: Alan Sylte, Twenty-Five

At around 8:30 a.m. on December 19, 2011, Officer Shawn Schneider and his partner responded to a domestic disturbance between Alan Sylte, Jr., and his seventeen-year-old girlfriend. The complainant reported that the man had a gun. When police arrived, both Sylte and the girlfriend were inside the home, which was rented by the girlfriend's parents. As the officers approached the home, the girl ran outside. Officers told her to get into the patrol car for her safety and then walked toward the home to confront the suspect.

Sylte then opened fire on the officers from the basement, striking Officer Schneider once in the head. He then engaged in a standoff with police for several hours before committing suicide.

Little is known about Alan Sylte's early history. A Wisconsin native, he played football in high school, but apparently dropped out before earning his diploma. In 2005, Sylte's father died from lung failure. After this time, Sylte had difficulty remaining stable in his own life.

In November 2006, Sylte was the subject of a domestic disturbance call in Somerset, Wisconsin. The call notes indicated:

Possible suicidal male and shotgun involved.

At the time, Sylte's live-in girlfriend told deputies that he pushed her down, punched her in the stomach, and kicked her during the fight. She called police when Sylte went to get a shotgun from the bedroom. Sylte was arrested and charged with misdemeanor battery and disorderly conduct, but the charges were later dismissed. It is likely that the victim refused to cooperate with the prosecution in this case.

Sylte joined the Wisconsin National Guard in 2009. He completed a three-month tour in Iraq just a few months before the shooting occurred. During his deployment, Sylte was assigned to escort a battalion commander, who later said:

He was a smart kid . . . he seemed like a very competent individual.

The commander characterized the zone where Sylte was assigned in Iraq as "very calm," minimizing the possibility that Sylte had been exposed to combat conditions that led to his violent behavior. However, at the time of the shooting, he was being discharged from the Guard for failing to report for required duty each month.

In April 2011, twenty-five-year-old Sylte began dating a seventeen-year-old girl in Lake City, Minnesota. She later described the relationship as occasionally violent and unstable. The week before the shooting, she broke up with Sylte. Over the weekend, Sylte sent a total of 282 text messages to the girl. The day before the shooting, Sylte posted cryptic messages on his Facebook page, calling himself a "wreck" and writing another ominous message:

If I mean anything to anyone, thanks and I love you.

On the morning of the shooting, Sylte showed up unannounced at his ex-girlfriend's house. As they argued, she called a friend, who overheard the argument through the phone. The friend called a third person, who finally notified police of the disturbance, triggering the police response to the scene.

After shooting Officer Schneider, Sylte remained barricaded, alone inside his ex-girlfriend's residence. Recognizing that Sylte had been trained in the use and creation of explosives during his time in the Wisconsin National Guard, police investigators requested assistance of the bomb squad to use a tactical bobcat and robot to see inside the home prior to SWAT entry. After a ten-hour standoff, the SWAT team made entry around 3:30 p.m., finding Sylte dead of a self-inflicted gunshot wound to the head.

Sylte committed suicide just one day before the sixth anniversary of his father's death on December 22, 2005.

In this study, fifteen percent of officers slain were engaged in the same behavior as the officer in this case: confronting a suspect involved in a volatile, obsessive romantic relationship with a woman.* From this analysis, a profile emerges one kind of suspect who is driven to kill police officers—a man who is engaged in an intense, controlling, and unstable relationship. As a suspect who became a cop-killer during a police response to a domestic violence situation, Alan Sylte presents a series of common traits shared with the others: suicidal, angry, violent, and unwilling to be controlled by law enforcement.

Sylte also shares mental illness symptoms with many of the other shooters in this study. He was deeply affected by personal trauma from enduring the loss of his father in young adulthood. He had been intermittently suicidal and had been the subject of a call to police under similar circumstances in the past. In truth, it will never be known if Sylte intentionally killed a police officer. What is known is that he fired from the basement in the direction of the officer as his girlfriend walked toward the officer's patrol car. Officer Schneider was approaching the house on foot and was struck by the first bullet. However, Sylte may have been aiming at his girlfriend and simply missed.

Sylte's case can be summarized as follows:

Name	Sylte, A.
Age	25

---

* The shooters of Officers Yaslowitz, Baitinger, Falcone, Birkholz, Bellar, Warren, Kenner, Paugh, and Rhyne were involved in unstable relationships that required police intervention, leading to the deaths of the officers who responded.

Race	W
Gang affiliation or criminal HX	None
Social factors	High school dropout
	Military training
	Obsessive relationship
Mental factors	Anniversary marker (death of father)
Motive	Unknown
Circumstances	Domestic disturbance
Outcome	Committed suicide

Discussion: Age

This group of shooters, aged twenty-five to twenty-nine, represents the changing faces of offenders from youthful to adult in nature. However similar their deadly encounters are, these men faced different struggles and challenges than their younger counterparts did. This age group also comprises the largest number of cop-killers in our study.

Recalling the previous peaks at ages sixteen, nineteen, and twenty-two, we can see new peaks with this age group across the spread of all offenders in their twenties. Again, we see clusters of offenders at particular ages. Let us examine the spread of offenders we have discussed so far by age:

Age of Shooter (under 30)

In this case, offenders aged twenty-five and twenty-seven account for all but one cop-killer in this group. Thus, it appears the risk for exhibiting cop-killer behavior under age thirty is highest among males aged twenty-two or twenty-five years of age.

As with younger offenders, this is also the threshold age of diagnosis for a number of mental illnesses. However, we will also see that offenders in the age group of twenty-five to twenty-nine begin to show different patterns of engagement with police—motives involving relationships and outcome trends that differ from those of other offenders we have studied so far.

Unlike teen offenders, the struggle for individuals in the age range of twenty-five to twenty-nine focuses more acutely on establishing and maintaining relationships with others, especially intimate relationships. This struggle is reflected in the underlying pathology and triggers that lead to police confrontations—including deteriorating romantic relationships and domestic violence. This new feature in our study of cop-killers begins to appear with this age group.

Discussion: Race

In this age group, white shooters accounted for nearly half of the cop-killers. Recalling the trend that was heavily weighted toward black shooters beginning with teen offenders, we will now begin to note a continuing shift in the race of cop-killers that reflects a more equitable inclusion of white shooters, along with other minority groups.

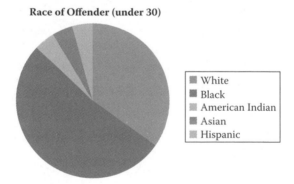

However, when examined on a larger scale of all cop-killers under age thirty, blacks are still seen as outnumbering other offenders. This group also includes the first Hispanic shooter in our study.

For comparison with offenders, we should also briefly examine the role of the officers' races:

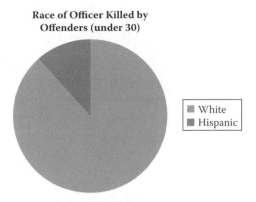

Race of Officer Killed by
Offenders (under 30)

■ White
■ Hispanic

Of the twenty-six officers killed by offenders under age thirty, twenty-three (eighty-eight percent) were white. Three were Hispanic.

Discussion: Gang Affiliation

Only two of the ten cop-killers (twenty percent) in this group were affiliated with a gang. Both gang members in this age group had served time in prison, where they had become involved with prison-based gangs, before they became cop-killers.

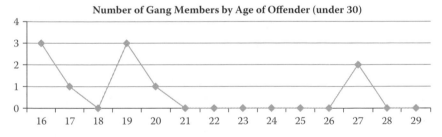

Number of Gang Members by Age of Offender (under 30)

Thus, with this age group, we see a continuing lack of number of offenders associated with gangs.

Discussion: Criminal History

Once again, we have offenders in this age group whose criminal histories align. However, along with three offenders in the last age group, two offenders (twenty percent) in this group had no criminal history.

The top five offenses are shown in the following chart:

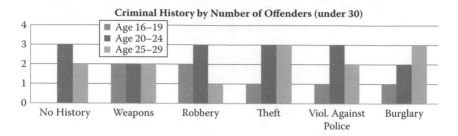

Among cop-killers under age thirty, most have prior arrests for robbery, theft, violence against police, and/or burglary. This trend illustrates the movement of these offenders toward a lifestyle of high-risk, high-reward activities common to hard-core criminal behavior. This trend is especially visible with regard to attaining the criminal history of a burglary offense as the offenders in the study age. Seen as a less violent crime, burglary represents the quintessential disregard of the rights of others to have property secure from theft. Perhaps this shared criminal history reflects the low regard for other human beings that may be the hallmark of cop-killer behavior.

Offenders in this group with a past history of violence against the police are usually characterized as offering resistance during arrest or attempting to flee from imminent arrest in the past, rather than overt and brutal acts against police.

Discussion: Social Factors

Let us look at the comparisons of offenders in this group:

Welch	Separated from wife
	Obsessive relationship
Mathews	High school dropout
	Teen offender
	On parole
Leon	On parole
Eggenberg	Separated from wife
	Obsessive relationship
Connor	High school dropout
	Teen offender
Russell	Alone with officer
Hodges	Military training
Barbee	Troubled childhood
Pride	Hard-core criminal

Sylte   High school dropout
               Military training
               Obsessive relationship

Three offenders in this group were involved in obsessive relationships, including two that were separated from their wives at the time
of the offense. Obsessive relationships are seen as highly intense yet
unstable and often violent intimate relationships, including marriages.
The trauma associated with the losses of these primary relationships
cannot be overestimated. Welch, Eggenberg, and Sylte are the first
offenders with this profile. Like these cop-killers, several offenders in
later groups will mark their descent into the lethal confrontation with
law enforcement over the actual or perceived dissolution of a romantic
relationship.

One-third of the offenders in this group are confirmed high school
dropouts. Two offenders were teenagers at the time of their first arrest.
Two were on parole.

We also have two offenders—Hodges and Sylte—who were
trained by the military. This trend will continue with offenders in
later categories.

Discussion: Mental Factors

Examining the mental factors, we can see some definite trends in the
behaviors and functioning states of these offenders.

Let us examine them side by side:

Welch   Bloodlust—committed recent murder of civilian
               Had shot self in chest (suicide attempt)
Mathews   Crime in progress
               Affinity for guns
Leon   None
Eggenberg   Bipolar
Connor   Schizophrenia
               Drug user (unknown type)
               Family members present
               Anniversary marker (death of mother)
               Affinity for guns
Russell   None
Hodges   Girlfriend present
               High on alcohol

Barbee	None
Pride	Other suspects present
	Involved in escape from crime scene
Sylte	Anniversary marker (death of father)

Like the two offenders who initiated the deadly encounter with police in the last group, Barbee approached and murdered a police officer without warning during an incident in which he was not involved. We should also note that alcohol and drugs play less of a role in this group's encounters with law enforcement.

The top factors are noted in the following chart:

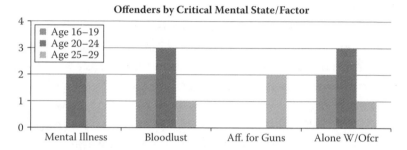

Compared with the other offenders, we begin to see two new trends in this group: anniversary markers and affinity for guns. Anniversary markers are critical dates marking the death of a significant person in the offender's life, usually a parent. These markers denote the relationship between the date of the anniversary and the date of the murder of the law enforcement officer. Affinity for guns describes a history of acquiring three or more firearms or significant history of weapons violations. We see two offenders (twenty percent) in each of these categories with this age group.

In this group, thirty percent of the cop-killers had no identified mental factors. This suggests that shooters in their late twenties are motivated by something different from what motivated the other groups already examined.

Discussion: Motives

Like other offenders, most of the offenders in this group were facing imminent arrest for a warrant or active crime in progress. Let us examine them together:

Welch	Suicide by cop
Mathews	Avoid arrest for armed robbery; felon in possession of firearm
Leon	Avoid arrest for felon in possession of firearm
Eggenberg	Unknown
Connor	Avoid imminent arrest for warrant
	Suicide by cop
Russell	Avoid imminent arrest for warrant
Hodges	Unknown
Barbee	Unknown
Pride	Avoid arrest for crime in progress
Sylte	Unknown

Clearly, there is a trend. The most common motive in the under-thirty age group is to avoid imminent arrest for a crime or warrant. These offenders are wanted by police as a result of an arrest warrant, extant illegal conduct (e.g., felon carrying a handgun), or during a crime in progress.

Motive of Offender (under 30)

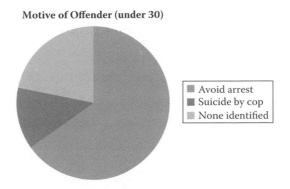

■ Avoid arrest
■ Suicide by cop
■ None identified

Two offenders in this group can be classified as having suicide-by-cop motives. This motive reflects the offender's desire for self-annihilation at the hands of the police.

Nearly one-quarter of offenders in the under-thirty age group have no definitive motive for killing a police officer. This reflects the very private decision made by these offenders who, most of the time, choose to commit suicide. All of the offenders in this age group with unknown motives did, in fact, commit suicide.

Discussion: Circumstances

What were the circumstances of the encounters with police that led to the deadly outcomes in this group? Let us examine these events side by side:

Welch	Shots fired
	Domestic disturbance
Mathews	Robbery in progress
Leon	Traffic stop
Eggenberg	Minor accident
	Domestic disturbance
Connor	Warrant service
Russell	Pedestrian stop
	Foot pursuit
Hodges	Disabled vehicle
	Domestic disturbance
Barbee	Ambush and execution
Pride	Robbery in progress
Sylte	Domestic disturbance

Most of the offenders in this age group (sixty percent) were the subjects of calls to police and/or engaged in a domestic disturbance outside the home (e.g., in a vehicle, on a roadway, etc.):

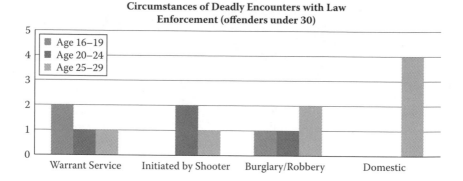

The most common circumstance for this age group leading to contact with law enforcement was a call to police, in particular domestic disturbances (forty percent).

Only one offender in this group was the subject of a warrant service operation. One was a pedestrian stop.

Discussion: Outcomes

Although every officer in this study was killed, an examination of the outcome of the incident for offenders provides some interesting data. Let us examine the cases side by side:

Welch	Fled on foot; committed suicide
Mathews	Fled on foot; shot by police, captured
Leon	Killed by police
Eggenberg	Committed suicide
Connor	Killed by police
Russell	Fled on foot, captured
Hodges	Committed suicide
Barbee	Committed suicide
Pride	Fled on foot, captured
Sylte	Committed suicide

Only two offenders in this age group survived without injury. Half (fifty percent) committed suicide. The rest of the offenders were shot and/or killed by police.

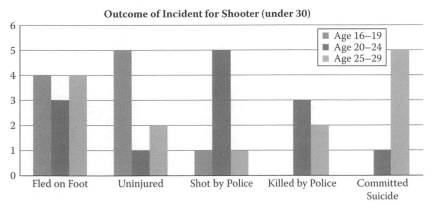

Outcome of Incident for Shooter (under 30)

Thus, the most common outcome for deadly encounters with this age group involved the shooter committing suicide after killing the police officer. Many offenders in this age group did flee on foot, but were either shot or killed by police.

A large number commit suicide with the same firearm used in the original shooting.

Conclusion

Among shooters in the twenty-five to twenty-nine age group:

- The majority were white or black males who were twenty-five or twenty-seven years of age.
- Three offenders used a long gun or automatic rifle in the incident; the majority used handguns.
- Most had a criminal history, including weapons, theft, robbery, and/or violence against police.
- Only two shooters were gang members.
- Most offenders were the subject of a call to police and/or involved in a domestic disturbance outside the home.
- Nearly half had an unknown motive for killing a police officer. All of the shooters with unknown motives committed suicide.
- One shooter initiated the encounter with police.
- Two shooters were mentally ill—one was bipolar and one was schizophrenic.
- Half of the shooters committed suicide.

References

Centers for Disease Control. 2009. Data, trends and maps of alcohol use in the United States [graph]. Retrieved May 9, 2012, from http://www.cdc.gov/alcohol/data-stats.htm

Gilgun, J. 2000. "Liquid courage" and "it don't matter." Retrieved May 9, 2012, from http://www.scribd.com/doc/24370107/Liquid-Courage-and-Other-Reasons-Convicted-Felons-Use-Alcohol-and-Other-Chemicals

Urban, M. "Gunman's Father Mourns Slain Deputy," *Reading Eagle,* July 1, 2011. Retrieved February 22, 2012, from http://readingeagle.com/article.aspx?id=317532

Bibliography

Adler, E., and Bormann, D. "Hundreds Gather to Remember Fallen Atchison Officer," *Kansas City Star,* December 10, 2011, Atchison, KS: TKCS.

Amelinckx, A. "Welch Had a Troubled, Violent Past," *Hudson-Catskill Papers,* February 22, 2011. Retrieved December 20, 2011, from http://www.registerstar.com/articles/2011/02/22/news/doc4d63395370646869217851.txt

Anderson, B. "Murder Suspect Charged Also with Burglary," *Anniston Star*, March 22, 2012. Retrieved April 18, 2012, from http://www.annistonstar.com/printer_friendly/17964069

Associated Press. "Police Identify Officer Slain by Gunman in NY," February 20, 2011, Poughkeepsie, NY: AP.

———. "Police: Wounded Gunman Kills Wife, NY Officer, February 21, 2011, Poughkeepsie, NY: AP.

———. "Tennessee Deputy Dies a Day after Being Shot in the Head," June 7, 2011, Nashville, TN: APO.

———. "Pennsylvania Sheriff's Deputy Killed, Suspect Dead," June 30, 2011, Albany, NY: APO.

———. "Sheriff Killed, Suspect Dead in Eastern Pennsylvania," June 30, 2011, Albany, NY: APO.

———. "Officer Critically Wounded; Hunt Is on for Suspect," August 24, 2011, Anniston, AL: APO.

———. "Police Officer Dies of Injuries after Being Shot," August 25, 2011, Anniston, AL: APO.

———. "Man Charged in Officer's Death Got Early Release," September 1, 2011, Anniston, AL: APO.

———. "Hearing Set for Alabama Man Charged in Officer's Death," October 23, 2011, Anniston, AL: APO.

———. "Man Who Killed Officer Was Angry at System," December 12, 2011, Atchison, KS: APO.

———. "Body Found of Man Suspected of Shooting Minnesota Cop," December 20, 2011, Lake City, MN: APO.

———. "Many Leave Lights on for Wounded Lake City Officer," December 21, 2011, Lake City, MN: APO.

———. "Officer's Shooter Was Being Discharged from Guard," December 21, 2011, Lake City, MN: APO.

———. "Mayo: Wounded Lake City Police Officer Dies," December 31, 2011, Rochester, MN: APO.

"Atchison KS Police Sergeant David Enzbrenner Killed by Skyler Barbee While Serving Nuisance Order in Apparent Murder–Suicide," *Hinterland Gazette* [web blog], December 11, 2011, Newstex.

Barrett, M. "Family of Alleged Cop Killer Has Area Ties," *Asheville Citizen-Times*, April 19, 2011, Asheville, NC: ACT.

Benfield, J. "Only Witness Who Saw Suspect Shoot and Kill Deputy Speaks" [video], October 25, 2011. Retrieved April 20, 2012, from http://www.wjbf.com/news/2011/oct/25/6/2606194

———. "WJBF News Channel 6 Obtains Christopher Hodges' Military Personnel File," November 7, 2011. Retrieved April 20, 2012, from http://www.wjbf.com/news/2011/nov/07/4/2668642

Benzel, L. "DOC Checks for Red Flags with Inmate Accused in Cop Killing," *Gazette*, April 5, 2011, Colorado Springs, CO: ProQuest.

"Berks County Deputy Sheriff Killed in Shootout," ABC News, June 30, 2011. Retrieved February 22, 2012, from http://abclocal.go.com/wpvi/story?section=news/local&id=8222882

Burger, B. "A City Mourns," *Chattanooga Times Free Press,* April 3, 2011, p. A1.
———. "Touched by Tragedy," *Chattanooga Times Free Press,* April 4, 2011, p. A1.
———. "Witness Describes Shooting Scene," *Chattanooga Times Free Press,* April 6, 2011, p. A1.
———. "Medical Examiner's Report on Slain Officer Released," *Chattanooga Times Free Press,* April 13, 2011, p. B1.
Bynum, R., and Martin, J. "Sheriff: Georgia Deputy's Killer Had Drinking Problem," Associated Press, October 24, 2011, Atlanta, GA: APO.
———. "Suspect in Shooting of Georgia Deputy Served in Iraq," Associated Press, October 24, 2011, Atlanta, GA: APO.
———. "Sheriff: Woman Says Georgia Deputy's Killer Was Drunk," Associated Press, October 24, 2011, Atlanta, GA: APO.
Celona, L., Marsh, J., and Martinez, J. "Fallen Finest Devastated Partner Sprang into Action," *New York Post,* December 13, 2011, p. 7.
Chanen, D. "Lake City Officer Loses Fight for His Life," *Star Tribune,* December 30, 2011, p. 1A.
Chattanooga Times Free Press. No title, April 9, 2011, p. A7.
CNN. "Georgia Sheriff's Deputy Killed with Assault Rifle, Sheriff Says," October 23, 2011, Richmond County, GA: Cable News Network.
CNN Wire Staff. "Alleged Killer of Wife, N.Y. Officer, Had Previous Abuse Arrest," CNN.com, February 19, 2011, New York: CNN.
Coe, J. "Buckeye Officer 'Executed,'" *Arizona Republic,* May 3, 2011, p. B1.
———. "Man Questioned in Policeman's Killing," *Arizona Republic,* May 4, 2011, p. B3.
———. "Officer Is out of Hospital," *Arizona Republic,* May 11, 2011, p. 4.
———. "Slain Buckeye Officer's Kin to Get Full Benefits," *Arizona Republic,* May 18, 2011, p. 12.
———. "Buckeye Officer Says He's No Hero," *Arizona Republic,* June 1, 2011, p. B1.
DeVries, C. "Poughkeepsie Shooter, Victim Described by Catskill Neighbors as 'Good Tenants,'" *Register-Star,* February 20, 2011.
Doyle, J., Yaniv, O., Parascandola, R., and Kennedy, H. "Path to Justice Begins Right Here," *Daily News,* December 14, 2011, p. 3.
Draper, B. "Kansas Officer Slain by Man Who Then Killed Himself," Associated Press, December 11, 2011, Kansas City, KS: APO.
Ford, J. "Slain Cop Was 22-Year NYPD Veteran," WPIX-TV, December 12, 2011, New York: McClatchey-Tribune Business News.
Gamiz, M. "Cop Killer's Dad Charged with Supplying Him with Weapons; Two Others Also Charged with Giving Matthew Connor Guns," *Morning Call,* August 20, 2011, p. A5.
Gebhart, L. "Florida Officer Takes 10 Rounds to Save Children, Her Own Life," *Police One,* November 2, 2011. Retrieved May 17, 2012, from http://www.policeone.com/pc_print?via=120351
Gilliam, M. "Veteran NYPD Cop Dead after Being Shot in Face during Brooklyn Break-In," WPIX-TV, December 12, 2011, New York: McClatchey-Tribune Business News.

Greenberg, P. "County Deputy Shot, Shooter Dead after Turning Gun on Self, Officials Say," *Tennessean,* June 6, 2011, Nashville, TN: TT.

———. "Eggenberg in 'Good Spirits' before Shooting," *Tennessean,* June 10, 2011, Nashville, TN: TT.

Hays, T. "4 More in Custody after NYC Officer's Death," Associated Press, December 13, 2011, New York: APO.

Hertz, L. "City Mourns Officer John Falcone, 'an Outstanding Member' of Police Department," *Poughkeepsie Journal,* February 19, 2011, p. APJ1.

———. "Police: Domestic-Violence Cases Are among Riskiest," *Poughkeepsie Journal,* February 20, 2011, p. APJ2.

Hoppa, K. "Community Reflects, Honors Fallen Officer," *St. Joseph News-Press,* December 11, 2011, Atchison, KS: ProQuest.

———. "Probe Continues in Fatal Shooting of Atchison Officer," *St. Joseph News-Press,* December 13, 2011, Atchison, KS: ProQuest.

Hudson-Catskill Papers. Retrieved December 20, 2011, from http://www .thedailymail.net/articles/2011/02/19/news/doc4d03330a830022075 5828.txt

Humbles, A. "Dickson County Deputy Dies from Shooting," *Tennessean,* June 8, 2011, Nashville, TN: TT.

Humphrey, K., and Walsh, P. "Officer Gravely Injured, Shooter Dead in Lake City," *Star Tribune,* December 20, 2011, p. 1A.

Kahl, J. "Police Dog Jynx Tried to Save Stricken Partner," *York Dispatch,* July 1, 2011, Reading, PA: York Newpapers, LLC.

"Lake City Shooting: Officer Shawn Schneider in Critical Condition after Shooting in Minnesota," *International Business Times,* December 20, 2011, Lake City, MN: Newstex, LLC.

Lambe, J. "Atchison Shooter Was Angry at Justice System, Grandfather Says," *Kansas City Star,* December 11, 2011, Kansas City, KS: TKCS.

Long, C., and Peltz, J. "2nd Suspect Sought in NYC Officer's Shooting Death," Associated Press, December 13, 2011, New York: APO.

Louwagie, P. "Shooter Was Iraqi Vet Facing Discharge," *Star Tribune,* December 21, 2011, p. 1A.

Louwagie, P., and Chanen, D. "Before Shooting in Lake City: 282 Messages and Fight with Ex," *Star Tribune,* December 22, 2011, p. 1B.

"Man Accused of Killing Officer Was Wanted," *Huntsville Times,* August 28, 2011, Anniston, AL.

Martin, K. "Officer Fired Three Bullets; One Hit," *Augusta Chronicle,* October 26, 2011, p. A01.

McManus, T. "Soldier Kills Deputy, Self; Gunman Shot from Car after Argument," *Augusta Chronicle,* October 24, 2011, p. A01.

Merrill, L., and Woodfill, D. "Buckeye Officer Is Killed in Shootout," *Arizona Republic,* May 2, 2011, p. A10.

Moore, T. "Tragedy of Gunman Who Killed Wife, Cop & Himself," *Daily News,* February 20, 2011, p. 10.

Murphy, M. "Suspect Who Fatally Shot NYPD Cop in Face in Custody," WPIX-TV, December 12, 2011, New York: McClatchey-Tribune Business News.

Newman, A. "NY Police Officer Fatally Shot Responding to Apartment Robbery," *Boston Globe,* December 13, 2011, p. 9.

Ngo, E., and Lam, C. "LI Officer Gunned Down," *Newsday,* December 13, 2011, p. A03.

Norvell, K. "Officer Killed in Atchison," *St. Joseph News-Press,* December 9, 2011, Atchison, KS: ProQuest.

"NYPD Officer Peter Figoski Killed by Robbery Suspect Lamont Pride in Cypress Hills Brooklyn," *Hinterland Gazette,* December 12, 2011, New York: Newstex, LLC.

Parascandola, R., and Kennedy, H. "Deathtrap for Brooklyn Cop," *Daily News,* December 13, 2011, p. 3.

"Police Seek 30-Year Old Who Shot Officer," *Anniston Star,* August 24, 2011, Anniston, AL: McClatchey-Tribune Business News.

Poovey, B. "Grand Jury Gets Fatal Shooting of Police Officer," Associated Press, April 13, 2011, Chattanooga, TN: AP.

Schram, J., and Martinez, J. "Fallen Finest Cop 'Killer' Left Trail of Victims," *New York Post,* December 13, 2011, p. 6.

"Sgt. Tim Chapin and Two Sides of the Law," *Denver Post,* May 22, 2011.

Shuster, B. "Bank Robber Bled to Death, Autopsy Finds," *Los Angeles Times,* April 1, 2007. Retrieved January 17, 2012, from http://articles.latimes.com/1997-04-11/local/me-47591_1_bank-robber

South, T. "Eyewitness Describes Officer Shooting during Defendant's First Court Appearance," *Chattanooga Times Free Press,* April 14, 2011, p. A1.

———. "Parents of Man Charged in Police Slaying Plead Guilty," *Chattanooga Times Free Press,* September 22, 2011, p. A1.

Steele, C. "Loved Ones Shine the Spotlight on Justin Sollhub's Selfless Personality," *Anniston Star,* August 25, 2011. Retrieved April 18, 2012, from http://www.annistonstar.com/printer-friendly/15208826

Stewart, E. (2011, February 21). "Mothers of Welches Recall Pattern of Abuse," *Poughkeepsie Journal,* February 21, 2011. Retrieved December 20, 2011, from http://www.poughkeepsiejournal.com/article/20110222/NEWS05/102220327/Mothers-Welches-recall-pattern-abuse

Stewart, K. "Sollohub Justice Center," ABC 33/40, September 28, 2011. Retrieved April 18, 2012, from http://www.abc3340.com/story/15564976/sollohub-justice-center

Turner, D., and Sainz, A. "Officials: Soldier Kills Deputy, Then Self in Georgia," Associated Press, October 23, 2011, Atlanta, GA: APO.

"Watch: Alleged NYPD Cop Killer Lamont Pride Confesses to Shooting" [video], *New York Post,* February 9, 2011. Retrieved May 1, 2012, from http://tinyurl.com/figoski

4

SELF-DESTRUCTION: COP-KILLERS IN THEIR EARLY THIRTIES

Overview

In this section, we will examine six cases involving cop-killers aged thirty to thirty-four. The cases in this chapter include:

- **James Cruckson**, who executed an officer investigating a rape by firing on police from a concealed position inside a home
- **Jamie Hood**, who executed an officer during a traffic stop
- **Leonard Statler**, who killed an officer investigating a shots-fired call
- **Shaun Seeley**, who executed an officer who was searching his home during a warrant service operation
- **Charles Post**, who killed an officer who approached him in a parking lot to arrest him on an attempted murder warrant
- **Martin Poynter**, who murdered an officer about to arrest him on a child support warrant

We will see that this group is influenced by the three major themes: failure of both interpersonal and professional relationships, engagement in criminal lifestyles, and/or drug addiction.

Every offender in this group was facing the same set of consequences: imminent arrest. Only one offender in this group survived his encounter with police; all of the others (eighty-three percent) committed suicide.

Case 24: James Cruckson, Thirty

In the early morning hours of March 20, 2011, three officers made entry into James Cruckson's home through the basement of a duplex. Cruckson was suspected of committing a rape of his girlfriend only two hours before. Announcing their presence, officers made their way through the first floor of the residence shouting "police!" Approaching the stairwell to the second floor, the officers began to ascend. On the stairway, one officer was shot twice in the shoulders by Cruckson, firing from a concealed position on the second floor. A police K-9 was also shot.

Cruckson continued firing multiple rounds from the second floor as officers began to arrive to set up a perimeter outside. Officer Craig Birkholz arrived on scene, positioning his vehicle on the north side of the perimeter. He grabbed his patrol rifle and began running southbound along the west wall of a tavern parking lot across from the suspect's residence. However, the officer did not realize he was running in the path of an unobstructed sightline from the suspect's second story window, a mere seventy-five yards away. Officer Birkholz was shot twice with a high-powered rifle. Both were fatal shots. After a six-hour standoff, Cruckson committed suicide with a handgun.

Cruckson had served honorably in the National Guard for several years and had one son, but was estranged from the child's mother. Near the time of the shooting, he had recently returned from a military training deployment on the West Coast. One report indicated that when Cruckson returned, his friends informed him that his girlfriend, Josephine Warner, had been cheating on him with other men.

Cruckson and Warner had been involved in a physically and emotionally volatile relationship for around three years. Both he and Warner often accused each other and admitted to sexual infidelities. Both parties had also been violent toward each other, resulting in one conviction for domestic violence for Cruckson. The relationship had ended recently again. However, in the two weeks before the incident, Warner left her six-year-old daughter with Cruckson and went to Florida for what may have been a "photo shoot." During this time apart, Cruckson came to believe that Warner was cheating on him with a foreign exchange student.

Four days before the shooting, Cruckson told his best friend that Warner had admitted to cheating on him in Florida. Text message records indicated that Cruckson was very angry about the situation. The messages he sent to Warner included a photo of a stuffed animal belonging to Warner with a large kitchen knife pointed at its throat. The next picture showed the stuffed animal cut to pieces on the floor.

Throughout Warner's time in Florida, Cruckson continued sending texts that were both aggressive and controlling. On the day before the shooting, Cruckson sent this message:

> Just start over with me . . . I love you and we hate each other. There is no breaking up when you get home. I will show you.

At around 4:45 a.m. on the day of the shooting, Warner arrived home from Florida and was met by Cruckson in the driveway of the duplex. After she went inside the house with Cruckson to retrieve her daughter, whom she believed was sleeping inside, Cruckson began making sexual advances. When Warner refused, Cruckson became angry and raped her. Afterward, Warner stated that she armed herself with a pair of scissors. Cruckson disarmed her easily. She then negotiated her way out of the house by claiming she would not go to the police, but to her mother's home.

After shooting Officer Birkholz, Cruckson remained barricaded for several hours. During this time, he fired rounds from a .308 hunting rifle and a .45 caliber handgun. He also retrieved a police tactical shotgun from the stairwell inside the home that an officer had dropped when he was shot. Cruckson fired six rounds from Williams's police shotgun during the incident.

While he was barricaded, Cruckson left two voice-mail messages on the victim's phone. In these calls, Cruckson admitted raping her and blamed her for the shooting. He also claimed that the reason for the incident was her infidelity with a foreign exchange student. One message was

> This is all your fault. I should have killed you. You deserve to die. You're an evil person.

Dawn began to break about thirty minutes after the shooting. At around 7:40 a.m., an officer who had taken up a position on the perimeter spotted Cruckson's rifle leaning out the window of the residence. The officer fired twice at Cruckson, striking him once in the left hand.

The police negotiator was able to speak with Cruckson several times during the incident. Cruckson admitted raping Warner, stated he was going to kill himself, and stated he knew he had killed a police officer. He emphatically stated he was not going to prison and nothing would convince him to put down his weapons and surrender. Cruckson also spoke with relatives, who were unable to convince him to give up. After Cruckson was wounded by police, he fired only one more round from the handgun, a self-inflicted wound several hours later.

After deploying tear gas, the SWAT team entered Cruckson's residence at 11:37 a.m., finding Cruckson dead. He had a single gunshot wound to the head and a grazing gunshot wound to his left hand. He had no alcohol or drugs in his system.

Warner's six-year-old daughter was not located inside the house. She was later found with one of Cruckson's relatives. After the incident, Cruckson's family reported that Cruckson, a military veteran, may have been suffering from post-traumatic stress syndrome.

Following the shooting, Officer Jay Salzmann—who was off-duty at the time of the incident—was placed on administrative leave. Subsequent investigation revealed that Officer Salzmann had been involved in a sexual relationship with the victim, Josephine Warner, which had ended just three months before the shooting. The morning of the shooting, Warner called Officer Salzmann before she went to the police station to report the sexual assault. Officer Salzmann reported that he counseled Warner to report any abuse to the police. Warner later insisted that Salzmann played no role in the incident. Six weeks later, under intense media scrutiny, he resigned from the police department.

Warner, excited by the limelight from the incident, gave several television interviews in the weeks after the shooting and even created a Facebook "fan page" for herself. During one interview, she flippantly claimed that the suspect had recommended she pursue a law enforcement career.

Cruckson's case can be summarized as follows:

Name	Cruckson, J.
Age	30
Race	W
Gang affiliation or criminal HX	Domestic violence

Social factors	Military training
	Obsessive relationship
Mental factors	None
Motive	Avoid arrest for sexual assault
Circumstances	Sexual assault call
Outcome	Committed suicide

Case 25: Jamie Hood, Thirty-Three

On March 22, 2011, police received a report of a carjacking, kidnapping, and shooting involving a known suspect, Jamie Hood. Hood had lured an acquaintance named Judon Brooks to a house, where several armed associates wearing ski masks were waiting. When Brooks entered, the men forced him to the ground and demanded addresses of several people. Hood told Brooks he would be killed if he did not bring them money. Brooks was then bound with zip ties and bundled into the trunk of his Cadillac. As Hood and the armed men drove around in the Cadillac, Brooks freed his hands and escaped from the trunk. Brooks called police and reported the incident, naming Hood as the suspect.

Officer Tony Howard recognized Hood's name and headed to an apartment where he knew Hood might be staying. On the way there, Officer Howard spotted a distinctive red Chevrolet Suburban, which he recognized as belonging to Hood's brother, Matthew. Believing Hood was inside the vehicle, Officer Howard conducted a stop of the vehicle. Officer Elmer "Buddy" Christian went to provide him with backup.

Once the vehicle stopped, the passenger—the wanted suspect Jamie Hood—got out of the vehicle. As Officer Howard opened his patrol car door to exit the vehicle, Hood pulled out a handgun and shot Officer Howard in the face. Officer Howard was struck by two bullets—one that entered through his left cheek and exited through his right cheek, and the other in the chest. As Officer Christian pulled up to the scene in his vehicle to assist Officer Howard, Hood ran toward Officer Christian and shot him through the patrol car window, killing him.

Hood then ran from the scene, through the woods, emerging on a nearby residential street. Hood then ran into the street and carjacked a vehicle driven by an elderly woman. Hood forced her to drive him away from the location for a few miles before pushing her out of the vehicle and taking the car. She was not harmed.

Hood became the subject of a massive manhunt. Three days after the shootings, Hood contacted police and told them he was afraid he would be killed by police and had taken several hostages. Hood told police that he would injure the hostages if his demands were not met. Seeking the spotlight, he demanded live television coverage of his surrender to ensure his safety.

With cameras trained on him, Hood walked out of an apartment, shirtless, with five hostages, including an infant, a toddler, and a thirteen-year-old girl. He was taken into custody without incident. When interviewed by the media, one of the hostages defended Hood, saying:

> Jamie didn't do no harm to none of us. He treated us like family.

Investigators reported that Hood had likely been using cocaine before he surrendered. By the time he shot two police officers, he was clearly involved in a violent, criminal lifestyle associated with drug trafficking. In 1997, eighteen-year-old Hood used a handgun to rob a pizza delivery man at an apartment complex. He managed to steal three dollars from the victim. He was sentenced to more than eleven years in prison and was released in 2009. After his release, he went to work on the streets as "muscle for hire" for a drug trafficking organization.

Investigations conducted after Hood was in custody revealed he had been on a violent crime spree in the criminal underworld. The grand jury indicted him on seventy counts, including two counts of murder, attempted murder, eleven counts of kidnapping, twelve counts of aggravated assault, and fifteen counts of firearms possession. In addition to the murder charge for Officer Christian, Hood was the only suspect in the murder of Kenneth Wray, a public works employee. The indictment stated that three months before becoming a cop-killer, Hood shot and killed Wray outside Wray's home in Athens, Georgia. Wray, who lived with his mother, was shot five times. The incident was described as drug related.

In October 2011, Hood petitioned to have his court-appointed attorneys removed from his defense team. Video of Hood shows him winking at the prosecutor and defiantly shouting down the judge in the hearing, refusing to cooperate. Despite being warned by the judge to be silent, Hood was also videotaped admitting to the killing of Officer Christian during pretrial hearings.

Hood's case can be summarized as follows:

Name	Hood, J.
Age	33
Race	B
Gang affiliation or criminal HX	Armed robbery, drug trafficking
Social factors	Hard-core criminal
	Drug user (cocaine)
Mental factors	Bloodlust (committed recent murder of civilian)
	Involved in escape from crime scene
	High on drugs (suspected)
Motive	Avoid arrest for kidnapping
Circumstances	Traffic stop—passenger
Outcome	Fled on foot and took hostages (child and adult); captured

Case 26: Leonard Statler, Thirty-One

On April 18, 2011, police responded to a call of shots fired in a residential neighborhood. Upon arrival, an officer observed Leonard Statler standing alone on the front porch of a home. Believing Statler was a mere bystander, the officer approached on foot and asked Statler if he had heard any shots being fired. Statler responded by pulling out a .357 revolver and firing at the officer, who took cover and returned fire. Statler then retrieved an SKS rifle and continued shooting, before fleeing into an alley between two houses. Statler encountered Officer Eric Zapata in the alley. He opened fire, striking Officer Zapata in the head and chest, killing him.

Statler was heavily intoxicated at the time of the incident. He had a criminal history, including violence toward police, and had recently been involved in a custody dispute involving his four-year-old daughter. He committed suicide immediately after the incident.

Statler was a local man who graduated from high school in 1998. His criminal history began in 2001, when Statler pled guilty to driving while intoxicated and received probation. In 2003, Statler pled guilty to a felony charge of property destruction after kicking out the window and door frame of a police cruiser after resisting arrest. One report suggested this arrest may have stemmed from an incident of domestic violence. In 2007, Statler pled guilty to carrying a concealed weapon and spent ninety days in jail. The felony charge stemmed from an incident in which Statler was carrying a knife with intent to use it.

Three days before the shooting, Statler appeared in court to contest primary custody of his four-year-old daughter being given to the child's mother. The mother's attorney later said:

> He was very passionate about wanting to raise his daughter.

Statler had also petitioned to prevent the mother's boyfriend from being allowed to spend time with his daughter. Statler's request was denied.

On the day of the incident, Statler spent the day drinking alcohol and playing a video game with his brother. Around 11:15 p.m., the men went outside and Statler fired a couple of shots into the air. The brothers joked that the shots would bring the police. They were right. Unfortunately, the consequences were fatal for both the officer and the suspect. After the shooting, Statler's brother became agitated and irate, walking around the neighborhood shouting obscenities and continuing to drink alcohol. He abruptly told a police officer near the scene:

> I am a convicted felon and there are some rifles in my house, and I know they shouldn't be there. I ain't going back to jail over them.

Officers seized twelve firearms and 207 rounds of ammunition from inside the home, where the suspect's brother lived with his father. Although the suspect lived in his own home across the street, he spent much of his time with his brother at the family home. Subsequent investigation revealed that the guns that were used in the incident had come from inside the home and belonged to the father of the suspect. The father admitted to police that he allowed his sons easy access to the weapons, even though he knew they were both convicted felons.

Statler, in an alcohol-driven frenzy, fired gunshots into the air and then joked with his brother that the police would soon respond. He then opened fire with a handgun and rifle at the first officer who responded. Why? The answer may be that the line between reality and fantasy had become quite distorted for Statler that night—not because of mental illness or animosity toward police, but rather because of the combination of alcohol and gaming.

Alcohol use lowers inhibitions, prevents users from clearly considering the consequences of their actions, and can contribute to suicidal action. Thus, users who are already depressed, angry, or frustrated become less able to control the inclination to commit acts of violence against others and themselves. Like Statler, people under the influence of alcohol do things they might not otherwise do.

Although gaming is generally perceived as an innocuous pastime, the link between practicing skills in the virtual world and transferring those same skills into the real world is very well documented. Thousands of organizations use online learning, including universities, governments, and medical centers worldwide, to train workers in new skills successfully. Gaming simulation in particular is also highly regarded as an effective training method. Narrowing the scope to simulations with a more violence-oriented emphasis (for example, warfare, street crime, and fantasy simulations) reveals that gaming scenarios involving killing people are a widely accepted genre, played by millions of people. In fact, military organizations, including the US Army, currently utilize warfare simulation games as their most effective recruitment tools.

Simulations are increasing in number and realism. With the dramatic increase in diagnoses of post-traumatic stress disorder brought on by modern combat fatigue, a project funded by the US military in 2010 focused on preparing soldiers for the emotional trauma of warfare through simulations. The project leader, a psychologist, described the simulation in development:

> What we want to create is something that pulls at the hearts of people. Maybe there's a child laying [sic] there with arms blown off, screaming and crying. Maybe your action kills an innocent civilian, or you see a guy next to you get shot in the eye, with blood spurting out of his face.

It seems clear that desensitization to violence through exposure is seen as the aim of the warfare simulation games for future soldiers. However, desensitization to violence is already occurring on a large scale among casual civilian gamers, including children and teens, creating a potential violent criminal with virtual experience beyond the current level of law enforcement tactical training or preparedness. Indeed, the executive producer of the US military's "America's

Army 3" admitted that it specifically targets the games to young teens. She said:

We want kids to be able to start playing at 13.

Now, imagine a highly realistic game that rewards players for decapitating police officers, killing them with a sniper rifle, massacring them with a chainsaw, or setting them on fire—complete with vivid and violent imagery. This game exists and has been highly successful worldwide with almost two billion dollars in sales. Its title: the Grand Theft Auto series, or simply "GTA." The official investigation revealed that Statler and his brother had been immersed in hours of playing GTA on the day of the shooting.

Described by one attorney as a "murder simulator," the game is infamous for glorifying depravity and violence, as well as encouraging police executions. Sadly, Statler is not the first suspect to play GTA at length and then subsequently kill police officers. In 2003, an eighteen-year-old suspect disarmed and killed two police officers and a 911 dispatcher in an Alabama police station after being arrested for stealing a car. He then fled in a stolen police car. Later investigation revealed that the suspect had spent months playing GTA III.[*]

When apprehended, the suspect in that case stated:

Life is a video game. You've got to die sometime.

The suspect in the 2003 case was given the death penalty. Of course, Statler's suicide negated the need for a trial in his case. Leonard Statler was not the only suspect in this study who was involved in a shots-fired call. Similar cases include Lee Welch (Case 14) and Michael Ferryman (Case 47).

Statler's case can be summarized as follows:

Name	Statler, L.
Age	31
Race	W

---

[*] The actions taken by suspect Devin Moore (AKA Devin Thompson) were reminiscent of actions available in the GTA III game, including killing police officers inside a police station, taking head shots, and stealing police cars with impunity. All three of the victims were shot in the head. The attorney in his case argued that Moore had done "just what he had been trained to do" in the hundreds of hours spent playing GTA III.

Gang affiliation or criminal HX	DWI, property crime, resisting arrest, domestic violence, weapons
Social factors	Family member present
	Video gaming
	Child custody dispute
Mental factors	Affinity for guns
	High on alcohol
	Alone with officer
Motive	Avoid arrest for attempted murder
Circumstances	Shots-fired call
Outcome	Fled on foot; committed suicide

Case 27: Shaun Seeley, Thirty-Three

On July 11, 2011, Officer Brent Long and his K-9 partner, Shadow, arrived at a house to serve a warrant with the US Marshals fugitive task force. The subject of the warrant was a longtime offender, Shaun Seeley, who was wanted for a probation violation. They approached the residence and knocked on the back door.

Subsequent investigation revealed that Seeley had installed video surveillance cameras outside the home. As the arrest team was staging outside the residence, Seeley may have watched their movements on a closed-circuit television. After a few minutes, two women came to the door. Both denied Seeley was inside. Police entered the home and located two men and another woman. All of them were shown a photo of Seeley and questioned about whether he was inside. All five occupants denied knowing Seeley and stated he was not inside.

Officer Long and Shadow began a search of the residence with another officer. Shadow indicated that someone was hiding in the bedroom closet. Officer Long opened the closet and discovered it was empty. As the team continued to search, they passed the closet a second time. Shadow again indicated that someone was hiding inside. Officer Long went into the closet and, this time, located a false wall from the back of the closet. Seeley was hidden behind the panel and began firing a handgun at police.

As Seeley fired on police, Officer Long and Shadow backed out of the closet, returning fire at the suspect behind the false closet wall. Seeley continued to fire, striking Long twice in the head and killing him. Shadow was also struck by gunfire. Facing continuing gunfire, the officers were forced to retreat from the home to defensive positions outside the residence. While he was barricaded, Seeley stripped Officer Long's body of his police firearm and ammunition, which were found on his person. The SWAT team eventually discovered Seeley dead from a single self-inflicted gunshot wound to the head.

Seeley had a lengthy criminal history and was a user and dealer of methamphetamine at the time of the incident. He had been a substance abuse addict since he was seventeen years old. However, Seeley was also a local man who had a remarkable history of violence in his family. In fact, his great-grandfather was killed in a similar encounter with police. In 1954, Elmer Seeley, sixty-eight, killed his estranged wife and eighteen-year-old daughter at their home by shooting them both in the back. He also shot his daughter-in-law during this incident, striking her in the back as she ran away. The daughter-in-law survived by falling to the ground and pretending to be dead until Elmer left the scene for his wife's workplace, Tulips Incorporated.

As police began searching the manufacturing plant for Elmer, he emerged from a hiding place and fired on officers. Officers returned fire, shooting Elmer in the head and killing him. The officers were unharmed. Shaun Seeley was Elmer's great-grandson. Both men lived and died in Terre Haute, Indiana, after an encounter with police.

Seeley's childhood experience is not known. However, in 1995—when Seeley was seventeen—he was arrested for burglary, theft, possession of a controlled substance, and a nuisance crime. He was given a light sentence and stayed out of trouble until 1998, when Seeley was implicated in helping a man, William Burns, to burn the body of a man he had killed in a drug-related murder. Just before he turned twenty-one, Seeley was charged as an accomplice in the murder. After giving a statement to police, he was released pending his trial date. While out on bond, Seeley was arrested for possession of marijuana, carrying a handgun, and driving with a suspended license. Unfortunately, Seeley had developed a serious drug problem by this time.

Seeley eventually pled guilty to helping burn and then bury the body of the victim Burns had killed. Seeley testified at Burns's trial that they smoked marijuana and snorted methamphetamine during the desecration of the victim. He was sentenced to four years in prison.

In 2001, just months after his release from prison, Seeley was found guilty of criminal mischief in a neighboring county. In 2002, Seeley was twice charged with driving on a suspended license. In 2005, he was charged with selling methamphetamine and possession of marijuana. This case was unresolved at the time of Seeley's death.

In 2010, Seeley was accused of bringing a stolen truck to a relative's home, dismantling it for parts, and then setting it on fire. This case led to the issuance of the arrest warrant for Seeley that resulted in the shooting.

The other five inhabitants of the residence were taken into custody for questioning. Two of the men refused to be interviewed, but one of the women stated she was married to the suspect and knew he was inside the apartment but that he was planning to hide from police. She also received several text messages from the suspect during the incident that indicated she knew he was hidden inside the residence.

The other woman told police she saw Seeley looking for something, possibly a gun, before police entered the residence. However, all five lied to police who questioned them before entering the house, leading to the death of Officer Long. All of the defendants accepted plea deals in December 2011; they each face sentences of up to ten years in prison. The US Attorney in this case said:

> The message is universal...Whether or not you actually pulled the trigger, if you are in any way, shape or form collaterally responsible for the...death of an officer of peace, you will be held accountable for your actions.

Ironically, Seeley's death echoed that of his own great-grandfather, Elmer Seeley, another violent murderer. Although it was always controversial, nineteenth century ideas of the so-called "criminal mind" were rife with references to the genetic predisposition of families with criminality to pass this trait on to their children and grandchildren. Eventually, more forward-thinking criminologists found this theory flawed, basing the development of criminal deviance on social, peer, and environmental factors. However, the remaining coincidence between the behaviors of these two men, separated by three generations within the same family, is striking.

Another observation: The suspect in this case is also not the first to have been hidden inside a residence when a warrant service team arrived. Like the circumstances of the Dail case, those who knew the shooter's whereabouts blatantly lied to police about the suspect's presence inside the home.

Seeley's case can be summarized as follows:

Name	Seeley, S.
Age	33
Race	W
Gang affiliation or criminal HX	Burglary, theft, drugs, accessory to murder, weapons, criminal mischief
Social factors	Other suspects present
	Family member (wife) present
	Hard-core criminal
Mental factors	Drug user (methamphetamine and marijuana)
Motive	Avoid arrest for probation violation
Circumstances	Warrant service
Outcome	Committed suicide

Case 28: Charles Post, Thirty-Three

On the evening of October 13, 2011, Officer Derek Kotecki responded to a local restaurant where, according to a tipster, a wanted man was waiting. The wanted man was suspect Charles Post. The tipster described Post's location as inside a white Jeep parked at the Dairy Queen. Officer Kotecki and his K-9 partner, Odin, arrived at the location first. After seeing the white Jeep, he got out of the patrol SUV to approach Post, leaving Odin in the patrol vehicle. Before Officer Kotecki could reach the suspect, Post fired. Officer Kotecki was struck fatally—once in the head, left arm, and abdomen.

After killing Officer Kotecki, Post exited the parked vehicle and ran behind the Dairy Queen, where he found a tall fence. He was pursued by arriving officers, some of whom rushed to aid the fallen officer. After failing to scale the fence, Post turned back to face the officers. Pointing their guns at Post, the officers gave him verbal commands to drop his weapon. Post then shot himself once in the head.

Charles Post was a local man who graduated from the same Lower Burrell, Pennsylvania, high school as the officer he eventually killed. Post graduated in 1996; Officer Kotecki graduated in 1989. Post's early history is not known, but his contact with police began in 1997, when nineteen-year-old Post was arrested for driving while intoxicated and possession of alcohol by a minor. In 1999, Post was arrested a second time for driving while intoxicated with a suspended license. He pled guilty.

In 2001, Officer Kotecki—the victim officer in this incident—charged Post with criminal mischief. Other details relating to this event were not available. Post was later found not guilty of this offense.

In 2002, Post was charged with aggravated assault, simple assault, and reckless endangerment for his role in a bar fight in Lower Burrell. Six witnesses reported that Post started the fight. Officer Kotecki was one of the officers who responded to the scene. In 2003, Post pled guilty and was sentenced to more than a year in jail.

After his release, Post was put into community supervision, which required periodic drug tests. By 2005, he had tested positive for opiates and cocaine at least sixteen times and was returned to custody. In 2006, after he was again returned to the community, Post was charged with fleeing police after they spotted him driving with a suspended license. He was fined and released. In December 2010, Post was arrested for possession of drug paraphernalia and six driving citations. However, Post was just becoming truly unstable. He was also reported to be a heroin addict.

On October 2, just ten days before the shooting, Post argued with his boss on the telephone. When his boss arrived at the Clarion Hotel where Post was staying to talk with him, Post opened fire on his truck. Twelve shell casings were recovered from the scene and a warrant for Post was issued. The charges from this incident included attempted homicide, aggravated assault, theft, and other charges. It is unclear what the two men argued about. The victim reported that Post was distraught about a situation involving his girlfriend.

When a detective contacted Post by cell phone to discuss the incident, Post told him he would never surrender to police. He also stated he had a loaded gun with fourteen bullets:

[I've got] thirteen for the cops and one for me.

Ten days later, he would kill Officer Kotecki to prevent his capture.

After the shooting, friends and relatives of the suspect reported that Post had become suicidal after the confrontation with his boss. During this period, he had repeatedly threatened to kill himself. No one reported his behavior to police.

Post's case can be summarized as follows:

Name	Post, C.
Age	33
Race	W
Gang affiliation or criminal HX	DWI, criminal mischief, aggravated assault, drugs, attempted murder
Social factors	Obsessive relationship
	Hard-core criminal
	Drug user (opiates, cocaine, heroin)
Mental factors	High on heroin (suspected)
	Prior contact with officer victim
	Suicidal ideation
Motive	Avoid arrest for attempted murder
Circumstances	Warrant service
Outcome	Fled on foot; committed suicide

Case 29: Martin Poynter, Thirty-Three

Around 12 p.m. on a Thursday afternoon, Deputy Rick Rhyne responded to a call of trespassing at a rural home on acreage. When he arrived, Deputy Rhyne encountered two men in the yard near a barn. Following standard procedure, the officer checked the suspects' identification and radioed in to see if either of the men, who were brothers, had outstanding warrants.

The officer learned that one of the men, Martin Poynter, was wanted for failure to pay child support. When Deputy Rhyne tried to arrest Poynter, the suspect drew a gun and shot the officer. Poynter then shot himself in the head, as his brother looked on in horror.

Poynter had an unusual history in that he was a decorated soldier before he became a murderer. Although little is known about his early life, he enlisted in the military and had earned the honor of Green Beret prior to his deployment to Iraq with the seventh Special Forces Group as a Special Forces medic in 2005. When he returned home in 2006, Poynter apparently suffered a psychotic break.

Martin Poynter was described by a neighbor:

He was weird. He dressed like military-style, like he wanted to hide.

Another neighbor reported that Poynter once ran into her home because he thought the police were after him. She reported that he only traveled at night.

Court documents paint a disturbing picture of Poynter, as he tried to readjust to life back home with his wife and four children. On April 19, 2007, Poynter was arrested for desertion from the Army. Warrant paperwork that was issued gave an ominous warning:

> [Poynter] is a soldier in the Army Special Forces Group and may be trained in martial arts.

Although the Army requested no bail, a local magistrate set Poynter's bail at two million dollars. Poynter was transferred from local law enforcement custody to the Army the same day he was arrested. No further information was available on what was done with Poynter while he was in the Army's custody. However, one month later, Poynter returned to the Moore County, North Carolina, home.

On May 29, 2007, Poynter's father-in-law requested a welfare check at the Poynters' home, reporting that he had been unable to reach anyone in the family for some time. Police were briefed about Poynter's military training and made the decision to send the special response team to the residence as a precaution. Poynter answered the door, but became uncooperative when officers asked him to step outside. Officers used a stun gun to subdue him. He was taken into custody and committed involuntarily to a psychological ward at the Army medical center at Fort Bragg for a mental evaluation.

The same day, Poynter's wife filed paperwork seeking a domestic violence protective order. The details of the report indicated that Poynter had become very ill, indeed. Susan Poynter wrote:

> He is convinced that we are helping someone spy on him and [he] has used the children to keep me hostage. He has become violent several times, once attempting to shoot my dog when he tried to protect me.

Susan Poynter went on to describe how her husband forced their oldest child to do pushups until he experienced muscle failure and confessed to being a spy. The children were also prevented from being alone with their mother, and their school supplies were seized by Poynter and destroyed because he believed:

[They] had been tampered with or planted to brainwash the children against him.

A Moore County judge approved the order, requiring Poynter not to return to the residence.

Four months later, on October 3, 2007, Susan Poynter applied for another protective order, in which she reported that her husband had been diagnosed with schizoaffective disorder, sexual addiction, and emotional disconnectedness that prevented the forming of healthy relationships with others. She also wrote that Poynter had held newly sharpened knives to the corner of her eye and her throat as he threatened her, and she feared for her safety upon his impending release from the mental hospital. She also filed for temporary custody of the children.

On November 15, 2007, the motion for custody was dismissed when Susan did not appear in court. Poynter did not return to the family home in North Carolina and went to Missouri instead, to live with his extended family. For the next four years, he simply disappeared from law enforcement's radar.

Around December 5, 2011, Poynter and his brother made the trip from Missouri to North Carolina. After they arrived, Poynter contacted his wife's grandfather asking to see his children. It is not known whether Poynter received an answer to his request, but several days later, he and his brother went to the property where he had lived with his wife and children years before. A neighbor spotted the two men on the property and notified the sheriff's office that the men were trespassing. Unfortunately, neither the officer not the suspect would survive the encounter.

A neighbor who was interviewed the day after the shooting said that, years before, the suspect had told her that he would never be taken back into custody by police:

He said he will kill his self [*sic*] before he goes back.

The same week that Poynter committed this offense, a similar incident occurred in nearby Raeford, North Carolina. In that incident, another Special Forces soldier just back from Afghanistan killed his wife and then committed suicide. Did Poynter hear about this incident and seek to do the same? Sadly, this may have been the case.

According to the media reports, Poynter was the owner of the deed to the home and had a legal right to be on the property. On the day of the shooting, what was his plan? There are many possibilities. Perhaps he was curious how his family was doing without him. Perhaps he simply wanted a reunion with his wife and the children he had not seen in, perhaps, more than four years. If his intentions were good, then the question becomes: Why did he bring a gun?

No, the most likely scenario is much darker. A 2005 study of familial murder–suicides indicated that eighty percent of parents who kill their spouses and children and then commit suicide have a diagnosis history of mood or thought disorders, *exactly like* Poynter. Poynter's diagnosis of schizoaffective disorder is symptomatic of the diagnosis of schizophrenia, characterized by hallucinations, delusions, and thinking disorder.

As we learned from the Connor case, schizophrenic subjects can be highly dangerous to their families and to law enforcement—not because they are simply mentally ill, but rather because they are, often, completely out of touch with reality. Thinking disorders like schizophrenia lead to gross misinterpretations of what is perceived by the schizophrenic patient. Martin Poynter brought the gun to the family home because he planned to kill them all.

Poynter's case can be summarized as follows:

Name	Poynter, M.
Age	33
Race	W
Gang affiliation or criminal HX	Mental commitment, domestic violence
Social factors	Military training
	Obsessive relationship
	Separated from wife
Mental factors	Schizoaffective disorder
	Sex addiction
Motive	Avoid arrest for child support enforcement
Circumstances	Trespassing call
Outcome	Committed suicide

Discussion: Age

After seeing a significant increase in the number of cop-killers in the twenty to twenty-nine age group, we now begin to see a decrease in the number of offenders aged thirty to thirty-four. Examining the following graph, we can see another spike in the number of cop-killers occurs around a particular age:

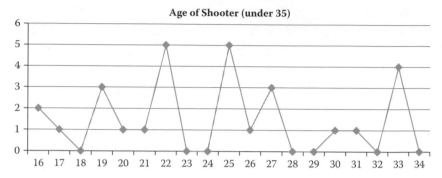

Age of Shooter (under 35)

Most cop-killers in this group (seventy-one percent) were males thirty-three years of age.

Discussion: Race

All but one shooter in this group were white males. Note the dramatic shift in the offenders' races by the time all shooters under age thirty-five are considered. Examining all shooters in the study under age thirty-five, the number of both black and white cop-killers is equal:

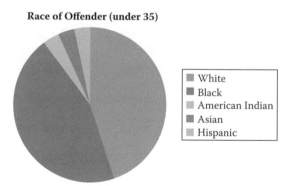

Race of Offender (under 35)

- White
- Black
- American Indian
- Asian
- Hispanic

One shooter from each of the following minority groups is also included: American Indian, Asian, and Hispanic.

For comparison with offenders, we should also briefly examine the role of the officers' races. This distribution remains relatively unchanged:

Race of Officer Killed by
Offenders (under 35)

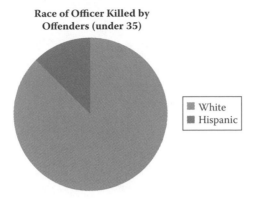

Of the thirty-two officers killed by offenders under age thirty-five, twenty-eight (eighty-eight percent) were white. Four were Hispanic. We have no black officers yet included in this study.

Discussion: Gang Affiliation

None of the cop-killers in this group were affiliated with a gang.

Discussion: Criminal History

All of the shooters in this age group had a criminal history. However, little or no overlap with offenders under age thirty is seen. The top three offenses reflecting the comparative trends among this age group are shown in the following:

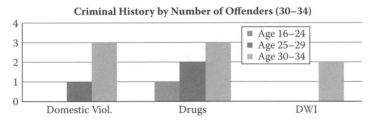

Criminal History by Number of Offenders (30–34)

Offenders in this group demonstrate a new profile from their more youthful counterparts. These offenders are influenced more deeply by deteriorating intimate relationships and poor lifestyle choices, especially with regard to substance abuse. Half were involved in violent relationships that directly or indirectly led to their fatal confrontations with police.

Discussion: Social Factors

Let us look at the comparisons of offenders in this group:

Cruckson	Military training
	Obsessive relationship
Hood	Hard-core criminal
	Drug user (cocaine)
Statler	Family member present
	Video gaming
	Child custody dispute
Seeley	Other suspects present
	Family member (wife) present
	Hard-core criminal
Post	Obsessive relationship
	Hard-core criminal
	Drug user (opiates, cocaine, heroin)
Poynter	Military training
	Obsessive relationship
	Separated from wife

Like three offenders in the previous group, three in this group were involved in obsessive relationships, including one that was separated from his wife. Half of the shooters could be classified as hard-core criminals, with lengthy histories of criminal conduct, including robbery, burglary, theft, and assault.

We also have two offenders—Cruckson and Poynter—who were trained by the military. This brings the total number of shooters trained by the military to four offenders.

Discussion: Mental Factors

Examining the mental factors, we can see some definite trends in the behaviors and functioning states of these offenders. Let us examine them side by side:

Cruckson	None
Hood	Bloodlust (committed recent murder of civilian)
	Involved in escape from crime scene
	High on drugs (suspected)
Statler	Affinity for guns
	High on alcohol
	Alone with officer

Seeley	Drug user (methamphetamine and marijuana)
Post	High on heroin (suspected)
	Prior contact with officer victim
	Suicidal ideation
Poynter	Schizoaffective disorder
	Sex addiction

We should note that alcohol and drugs play a more significant role in this group's encounters with law enforcement. The top factors are noted in the following:

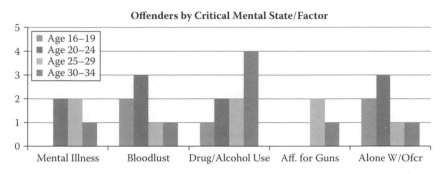

Cop-killers aged thirty to thirty-four have twice the rate of drug and alcohol use at the time of the shooting than previous groups.

Discussion: Motives

All of the offenders in this group were facing imminent arrest for a warrant or active crime in progress:

Cruckson	Avoid arrest for sexual assault
Hood	Avoid arrest for kidnapping
Statler	Avoid arrest for attempted murder
Seeley	Avoid arrest for probation violation
Post	Avoid arrest for attempted murder
Poynter	Avoid arrest for child support enforcement

The only motive in this group was to avoid imminent arrest for a serious crime, including two offenders who were wanted for attempted murder:

Motive of Offender (under 35)

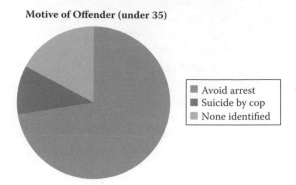

Avoid arrest
Suicide by cop
None identified

All offenders in this group were wanted by police either as a result of a warrant or a crime in progress.

Discussion: Circumstances

What were the circumstances of the encounters with police that led to the deadly outcomes in this group? Let us examine these events side by side:

Cruckson	Sexual assault call
Hood	Traffic stop—passenger
Statler	Shots fired call
Seeley	Warrant service
Post	Warrant service
Poynter	Trespassing call

Most of the offenders in this age group were either the subjects of calls to police or a warrant service operation at the offender's home; yet the circumstances are not clearly trends in this group:

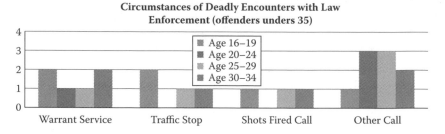

Circumstances of Deadly Encounters with Law Enforcement (offenders unders 35)

Like other groups, a distribution of circumstances is seen: Two offenders were the subject of warrant service and two were reported in other calls to police. One offender each was the subject of a traffic stop and shots-fired call.

Discussion: Outcomes

Although every officer in this study was killed, an examination of the outcome of the incident for offenders provides some interesting data. Let us examine the cases side by side:

Cruckson	Committed suicide
Hood	Fled on foot; captured
Statler	Committed suicide
Seeley	Committed suicide
Post	Committed suicide
Poynter	Committed suicide

Only one offender survived without injury; however, none were killed by police. Five of the six cop-killers in this age group (eighty-three percent) committed suicide.

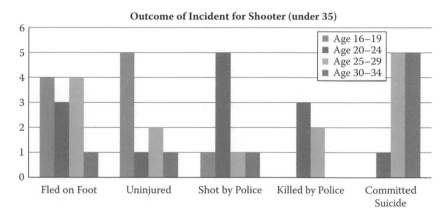

Outcome of Incident for Shooter (under 35)

Echoing the trend among those aged twenty-five to twenty-nine, the vast majority of cop-killers in this group shared the same outcome: self-annihilation.

Conclusion

Among shooters in the thirty to thirty-four age group:

- The majority were white males who were thirty-three years of age.
- Two offenders used a long gun or automatic rifle in the incident; the majority used handguns.

- All had a criminal history, including such offenses as robbery, domestic violence, drugs, or DWI.
- No shooters were gang members.
- All offenders were the subject of a call to police or the subject of a warrant service operation.
- All offenders shared the same motive: avoid imminent arrest for a serious crime, including such offenses as attempted murder and sexual assault.
- One shooter was diagnosed as schizophrenic.
- Most of the shooters committed suicide.

Bibliography

Associated Press. "'Grand Theft Auto' Led Teen to Kill, Lawyer Claims," April 1, 2005. Retrieved January 27, 2012, from http://www.msnbc.msn.com/id/6976676/ns/technology_and_science-games/t/lawsuit-blames-shootings-video-game/#

——. "Suspect Sought in Killing Ga. Police Officer," March 23, 2011, Athens, GA: AP.

Aubele, M., and Cholodofsky, R. "Fugitive Who Gunned Down Lower Burrell Officer Apparently Took His Own Life," *Valley News-Dispatch,* October 15, 2011, Tarentum, PA: McClatchey-Tribune Business News.

Ball, B. "Brief: Moore Deputy Killed in Vass," *Sanford Herald,* December 9, 2011, Vass, NC: McClatchey-Tribune Business News.

Barnes, G. "Records Paint Scary Picture of Man Who Killed Moore Deputy," *Fayetteville Observer,* December 10, 2011, Vass, NC: McClatchey-Tribune Business News.

Biedka, C. "Fugitive Post Had Boasted He Was Gunning for Police," *Valley News-Dispatch,* October 14, 2011, Tarentum, PA: McClatchey-Tribune Business News.

——. "Lower Burrell Officer Knew He Was Headed to Dangerous Situation," *Pittsburgh Tribune Review,* October 14, 2011, Lower Burrell, PA: Tribune Review Publishing Co.

——. "Brief: Investigation into Lower Burrell Shootings Resumes," *Valley News-Dispatch,* October 19, 2011, Tarentum, PA: McClatchey-Tribune Business News.

Biedka, C., and Skena, R. "Cornered Fugitive Kills Lower Burrell Officer, Dies," *Valley News Dispatch,* October 13, 2011, Tarentum, PA: McClatchey-Tribune Business News.

Boyce, B. "Six to Face Federal Charges in Officer Long Shooting," *Tribune-Star,* August 25, 2011, Terre Haute, IN: McClatchey-Tribune Business News.

Chappell, J. "Man Who Shot Deputy Underwent Change in Iraq," *Pilot,* December 16, 2011. Retrieved April 25, 2012, from http://www. thepilot.com/news/2011/dec/16/man-who-shot-deputy-underwent-change-in-iraq

CNN. "Funeral Services Held for Slain Officer," March 27, 2011, Athens, GA: CNN.

Federal Bureau of Investigation. "Hogsett Announces Another Federal Indictment in Death of Terre Haute Officer Brent Long," November 2, 2011, Terre Haute, IN: Justice Department Documents and Publications.

Foulkes, A. "Police Talk about Killing of THPD Officer Brent Long," *Tribune-Star,* July 12, 2011, Terre Haute, IN: McClatchey-Tribune Business News.

———. "Alleged Shooter Surrounded by Violence, Crime," *Tribune-Star,* July 16, 2011, Terre Haute, IN: McClatchey-Tribune Business News.

Fox 11 News. "Cruckson's Aunt Faces Allegations," May 13, 2011. Retrieved February 14, 2012, from http://www.fox11online.com/dpp/news/local/fox_cities/hlee-cruckson-faces-threat-charges

Friedman, S., Hrouda, D., Holden, C., Noffsinger, S., and Resnick, P. 2005. Filicide–suicide: Common factors in parents who kill their children and themselves. *Journal of the American Academy of Psychology and the Law.* Retrieved May 14, 2012, from http://www.jaapl.com/content/33/4/496.full

Gurman, S. "Answers Lost in Gunman's Death," *Pittsburgh Post-Gazette,* October 15, 2011, p. B1.

Gurman, S., and Navratil, L. "Community in Shock, Grief over Officer's Death," *Pittsburgh Post-Gazette,* October 14, 2011, p. A1.

Hall, R. "A Senseless Tragedy; Eric Zapata Is the First KDPS Officer Killed in the Line of Duty," *Kalamazoo Gazette,* April 20, 2011, p. A1.

———. "Officer's Death a Senseless Tragedy; Father of Three Is the First KDPS Officer Killed in the Line of Duty," *Grand Rapids Press,* April 20, 2011, p. A3.

———. "Brothers Played 'Grand Theft Auto,' Drank before Officer Was Killed," *Kalamazoo Gazette,* June 1, 2011, p. A1.

———. "Family Seeks Return of Guns Seized after Officer Killed; Prosecutors Oppose Return of Dozen Firearms," *Kalamazoo Gazette,* September 2, 2011, p. A2.

Halpin, J. "Man Kills Moore County Sheriff's Deputy, Then Shoots Self," *Fayetteville Observer,* December 9, 2011, Fayetteville, NC: McClatchey-Tribune Business News.

Hsu, J. "For the US Military, Games Get Serious," August 19, 2011. Retrieved January 27, 2012, from http://www.livescience.com/10022-military-video-games.html

Inaba, D., and Cohen, W. 2007. *Uppers, downers, all arounders: Physical and mental effects of psychoactive drugs.* Medford, OR: CNS Productions, Inc.

Johnson, J. "Athens Policeman Killed; Search Goes into Night after Double Shooting," *Augusta Chronicle,* March 23, 2011, p. B05.

————. "Athens Policeman Killed; Search Goes into Night after Double Shooting," October 27, 2011. Retrieved January 9, 2012, from http://onlineathens. com/local-news/2011-10-27/accused-cop-killer-demands-new-lawyers

Jones, M. "1 Officer Shot Dead; Another Wounded," *Milwaukee Journal Sentinel*, March 21, 2011, p. 7.

Kaminsky, D. "Press release: DA summary and findings," September 12, 2011, Fond du Lac County publication.

————. "Letter: Police Involved Shooting," September 13, 2011, Fond du Lac County publication.

King, M. "Athens: Jamie Hood Indicted on 70 Counts in Crime Spree," June 21, 2011. Retrieved January 9, 2012, from http://www.11alive. com/rss/article/195243/3/athens-jamie-hood-indicted-on-70-counts-in-crime-spree

Leamanczyk, L. "Voicemails from Fond du Lac Killer," April 27, 2011. Retrieved February 14, 2012, from http://www.todaystmj4.com/news/local/120832034.html

Leung, R. "Can a Video Game Lead to Murder?" October 6, 2009. Retrieved January 27, 2012, from http://www.cbsnews.com/2102-18560_162-678261.html?tag=contentMain;contentBody

Mandak, J. "DA: Man Who Killed Pennsylvania Officer Made Police Threats," October 14, 2011, Associated Press, Lower Burrell, PA: APO.

————. "Unclear if Man Who Killed Pennsylvania Officer Shot Self," Associated Press, October 14, 2011, Pittsburgh, PA: APO.

"Michigan: Kalamazoo Officer's Killer Was Drinking," *US Official News*, June 1, 2011, Detroit, MI: USON.

Milligan, M. "Wounded Athens Police Officer Returns to Work," October 11, 2011. Retrieved January 9, 2012, from http://www/cbsatlanta.com/story/15663547/wounded-athens-police-officer-returns-to-work

Navratil, L., and Gurman, S. "Lower Burrell Officer Slain; Gunman Also Found Dead at Scene outside Restaurant," *Pittsburgh Post-Gazette*, October 13, 2011, p. A1.

Nixon, A. "Suspect Had Previous Run-Ins with Police; Leonard Statler Also Was Involved in Custody Dispute," *Kalamazoo Gazette*, April 21, 2011, p. A2.

"One Fond du Lac Officer Killed; 1 in Critical Condition Following Morning Shooting," *Reporter*, March 20, 2011, Fond du Lac, WI: TR.

Plummer, R. "Officers Were Trapped inside Fond du Lac Shooter's Basement," *Oshkosh Northwestern*, March 22, 2011, Gannett, WI: OSH.

————. "Two Fond du Lac Police Officers Were Trapped inside Shooter's Home," *Post-Crescent*, March 22, 2011, p. A01.

————. "DA: Reason for Police Shooting Unknown," *Reporter*, May 26, 2011, Fond du Lac, WI: TR.

————. "Chief 'Regrets' Release of Info," *Reporter*, July 15, 2011, p. A01.

————. "State Probed Fond du Lac Shooting," *Reporter*, July 17, 2011, p. A04.

"Post's Acquaintances Have Little to Say in Wake of Killing," *Valley News-Dispatch*, October 14, 2011, Tarentum, PA: McClatchey-Tribune Business News.

Ramde, D. "Wisconsin DA Clears Officers in Battle That Left One Dead," Associated Press, September 12, 2011, Milwaukee, WI: APO.

Ritger, L. "Fond du Lac DA: Volatile Relationship Led to Officer Shooting," *Reporter,* September 17, 2011, Fond du Lac, WI: TR.

———. "Police Car Camera Captured Shots That Killed Fond du Lac Officer Craig Birkholz," *Reporter,* September 21, 2011, Fond du Lac, WI: TR.

Tagami, T. "Cop Dies in Shooting; Search on for Suspect," *Atlanta Journal-Constitution,* March 23, 2011, p. 1B.

———. "Alleged Killer of Athens Cop Bound Victim in Trunk," *Atlanta Journal-Constitution,* March 24, 2011, p. 1B.

Targeted News Service. "Hogsett Announces Federal Prosecution of Six Individuals in the Shooting Death of Terre Haute Officer Brent Long," August 25, 2011, Indianapolis, IN: TNS, LLC.

"Timeline Details Events of March 20 Officer Shooting," *Reporter,* September 14, 2011, Fond du Lac, WI: TR.

"Timeline of the March 20 FDL Police Shooting," *Reporter,* July 15, 2011, Fond du Lac, WI: TR.

Trigg, L. "Monday Afternoon Shooting Shakes Up Neighborhood," *Tribune-Star,* July 12, 2011, Terre Haute, IN: McClatchey-Tribune Business News.

———. "Shooter Was Hiding in Closet," *Tribune-Star,* July 13, 2011, Terre Haute, IN: McClatchey-Tribune Business News.

———. "Police: Shooter Took His Own Life," *Tribune-Star,* July 16, 2011, Terre Haute, IN: McClatchey-Tribune Business News.

———. "Federal Trial Date Set for Six Charged in Long Shooting," *Tribune-Star,* September 2, 2011, Terre Haute, IN: McClatchey-Tribune Business News.

———. "Feds Indict Another in Long Shooting," *Tribune-Star,* November 2, 2011, Terre Haute, IN: McClatchey-Tribune Business News.

Turner, D. "Police: Suspect in Ga. Officer's Death Surrenders," March 26, 2011, Athens, GA: AP.

Yeager, A. "Coroner: Terre Haute Officer Died from Gunshot Wound to the Head," WXIN-TV, July 12, 2011, Terre Haute, IN: McClatchey-Tribune Business News.

5

HARD-CORE: COP-KILLERS IN THEIR LATE THIRTIES

Overview

In this chapter, we will examine five cases involving cop-killers aged thirty-five to thirty-nine. The cases include:

- **Hydra Lacy, Jr.**, who killed an officer who found him hiding in the attic during a warrant service operation and then killed a second police officer who attempted to rescue his fallen colleague
- **Carlos Boles**, who killed an officer during a warrant service operation
- **Jerry Lard**, who executed an officer during a traffic stop
- **Bennie Brown**, who murdered an officer who came to his home to arrest him for murdering his girlfriend
- **Henry Smith, Jr.**, who killed an officer while fleeing from the scene of a bank robbery

We will see that this group continues to be influenced by two major themes: failure of both interpersonal and professional relationships and a history of engagement in criminal lifestyles. Every offender in this group was facing the same set of consequences: imminent arrest for a serious crime.

Case 30: Hydra Lacy, Jr., Thirty-Nine

On January 24, 2011, three members of a fugitive task force arrived at the home of Christine Lacy. They were seeking information on the whereabouts of a wanted felon, her off-and-on-again estranged husband, Hydra Lacy, Jr. A warrant had been issued for Lacy after he had failed to show up for his trial on domestic violence charges. Lacy and his wife had a romantic relationship characterized by a long history of mutual obsession, physical combat, and emotional abuse.

Three or four minutes after the officers began knocking on the door of the residence, Christine Lacy answered the door and acknowledged her husband was at home and had been in bed with her minutes before. She told police that Lacy was hiding in the attic. The three officers then called for backup and began formulating a plan to locate Lacy without compromising Christine's cooperation with police.

K-9 Officer Jeffrey Yaslowitz responded to the call for backup with his dog, Ace, to assist in the search of the house. After locating the sliding access panel to the attic in the hallway ceiling, one of the officers challenged Lacy to reveal himself. When they did not receive a response, Officer Yaslowitz and Marshal Scott Ley climbed into the attic. Seeing no sign of Lacy, Marshal Ley descended back down the ladder.

Alone in the attic, Officer Yaslowitz suddenly spotted Lacy, lying spread-eagle and clothed in his boxers only, on the attic rafters ten to fifteen feet away. He pointed his gun at Lacy, ordering him to show his hands, as Marshal Ley returned to the attic to provide assistance. When Lacy became uncooperative, Marshal Ley used an electricity-conducting weapon (ECW), striking Lacy in the shoulder and chest.

As Officer Yaslowitz moved in to handcuff him, Lacy fired a single shot from a concealed handgun. Lacy then shot Marshal Ley in the chest and once in the groin. Marshal Ley lost his footing and fell through the attic opening into the hallway below. Another officer dragged Marshal Ley into the bathroom and assessed his injuries.

The officers radioed their position from inside the bathroom and requested help. Sgt. Tom Baitinger, who had arrived outside the house with other officers, organized a four-man rescue team. Wielding a ballistic shield over his head, Baitinger led the team into the house. As he neared the bathroom, Baitinger was shot twice from above by the suspect.

Sgt. Baitinger fell face down and crawled into a nearby bedroom, wounded. Gesturing to Yaslowitz's boot, which was sticking out into the attic opening, Sgt. Baitinger told the other officers to rescue

Officer Yaslowitz from the attic as Baitinger provided cover fire from the floor of the bedroom with an AR-15 rifle. When they were unsuccessful, Lacy began firing again.

A few minutes later, Lacy phoned 911 and talked to police off and on for almost an hour. Still barricaded in the attic with Officer Yaslowitz, Lacy claimed that he was interested in surrendering and that he did not want to hurt anyone else. Lacy stated that if there were any additional rescue attempts, he would kill the officer in the attic. However, Officer Yaslowitz was no hostage; he was already dead.

Lacy texted and called several friends while he was barricaded, telling them he had shot police officers. Around 9:00 a.m., the SWAT team stormed the house, but was forced to retreat under gunfire. Minutes later, a second entry was made, and the team was able to extract the body of Yaslowitz. His body had been wrapped in cords and ductwork by Lacy to prevent his easy extraction. Police then cut off the electricity and water to the residence. With no further communication from Lacy, police used construction equipment, including a backhoe, to punch holes in the home. Lacy was found dead in the rubble, shot ten times.

Hydra Lacy, Jr., had a long and violent criminal history, including aggravated assault on a law enforcement officer, sexual assault, domestic violence, and kidnapping. At the time of the incident, Lacy was wanted on warrant for failing to appear at trial for aggravated battery on his estranged wife, Christine Lacy. Three weeks before the incident, Lacy told his wife and others that he would never go back to prison and that he would "shoot it out with police."

Lacy was the second of nine children born to Hydra Lacy, Sr., a former professional boxer, and his wife. Lacy's mother was ill much of the time, so Hydra and his brother often stayed with a neighbor who had six children of her own. By the age of seventeen, Lacy had a substantial criminal history including arrests for burglary, larceny, and auto theft. He then quickly progressed from theft to more violent, predatory crimes. In 1991, twenty-year-old Lacy dragged a seventeen-year-old neighborhood girl into a car and threatened to kill her. Driving for miles on the interstate, he finally pulled over onto the shoulder and raped her for over three hours. Afterward, he fell asleep atop her in the car.

Police found them by the side of the road and arrested Lacy for sexual assault. Lacy spent ten years in prison and was released in 2001. He seemed to be putting his life back together, working a steady job and achieving stability. In 2004, he married Christine and they purchased a home together. They began investing in real estate, purchasing seven homes over the next three years. Unfortunately, Lacy's troubles with the law would soon begin again.

In 2006, Lacy was involved in a serious motorcycle accident. He spent two months in the hospital. Christine worked two jobs to keep them afloat financially and spent her spare time visiting and caring for Lacy. During his time in the hospital, Christine discovered that Lacy had another girlfriend. Their relationship would never fully recover.

Christine had a history of grand theft and was physically abusive and emotionally volatile. She did not hesitate to use the police as a weapon against Lacy. During a 2010 deposition, she said:

> I'm the more aggressive person. Like I told him, he can't do nothing to me anyway . . . he's got a criminal history. He's a black man, I'm a white girl. They're going to believe me before they believe him.

Christine routinely came to Lacy's workplace to argue with him, often using profanity and calling him names like "asshole" and "nigger" more than once. In December 2007, Christine called Lacy's probation officer to report Lacy had slapped her and thrown her down on the floor. Despite Christine's wish to drop charges, Lacy was arrested for a parole violation as a result of this incident in April 2008; he spent a month in jail. During that month, Christine visited him in jail six times.

Then, one day he did not show for work. That day, in 2009, police were called to the Lacy home where Lacy admitted he had stabbed his wife in the face with a samurai sword during an argument. She had a broken nose and a broken bone in her face. Lacy was charged with domestic violence, posted bail, and was ordered to have no contact with Christine.

At her 2010 deposition, ten months before the incident that took the life of two officers, Christine described a scene where she, rather than Lacy, had started the argument. Lacy had asked Christine to leave "his house" over and over. Christine disputed Lacy's claim to the home and accused him of infidelity. She insisted on a physical confrontation and admitted she had brandished a sword first, and then progressed to hitting Lacy with unopened liquor bottles, before finally being struck by Lacy in self-defense. Prosecutors pressed ahead with the case and set a November 1 trial date. Lacy would never stand trial.

On November 9, Christine filed court paperwork to have Lacy's name removed from their home's deed. With the help of a female friend, a notary public and fellow criminal, Christine forged Lacy's signature on the quit-claim deed. Thus, Lacy was about to lose everything—his wife, his home, and his freedom in one fell swoop. He would not go peacefully.

Subsequent police reports revealed that Lacy had used his own 9mm handgun and Officer Yaslowitz's weapon. The three officers that were shot—Officer Yaslowitz, Sgt. Baitinger, and US Marshal Ley—were transported to the hospital. Ley was the sole survivor.

This case presented a startling sensation of déjà vu for the Florida law enforcement community. Four days before this event, two other Florida officers were killed in the line of duty by Johnny Simms (Case 8). Both suspects were hard-core repeat offenders facing a certain return to prison for a felony offense. Both suspects were confronted at home by a team of highly skilled, tactically trained police officers. Both suspects opened fire with handguns and were killed by police.

Lacy's case can be summarized as follows:

Name	Lacy, H.
Age	39
Race	B
Gang affiliation or criminal HX	Aggravated assault on law enforcement officer, burglary, theft, auto theft, sexual assault, kidnapping, domestic violence
Social factors	Hard-core offender
	On parole
	Obsessive relationship
Mental factors	None
Motive	Avoid arrest for domestic violence warrant
Circumstances	Warrant service
	Disarmed officer after death
	Booby-trapped officer's body
Outcome	Killed by police

Case 31: Carlos Boles, Thirty-Five

On March 8, 2011, a fugitive task force arrived at the residence of Carlos Boles to serve a warrant. Boles had a lengthy criminal history that included more than one assault on police officers. The home was located in a high-crime district. Due to the danger posed by Boles, St. Louis PD's Violent Offenders Unit had requested the assistance of the US Marshals in the takedown. Eight marshals, including John Perry, were assigned to the team to accompany two city officers.

When police entered, Boles was concealed on the second floor and immediately fired upon officers, striking Marshal Perry in the head and another marshal in the ankle in the initial attack. A third officer was grazed on the face and neck by a third bullet that ricocheted off his vest, sending him toppling down the stairs. Officers returned fire and then retreated from the residence, cordoning off the area and calling in the SWAT team.

As the SWAT team prepared to make entry, an angry mob of around a hundred people converged on the location, shouting obscenities and expressing anger at the police. Crowd control measures were used to keep order as SWAT entered and searched for the suspect. However, Boles was already dead, fatally wounded by the officers who had returned fire earlier.

Days after the shooting, an electronic photo of Boles's bullet-ridden corpse taken at the crime scene was circulated to news media. Under investigative pressure, a SWAT officer later admitted he had taken the photograph using his cell phone. The photo "went viral" after recipients had passed it along to others.

Boles had a lengthy criminal history. He began his criminal behavior in 1992, when he was charged with first-degree assault at the age of sixteen. He assaulted a detention officer while in custody and later escaped from the juvenile detention center. He pled guilty to assault and served four months in prison on a ten-year sentence. In 2005, he was returned to prison for another four months after being arrested on felony marijuana possession. His mother wrote a letter to the court that read, in part:

> Deep down in my heart, I feel my son never really had a chance in life. I know he's no Angel, yet he isn't the worse [*sic*] person either.

His mother went on to describe how Boles had been "shot ten times and left for dead" at the age of fifteen and was only carrying a pistol for protection in his own neighborhood when he was arrested. Clearly, Boles had also developed a substance abuse problem. The court seemed inclined to offer sympathy, giving Boles a second four-month sentence for a ten-year prison term and ordering drug rehabilitation services. Boles was put on probation until 2008 and seemed to stay out of legal trouble for the next few years.

In 2010, Boles was seen by police dealing drugs on a public street. When police tried to arrest him, he threw a pill bottle and tried to run. Boles then resisted arrest, punching a police officer in the neck, and threatened to kill them before being subdued by a stun gun. The pill bottle appeared to contain illegal drugs, which were sent to a lab for processing. Boles was released from custody pending the results of the lab tests.

A grand jury later indicted Boles on the charges and a warrant was issued. The delay in the indictment was due to the length of time required to identify the narcotics contained in the pill bottle positively as heroin, cocaine base, and a prescription antianxiety medication, alprazolam.

Boles had told his family that he would never be taken alive. Less than a month later, he kept his word. Like several other suspects in this study, Carlos Boles had a history of violence and antagonism toward police. He was a youthful offender, incarcerated early in life, from an impoverished background. Boles had become addicted to drugs, perhaps as a juvenile, and was trapped in a downward spiral of crime, violent behavior, and, eventually, death inflicted on and delivered by police.

Boles's case can be summarized as follows:

Name	Boles, C.
Age	35
Race	B
Gang affiliation or criminal HX	Escape from detention, assault on police, assault, drugs
Social factors	Impoverished family
	Gangster lifestyle
Mental factors	Drug user (marijuana)
Motive	Avoid arrest for warrant
Circumstances	Warrant service
Outcome	Killed by police

Case 32: Jerry Lard, Thirty-Seven

In the late evening hours of April 12, 2011, Officer Jonathan Schmidt conducted a traffic stop on a car driven by Brian Elumbaugh. Elumbaugh had three passengers: his girlfriend, another woman, and the suspect Jerry Lard. Elumbaugh was wanted on a misdemeanor warrant for violating the town's dog leash law; he was removed from the car and handcuffed by Officer Schmidt, who was smiling and joking with Elumbaugh and the others after mispronouncing the driver's name.

Sgt. Corey Overstreet arrived to provide backup for Officer Schmidt, who was checking the passengers for warrants. Dispatch reported a misdemeanor warrant on one of the females; Lard was also wanted on a rape warrant. Officer Schmidt approached the right rear passenger door and asked Lard to step out. As Lard stepped out, he turned and fired a single shot with a handgun, striking Officer Schmidt in the neck. Lard then pursued the two officers, firing repeatedly and shouting:

What you got? What you got, bitch?

After pushing his partner backward toward safety, Officer Schmidt returned fire, striking Lard several times. However, Lard also refused to go down. After both men were wounded, Officer Schmidt pleaded for Lard not to shoot him again. As he shot Officer Schmidt again, Lard responded:

Die, motherfucker!

Shot more than once, Officer Schmidt then collapsed against the right front fender of his patrol car. Although he was transported to the hospital, Officer Schmidt died a short time later. Lard survived and was arrested. The entire incident was captured on the patrol car's dash cam video.

Lard had a violent criminal history and was a methamphetamine user at the time of the incident. He had previously faced charges for punching a police officer in the face and domestic violence.

The Lard family had a long history in the Trumann, Arkansas, area. In 1993, eighteen-year-old Lard was arrested for felony burglary and sentenced to jail time. Lard's interpersonal relationships were also rocky. In 2000, he was arrested for domestic violence after his wife reported that Lard hit her and took off with their son. Lard eventually had five children. His wife later divorced him.

Lard also had a history of violence against police. In 2003, Officer Tony Rusher accompanied a social worker to the Lard home to conduct a welfare check, probably related to his children. Lard punched Officer Rusher in the face and was arrested. The officer said:

> This guy [Lard] literally attacked me in full uniform.

In an odd twist of fate, Officer Rusher later became the police chief of Officer Schmidt's department and was responsible for coordinating Schmidt's memorial service.

Lard also had been jailed for simple violations like failure to appear and child support enforcement. However, Lard was becoming involved in more predatory crimes. On November 1, 2010, a fifteen-year-old girl reported to police that she had been raped after going trick-or-treating the night before. A forensic exam of the girl's underwear revealed a DNA sample that was sent for analysis. She named Lard as the suspect, and a warrant was issued when Lard could not be located for questioning.*

The night of the incident, Lard showed up at Elumbaugh's home and requested a ride home. As Elumbaugh drove the streets, he was pulled over by Officer Schmidt and arrested. Inside the car, Elumbaugh's girlfriend, sitting in the front seat, heard Lard repeating a phrase over and over from the back seat:

> Today is the day. Today is the day.

Lard, high on methamphetamine, was determined that he would not go to jail willingly this time.

Illicit drug use can lead to horrific murders. Suspects who might never be homicidal can become deeply delusional under the influence of drugs that have unpredictable effects, are laced with secondary drugs, or are simply overly pure. Otherwise normal people can kill their spouses, children, and even themselves in a violent, meth-fueled rage. In one case, a defense attorney said:

---

* An unconfirmed report in social media suggested that Lard molested his daughter. It is unknown if his daughter was the same victim described in the rape affidavit.

[Meth] is not illegal because we don't want people to feel better. It's illegal because it makes good people do crazy things.

His client's crime: She stabbed and slashed her six-week-old infant while on a meth binge. Fortunately, the baby survived.

As a methamphetamine user, Jerry Lard was living on the razor's edge. As a result of his drug-induced state, it is almost certain that he experienced a very different reality from that of the other passengers in the car. Chronic use of meth can lead to complete loss of touch with reality, including full psychosis, hearing voices, and seeing hallucinations. Extreme paranoia brought on by the drug then leads to sleep deprivation as users stay awake for *up to ten days at a time* before crashing down hard. This paranoia can lead the user to experience irrational suspicion that he or she is being targeted, pursued, or attacked:

Once people who are on meth become psychotic [and] triggered to violence, there are not any limits or boundaries.

Like Officer Christian, killed by shooter Jamie Hood (Case 25) less than a month before, Officer Schmidt was shot and killed by a passenger who was wanted, high on drugs, and homicidal. Like Jerry Lard, the suspect in that case also fired on a second officer.

Lard's case can be summarized as follows:

Name	Lard, J.
Age	37
Race	W
Gang affiliation or criminal HX	Burglary, domestic violence, sexual assault
Social factors	None
Mental factors	Drug user (methamphetamine)
	Girlfriend present
Motive	Avoid arrest for sexual assault warrant
Circumstances	Traffic stop
Outcome	Shot by police; captured

Case 33: Bennie Brown, Thirty-Nine

On July 13, 2011, Deputy Roger Rice worked the day shift obtaining warrants. After completing his shift, he went home for a few hours of sleep before coming back into work to fill in for another officer. In the late evening, a man called 911 to report that a relative, Bennie Brown, had told him that he had shot and killed his girlfriend at her jobsite in nearby Fountain Inn, South Carolina. Local police went to the site, an auto parts manufacturing plant, where they discovered that Nicole Kingsborough had been murdered in the parking lot.

Around 11:30 p.m., a group of officers including Deputy Rice went to the home of the suspect in Clinton. Finding Brown outside, the officers attempted to place him under arrest. Instead, Brown opened fire on officers, striking Deputy Rice once in the chest just above his vest. Brown was then shot in the leg by other officers who returned fire. However, Brown was able to make it into his home, where he barricaded himself for several hours before surrendering without incident.

Brown's early history is not known, but he was a local man with a relatively stable life. As a young man in 1992, he went to prison for burglary and theft. Since his release, his main struggle had become more personal in nature. Brown and his girlfriend, Nicole Kingsborough, had been together for over seventeen years in a relationship that was often abusive. Together, he and Kingsborough had three children, including a 3-year-old.

In 2002, Brown pled guilty to a charge of domestic violence and was given a $425 fine. In 2005, he pled guilty to a second incident and was sentenced to domestic violence counseling. Brown completed twenty-six weeks of therapy for anger management and, as a result, the charges were dropped in this incident.

Just two weeks before the shootings, Brown was arrested again for domestic violence against Kingsborough. However, it appeared that this time, Kingsborough was finally ready to leave the relationship permanently. She and her three children went to stay with Kingsborough's mother after Brown's arrest.

Brown stayed in jail for several days and, due to a judicial error, was released on personal recognizance on July 2. Questioned later, the magistrate said he was not aware of the suspect's prior record at the time he set Brown's bond, despite the legal requirement to consider criminal history of the suspect. This would prove to be a fatal mistake.

On the night of the murders, Kingsborough arrived for her night shift job at the Fehrer auto plant. Brown either waited for her to arrive or followed her to work. As she sat in her vehicle with the driver's side window rolled down and the doors locked, perhaps smoking a last cigarette, Brown walked up to her car and shot her once in the face with a handgun, killing her.

Brown then drove away from the plant and returned home, calling a relative to confess what he had done. The relative called police, leading to the confrontation that took the life of Deputy Rice.

Like several other suspects, Bennie Brown was in the throes of a disintegrating relationship, undone by his violent acts toward his common-law wife. The suspect in this case is not the first to murder an estranged spouse with a firearm before being confronted by police. Officer Falcone's killer, Lee Welch (Case 14), also killed his wife after luring her to a parked car in a train station parking lot. Like Kingsborough, the victim in that case also had a long history of enduring abuse at the hands of the suspect.

Brown's history is also reminiscent of the suspects Jayson Eggenberg, James Cruckson, and Hydra Lacy, Jr. (Cases 17, 24, and 30). All of these shooters were witnessing the end of a volatile, unstable love relationship that gave them a distorted sense of identity and commitment. The suspects in these cases decided that death was preferable to losing control of the women who were the subject of their obsessions.

Brown's case can be summarized as follows:

Name	Brown, B.
Age	39
Race	B
Gang affiliation or criminal HX	Burglary, theft, domestic violence (× 2)
Social factors	Separated from wife
	Obsessive relationship
Mental factors	Bloodlust
	Out on bond/bail
Motive	Avoid arrest for murder
Circumstances	Arrest at suspect's home
Outcome	Shot by police; captured

Case 34: Henry Smith, Jr., Thirty-Seven

On November 17, 2011, suspect Henry Smith, Jr., committed a bank robbery using a handgun at the Bank of America. Escaping in a silver sport-utility vehicle with a sum of cash, Smith was spotted by Officer James Capoot a few minutes after the robbery occurred. Officer Capoot initiated a pursuit of Smith in his patrol car for approximately four miles before conducting a pursuit intervention technique (PIT) maneuver.

The PIT maneuver was successful, causing Smith's vehicle to spin out of control up onto a sidewalk in a densely populated residential area. Smith fled on foot and Officer Capoot got out of his car and pursued Smith, just as two other officers arrived in their patrol cars. As Officer Capoot disappeared from sight into the backyard of a home, backup officers heard several gunshots being fired. Officer Capoot had been shot in the head. Smith was apprehended soon after the shooting as he tried to break into a home near the scene, seeking a hiding place from pursuing officers. He survived the incident unharmed.

Not much is known about Smith beyond his criminal history and court paperwork. He was a local man and convicted felon who had served time in prison for weapons charges. However, despite his conviction, Smith subsequently lived an upper middle class lifestyle with a relatively stable family of his own.

Smith was married with three children. After facing foreclosure on their home in April 2011, he and his wife filed for bankruptcy, claiming to owe more than $1.1 million in their filing paperwork. The papers reported Smith as unemployed, but Smith's wife reported that she had worked for a local ministry run by her father for the past sixteen years. Smith's wife reported her income was less than fifty thousand dollars per year; however, they owned two homes that were heavily mortgaged and had student loans and extensive credit card debt, including charge cards at Macy's and Nordstrom department stores.

In August 2011, the Smiths were released from bankruptcy proceedings, meaning that they were no longer held responsible for the liabilities reported. The Smiths gave up their second home, a rental property, as a part of their bankruptcy proceeding. Whether they were able to remain in their own home is not known. At some point, Smith determined that bank robbery might be a more lucrative way to make ends meet. His decision was deadly for the victim officer.

Smith's case can be summarized as follows:

Name	Smith, H.
Age	37
Race	B
Gang affiliation or criminal HX	Weapons
Social factors	None
Mental factors	Escaping from crime scene (robbery)
	Affinity for guns
Motive	Avoid arrest for bank robbery
Circumstances	High-speed pursuit/foot pursuit
Outcome	Fled on foot; captured by police

Discussion: Age

With only five offenders, the age group thirty-five to thirty-nine contains fewer cop-killers than any other group studied so far.

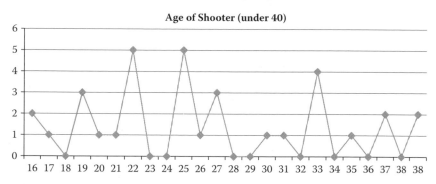

Thus, the downward trend in the number of shooters by age continues with this group.

Discussion: Race

Reversing the trend in the last group, all but one shooter in this group were black males. This tips the balance back to the majority of shooters sharing this trait:

Race of Offender (under 40)

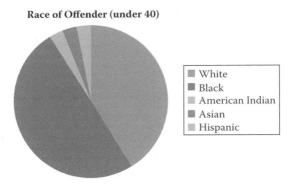

For comparison with offenders, we should also briefly examine the role of the officers' races. This distribution remains relatively unchanged throughout the study:

Race of Officer Killed by Offenders (under 40)

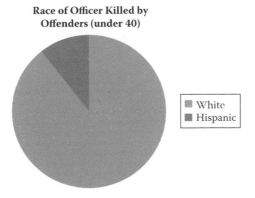

Of the thirty-eight officers killed by offenders under forty, thirty-four (eighty-nine percent) were white. Four were Hispanic. We have no black officers yet included in this study.

Discussion: Gang Affiliation

Like the previous group, none of the cop-killers in this group were affiliated with a gang.

Discussion: Criminal History

Like all of the offenders in the last group, all of the shooters in this group had a criminal history. Their profiles also return to a more typical criminal profile seen among cop-killers in their twenties:

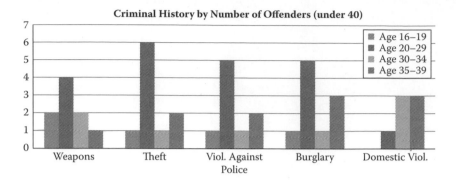

Criminal History by Number of Offenders (under 40)

Offenders in this group had criminal histories of committing burglaries, thefts, domestic violence, and violence against police, echoing that of offenders in their twenties. More than half had been convicted of domestic violence and/or burglary offenses.

Discussion: Social Factors

Let us look at the comparisons of offenders in this group:

Lacy	Hard-core offender
	On parole
	Obsessive relationship
Boles	Impoverished family
	Gangster lifestyle
Lard	None
Brown	Separated from wife
	Obsessive relationship
Smith	None

Like six of the offenders in the previous two groups, two in this group were involved in obsessive relationships, including one that was separated from his wife.

Discussion: Mental Factors

Examining the mental factors, we can see few trends. Let us examine them side by side:

Lacy	None
Boles	Drug user (marijuana)

Lard	Drug user (methamphetamine)
	Girlfriend present
Brown	Bloodlust
	Out on bond/bail
Smith	Escaping from crime scene (robbery)
	Affinity for guns

We have a truly mixed set of offenders in this group. However, cop-killers aged thirty-five to thirty-nine have a lower rate of drug and alcohol use than offenders in their twenties and early thirties.

The top factors, compared with previous groups, are noted in the following chart:

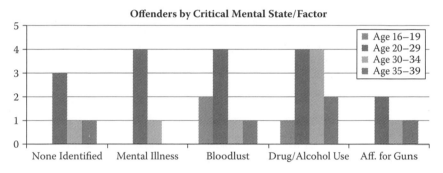

Offenders by Critical Mental State/Factor

Discussion: Motives

All of the offenders in this group were facing imminent arrest for a warrant or active crime in progress. Let us examine them together:

Lacy	Avoid arrest for warrant
Boles	Avoid arrest for warrant
Lard	Avoid arrest for warrant
Brown	Avoid arrest for murder
Smith	Avoid arrest for bank robbery

Like offenders in the last group, all offenders in this group were wanted by police either as a result of an arrest warrant or a crime in progress:

Motive of Offender (under 40)

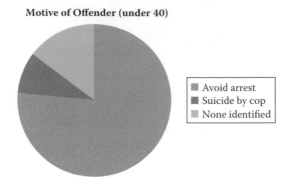

- Avoid arrest
- Suicide by cop
- None identified

The only motive in this group was to avoid imminent arrest for a serious crime, including two offenders who were engaged in crimes in progress. Seventy-five percent of offenders under age forty were facing imminent arrest at the time they killed a police officer.

Discussion: Circumstances

What were the circumstances of the encounters with police that led to the deadly outcomes in this group? Let us examine these events side by side:

Lacy	Warrant service
Boles	Warrant service
Lard	Traffic stop—passenger
Brown	Arrest for murder
Smith	High speed pursuit/foot pursuit

In contrast to offenders aged twenty to thirty-four, only one of the offenders in this age group was the subject of a call to police:

Circumstances of Deadly Encounters with Law Enforcement (offenders under 40)

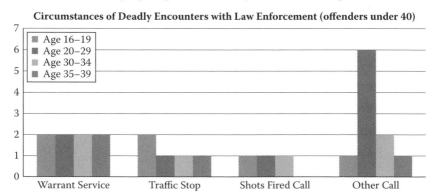

- Age 16–19
- Age 20–29
- Age 30–34
- Age 35–39

Warrant Service   Traffic Stop   Shots Fired Call   Other Call

Three offenders in this group were facing arrest at their homes, including two who were facing a felony warrant. Yet the circumstances that brought these offenders into contact with police show no other trends in common.

Discussion: Outcomes

Although every officer in this study was killed, an examination of the outcome of the incident for offenders provides some interesting data. Let us examine the cases side by side:

Lacy	Killed by police
Boles	Killed by police
Lard	Shot by police; captured
Brown	Shot by police; captured
Smith	Fled on foot; captured

Only one offender in this age group survived without injury; most (eighty percent) were shot by police, including two who were killed:

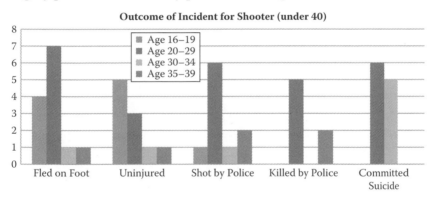

Unlike the majority of offenders aged twenty to thirty-four, none of the offenders in this group committed suicide.

Conclusion

Among shooters in the thirty-five to thirty-nine age group:

- The majority (eighty percent) were black males.
- All of the offenders used handguns.

- All had a criminal history, including such offenses as burglary, domestic violence, or violence against police.
- Drug and alcohol use was seen less often in this group, when compared with younger offenders.
- No shooters were gang members.
- All offenders shared the same motive: avoid imminent arrest for a serious crime, including such offenses as robbery, felony warrants, or murder.
- Most of the shooters (eighty percent) were shot by police, including two (forty percent) who were killed.

Reference

Nuss, J. "Witnesses Recall Fatal Shooting of Arkansas Policeman," Associated Press, April 14, 2011, Trumann, AR: APO.

Bibliography

Alongi, A. "A Dark Day," *Tampa Tribune*, January 25, 2011, p. 1.
———. "Tactics an Issue in Fatal Shootout," *Tampa Tribune*, January 26, 2011, p. 1.
———. "A Community in Mourning," *Tampa Tribune*, January 28, 2011, p. 1.
———. "Defense Seeks Gag Order in Deputy's Shooting," *Greenville News*, July 27, 2011, Clinton, SC: TGN.
———. "Solicitor to Seek Death Penalty in Laurens Deputy's Killing," *Greenville News*, November 11, 2011, Clinton, SC: TGN.
Amendola, K., Weisburd, D., Hamilton, E., Jones, G., and Slipka, M. 2012. The impact of shift length in policing on performance, health, quality of life, sleep, fatigue, and extra-duty employment. Washington, DC: US Department of Justice Report.
Bell, K. "'We Were All Shocked;' Deputy Marshal Killed in Shootout," *St. Louis Post-Dispatch*, March 9, 2011, p. A1.
BNO News. "Two St. Petersburg Police Officers Killed by Fugitive Barricaded inside House," January 24, 2011, St. Petersburg, FL: BNO.
Chalk, R. "Not Guilty Plea in Officer Shooting," *Reporter*, November 30, 2011, Vacaville, CA: McClatchey-Tribune Business News.
CNN. "2 Officers Killed, Man Found Dead after Shootout inside Florida Home," January 24, 2011, St Petersburg, FL: CNN.
Collins, J. "Laurens County Sheriff's Deputy Shot and Killed," Associated Press, July 14, 2011, Columbia, SC: APO.
Colwell, J., and Huth, C. 2010. *Unleashing the power of unconditional respect*. Boca Raton, FL: CRC Press.

Gay, M. "3 Law Officers Are Shot in St. Louis; One Dies," *New York Times*, March 9, 2011, p. 17.

Hale-Shelton, D. "Suspect Faced Arrest in Rape; Trumann Man Leaves Hospital," *Arkansas Democrat-Gazette*, April 21, 2011, Little Rock, AR: LRN, Inc.

Heard, K. "At Traffic Stop in Trumann, Officer Is Killed, Passenger Is Wounded in Gun Battle," *Arkansas Democrat-Gazette*, April 14, 2011, Little Rock, AR: LRN, Inc.

————. "Trumann Killing Charges Set in Officer's Death, Man to Face Capital-Murder Count," *Arkansas Democrat-Gazette*, April 27, 2011, Little Rock, AR: LRN, Inc.

————. "Sentence of Death Is the Aim; Officer's Slaying Labeled as Cruel," *Arkansas Democrat-Gazette*, August 18, 2011, Little Rock, AR: LRN, Inc.

Hundley, K., Valentine, D., and Thalji, J. "Questions and Grief," *St. Petersburg Times*, January 27, 2011, p. 1A.

Krueger, C., Nohlgren, S., and Hundley, K. "Report Details Officers' Heroics," St. Petersburg Times, February 25, 2011, p. 1A.

"Laurens County Deputy Killed in Shootout Is Buried Sunday," *Anderson Independent-Mail*, WSPA News Channel 7, July 17, 2011, Laurens, SC: Independent Publishing Co, LLC.

Lee, H. "Vallejo Officer—'True Champion,'" *San Francisco Chronicle*, November 19, 2011, p. A1.

————. "Cop's Accused Killer Pleads Not Guilty," *San Francisco Chronicle*, November 30, 2011, p. C4.

Lee, H., Kane, W., and Newton, C. "Officer Shot Dead Chasing Suspect," *San Francisco Chronicle*, November 18, 2011, p. A1.

Lush, T., and Stacy, M. "Officials ID Officers Killed in Florida Shootout," Associated Press Online, January 24, 2011, St. Petersburg, FL: APO.

————. "Grim Month for Police, 2 More Florida Officers Slain," Associated Press Online, January 25, 2011, St. Petersburg, FL: APO.

Mann, J. "Shots Not a Surprise; Fugitive Apprehension Team Knew Suspect Had Vowed Not to Be Taken Alive," *St. Louis Post-Dispatch*, March 10, 2011, p. A1.

Montgomery, B., Nohlgren, S., Anton, L., Stanley, K., and Kreuger, C. "A Love Spiraled into Tragedy," *St. Petersburg Times*, January 30, 2011, p. 1A.

Nohlgren, S. "Killer Eluded 3 Searches," *St. Petersburg Times*, February 2, 2011, p. 1A.

————. "If Officer Is Down, Loyalty Wins," *St. Petersburg Times*, February 5, 2011, p. 1A.

Nuss, J. "Arkansas Police Shooting Suspect Linked to '03 Attack," Associated Press, April 15, 2011, Trumann, AR: APO.

————. "Suspect in Arkansas Officer's Death Held without Bond," Associated Press, April 20, 2011, Trumann, AR: APO.

Perez, L. "In 911 Call, Lacy Sent Out Warning," *St. Petersburg Times*, April 16, 2011, p. 3B.

Pittman, C., and DeCamp, D. "On Police Radios, Gunfire and Urgency," *St. Petersburg Times*, January 30, 2011, p. 13A.

Reyes, R. "'Get Us out of Here,' a Voice Says," *Tampa Tribune*, February 1, 2011, p. 1.

"Shooting Time Line," *St. Petersburg Times*, January 25, 2011, p. 8A.

"Shootout Report Clarifies but Falls Short" [editorial]. *St. Petersburg Times*, February 25, 2011, p. 10A.

"Slain Officers Laid to Rest," *South Florida Times*, January 27, 2011, p. 1A, vol. 21, no. 5.

Stacy, M. "Florida Officer Slayings Underscore Warrant Risks," Associated Press Online, January 25, 2011, St. Petersburg, FL: APO.

———. "Police Cleared of Killing Man Who Shot 2 Officers," Associated Press Online, February 24, 2011, St. Petersburg, FL: APO.

Stanley, K. "As Bullets Flew, He Entered Fray," *St. Petersburg Times*, April 22, 2011, p. 1A.

Suhr, J. "Arrest Attempt on Risky Suspect Turns Deadly," Associated Press Online, March 9, 2011, St. Louis, MO: AP.

Sullivan, J. "Accused Cop Killer from Fairfield Was in Financial Trouble. *Daily Republic*, November 18, 2011. Retrieved April 25, 2012, from http://www.dailyrepublic.com/?p=109809

Thalji, J. "St. Petersburg Chief to Review Police Tactics," *St. Petersburg Times*, March 30, 2011, p. 1B.

Thalji, J., and Stanley, K. "Killer's Brother: Family Is Sorry," *St. Petersburg Times*, January 26, 2011, p. 1A.

Thompson, S. "Lacy Would 'Shoot It Out with Police,' Wife Had Warned," *Tampa Tribune*, February 3, 2011, p. 3.

———. "Report Details Chaos of Shootout," *Tampa Tribune*, February 25, 2011, p. 1.

———. "Ruling Made on Shooting," *Tampa Tribune*, April 15, 2011, p. 3.

Walker, M. "Shootout Exposes Raw Nerves," *St. Louis Post-Dispatch*, March 16, 2011, p. B1.

———. "Officer Admits Taking Crime Photo," *St. Louis Post-Dispatch*, March 22, 2011, p. A3.

Wosniacka, G. "Horrific Murder No Surprise in U.S. Meth Capital," Associated Press, January 21, 2012, Fresno, CA: AP.

York, J., and Burchyns, T. "Lone Suspect Identified in Vallejo Officer's Slaying," *Contra Costa Times*, November 18, 2011, Vallejo, CA: CCN.

———. "Fairfield Man Identified as Lone Suspect in Slaying of Officer Capoot," *Vallejo Times Herald*, November 19, 2011, Vallejo, CA: TTH.

6

Disturbed: Cop-Killers in Their Early Forties

Overview

In this chapter, we will examine three cases involving cop-killers aged forty to forty-four. The cases include:

- **David Bowling**, who killed an officer while trying to escape from a home burglary
- **Mark Gonzales**, who executed an officer he pulled alongside after being involved in a minor accident
- **Christian Patterson**, who barricaded himself in a garage and killed an officer investigating a domestic disturbance

This group shows a dramatic increase in the use of drugs and alcohol as a contributing factor that led to the death of police officers involved in confrontations with them.

Case 35: David Bowling, Forty-Four

During the first week in January 2011, police received a tip from an informant who reported that brothers David and Terry Bowling were involved in a series of more than thirty home burglaries and home invasion robberies across several suburban jurisdictions near Detroit, Michigan. Police initiated an undercover surveillance operation on the suspects, placing a global positioning system (GPS) tracker on the Bowlings' vehicle just days later.

On January 17, a team of undercover officers, including Officer Larry Nehasil, was trailing the suspects as they drove into an upscale residential neighborhood. Spotting a homeowner's vehicle pulling out of a cul-de-sac driveway about 5:15 p.m., the suspects made a quick decision to break into the home. Terry dropped off David, who ran around to the rear of the home. Wielding a pry bar, David broke in through a rear window and began gathering valuables while Terry circled the block. In addition to a locked safe, David found a loaded .45-caliber handgun. David then phoned his brother to return to the house and went into the garage of the home to wait. Terry backed the getaway car into the driveway. Police in unmarked units then moved to cut off their escape.

David ran through the garage and out a rear door into the fenced backyard of the home, leaving Terry behind the wheel of the getaway car to face police. Officer Nehasil chased David on foot. As David tried to scale the fence, the officer grabbed him from behind. David fired five shots, striking the officer in the head, back, buttocks, thigh, and hip; one round was stopped by the officer's vest. Officer Nehasil returned fire, striking the suspect twice in the chest. The suspect died from his injuries. Terry survived the incident unharmed and was arrested without incident.

Terry and David Bowling were brothers with long and violent criminal histories. At the time of the incident, both men were described by police as drug addicts fueling their habits by breaking into houses, engaging in home invasion robberies, and selling stolen property for cash and drugs. David was on probation for a violent offense when he shot and killed Officer Nehasil. Terry had been released from parole in 2009.

As a young man, David established a criminal history in Livonia, where he would eventually shoot and kill Officer Nehasil. In 1987, David was convicted of felonious assault in the city limits. However, his criminal history began in 1986, when the twenty-year-old was convicted of armed robbery in a nearby jurisdiction. David was later convicted of domestic violence and drug possession and, in 2010, he was convicted of causing serious injury while driving intoxicated. According to police, he crashed a car while on the way to a concert, causing a female passenger serious injury; she was in a coma for several days and sustained a traumatic brain injury.

In the weeks prior to the incident, David and his brother were evicted from a Detroit residence. They began breaking into homes and committing home invasion robberies numbering as many as fifty over the course of several months, until they encountered police during a home burglary.

David did not survive the incident. As the getaway driver and accessory to the criminal act committed, Terry Bowling pleaded no contest to the second-degree murder of Officer Nehasil in September 2011. In October 2011, he was sentenced to one hundred years in prison.

Bowling's case can be summarized as follows:

Name	Bowling, D.
Age	44
Race	W
Gang affiliation or criminal HX	Assault, armed robbery, domestic violence, drugs, DWI, burglary
Social factors	Hard-core offender
	On parole
	Crime in progress (burglary)
	Other suspect present
Mental factors	Drug use (heroin)
	Alone with officer
Motive	Avoid arrest for crime in progress (burglary)
Circumstances	Surveillance operation
	Escaping from crime in progress (burglary)
	Foot pursuit
Outcome	Killed by police

Case 36: Mark Gonzales, Forty-One

At around 2:15 a.m. on May 28, 2011, during the long Memorial Day holiday weekend, Sgt. Kenneth Vann was on the way to a call regarding an accidental shooting. As he stopped for a red light at a major intersection, a truck pulled up next to Sgt. Vann, on the passenger side. From inside the vehicle, the shooter immediately fired a barrage of bullets at Sgt. Vann, striking him twenty-five times and killing him instantly. The shooter's name was Mark Gonzales.

Gonzales was, in some ways, an atypical cop-killer. He and his wife lived together on the south side of San Antonio, Texas, in a peaceful trailer park surrounded by relatives who lived just a few doors down. They had two children together, ages seven and thirteen. In a strange coincidence, Gonzales had apparently admired law enforcement work years before. In 2003, he had applied to become a police officer. Although Gonzales passed the entrance exam, his name was placed on a waiting list that expired before his application could move forward.

Gonzales worked as a truck driver for several years until he was convicted of driving while intoxicated. In 2010, he began working as an aircraft mechanic on the night shift. He had no history of violence, but had been twice arrested for unlawful carrying of a weapon. He was described as reclusive, even with members of his own family.

On the day before the shooting, Gonzales drank heavily and spent the evening with a friend as they worked on tires at a third man's house. While at the home, Gonzales pulled out an MP-15 assault rifle and showed it off to his friends. Just before the shooting, Gonzales and his friend decided to drive to Denny's restaurant to eat. They took separate vehicles and Gonzales followed his friend. While on the way to Denny's, the intoxicated suspect rear-ended his friend's truck, causing minor damage.

Minutes later, Gonzales's friend turned right at a stoplight. Gonzales pulled up next to Sgt. Vann and, without saying a word, opened fire. Gonzales fired forty-six rounds total and then drove away.

As the reward for information grew to more than one hundred thousand dollars within one week of the killing, the community responded with information about the shooter. The day after Sgt. Vann was laid to rest, the US Marshals Service received a tip from an acquaintance of the suspect. The informant told police that he had been with the suspect, Mark Gonzales, on the day of the shooting. The informant reported the events that led up to the shooting, including the trip to Denny's involving two separate vehicles. After rear-ending his friend's truck, Gonzales stopped his truck right next to Sgt. Vann. As the informant turned the corner, he heard several loud "pops," but continued on to the Denny's.

Gonzales never arrived, but called him a short time later and said:

> I killed a cop. Don't tell no one, not even your wife.

The caller stated that he had been afraid to contact authorities, but had told his wife. In turn, his wife contacted the US Marshals. Surveillance tapes from local businesses and wireless phone records confirmed the informant's version of events.

The US Marshals executed a search warrant on Gonzales's home. Gonzales and his wife were taken into custody without incident. Hidden in the bathtub of the residence, police located a Smith & Wesson MP 15 assault rifle, two high-capacity drum magazine attachments, and two thousand rounds of .223 caliber ammunition. Police also seized a handgun. Gonzales's vehicle was found at a local body shop, where it was undergoing repairs from the minor accident. He was charged with capital murder.

Gonzales is not the first suspect to execute a police officer following an alcohol- or drug-fueled binge. Like Leonard Statler (Case 26) and Wesley Davis (Case 47), Gonzales had been drinking heavily just before the shooting.[*] He was clearly impaired as he drove the streets of San Antonio and was also under the influence of the antidepressant Prozac at the time he shot and killed Sgt. Vann.

Unlike most other cop-killers, Gonzales initiated the contact with the officer, like previous shooters Dejon White (Case 11) and Ross Ashley (Case 13).[†] The question is: Why did he kill Sgt. Vann? The only living person who knows exactly what transpired in the moments before the shooting is the suspect. However, circumstantial evidence points to the possibility that Sgt. Vann was killed because of what he saw. Did Sgt. Vann witness the minor accident between Gonzales and his friend? If so, did the suspect unsuccessfully attempt to wave him off, smiling in a friendly way while trying to convince Sgt. Vann that all was well? Gonzales knew he would face steep consequences for the third arrest for weapons and a second conviction for DWI. Perhaps he chose to become a murderer instead.

Gonzales's case can be summarized as follows:

Name	Gonzales, M.
Age	41
Race	H
Gang affiliation or criminal HX	DWI, weapons
Social factors	None
Mental factors	Alcohol use

---

[*] Statler had been drinking and playing violent video games in the hours before the shooting. He executed the officer in an alleyway after firing upon police from his front porch.

[†] Like White, Gonzales fired from inside his own vehicle when he pulled alongside the officer. Ashley approached an officer on foot as he wrote a traffic citation to a motorist.

	Drug use (Prozac)
	Affinity for firearms
	Alone with officer
Motive	Avoid arrest for DWI, weapons possession
Circumstances	Initiated by shooter
Outcome	Fled in vehicle; captured

Case 37: Christian Patterson, Forty

On June 6, 2011, deputies responded to a domestic disturbance at the home of the suspect, Christian Patterson. Patterson had threatened to kill his live-in girlfriend and himself. His girlfriend had fled the residence with her teenage son and sought help at a neighbor's home.

Two additional officers arrived to manage the negotiations with Patterson, who had barricaded himself in an attached garage with a shotgun. Negotiations with Patterson continued for nearly six hours. He repeatedly stated he only wanted to harm himself.

The emergency response team (ERT) commander determined that if the negotiations continued until 3 a.m., relief personnel and the state police would be notified. He later testified he ordered that less lethal rounds could be used if Patterson took his finger off the trigger. Around 2 a.m., Patterson tried to put on a jacket. Members of the ERT fired less lethal 40mm hard-foam impact rounds at Patterson, knocking him backward. Patterson then fell forward onto his knees with the shotgun across his legs.

Seizing what he saw as an opportunity to disarm Patterson, Deputy Kurt Wyman rushed into the garage with an electricity-conducting weapon (ECW) in his hands. Patterson quickly regained control of the shotgun and fired, striking Deputy Wyman fatally in the neck. Patterson was then shot multiple times by other officers. He survived the incident.

Almost nothing is known about Christian Patterson. He grew up in New York. After graduating from high school, he attended a local community college for two years. He studied criminal justice, but did not graduate. In 1992, he met Shannon Secor, who would become his longtime girlfriend and the mother of his sixteen-year-old son, Christian Jr. Patterson was erratically employed over the next fifteen years, finally working as a janitor at Utica College. Patterson had no criminal history.

At his trial, Patterson took the stand to offer his version of the events on the day of the shooting. He stated the disturbance at his home started when he realized his girlfriend of nearly twenty years no longer cared for him and refused to tell him where she was going. Patterson suspected Secor was having an affair with another man. He grabbed a shotgun from the gun cabinet and threatened to kill himself. Before barricading himself in the garage, Patterson also placed $4,500 in cash in a pillow case.

During his trial, Patterson recalled how the first officer to arrive spotted him and radioed a transmission:

The suspect has a gun.

The deputies backed off. Patterson testified that, as he remained in the garage for the next six hours, he was continually blinded by a spotlight from one of the officer's cars and could not see anyone. Officers asked him repeatedly to drop the weapon, and he repeatedly refused. He stated he had been suicidal but had no intent to kill police.

Patterson recalled that he was barricaded for several hours when, suddenly, he felt himself being fired upon by police. Unfamiliar with the less lethal rounds that police were firing, Patterson simply felt searing pain and stated he thought:

Why? Why are they shooting me?

He testified that he never saw anyone enter the garage and fired the shotgun accidentally. A psychologist testified that Patterson was clinically depressed but not delusional. Patterson was found guilty on all charges on February 9, 2012.

Just like Wesley Davis (Case 38), the suspect in this case had removed himself to a barricaded position—alone in a garage—where he contemplated harming himself. What might have happened if the officers had simply maintained a position of cover for six more hours and waited for the suspect to come out on his own terms? Perhaps Patterson would have committed suicide. While this would have been a sad outcome, it would have been preferable to Deputy Wyman's death.

Patterson's case is summarized as follows:

Name	Patterson, C.
Age	40
Race	W
Gang affiliation or criminal HX	None
Social factors	Obsessive relationship
	Family member present
Mental factors	Depression
	Suicidal ideation
Motive	Avoid arrest for domestic violence
Circumstances	Domestic disturbance call
	Barricaded in garage
Outcome	Shot by police; captured

Discussion: Age

Shooters in their forties make up the fewest number of cop-killers in this study.

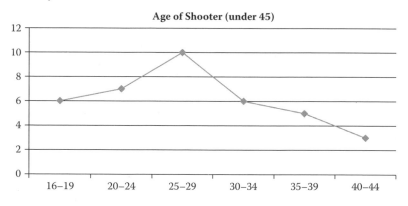

Thus, after peaking with the age group twenty-five to twenty-nine, the downward trend in the number of shooters by age continues with this group.

Discussion: Race

Reversing the trend in race from shooters in the last group, none of the offenders in this age group were black males.

Race of Offender (under 45)

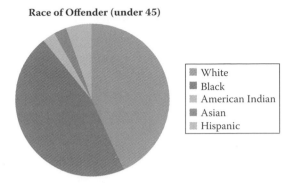

White
Black
American Indian
Asian
Hispanic

For comparison with offenders, we should also briefly examine the role of the officers' races. This distribution remains relatively unchanged throughout the study:

**Race of Officer Killed by
Offenders (under 45)**

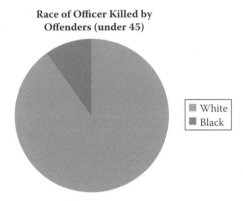

White
Black

Of the forty-one officers killed by offenders under age fifty, thirty-seven (ninety percent) were white. Four officers were Hispanic.

Discussion: Gang Affiliation

Like several of the previous groups, none of the cop-killers in this group were affiliated with a gang.

Discussion: Criminal History

The majority of the shooters in this group had a minor criminal history, including half who had been convicted of DWI. Their profiles look similar to other age groups in some ways:

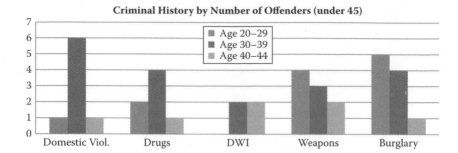

Generally, the offenders in this age group were historically less violent than those in other groups. With the exception of David Bowling, none of the offenders could be categorized as hard-core offenders. One had no criminal history.

Discussion: Social Factors

Let us look at the comparisons of offenders in this group:

Bowling	Hard-core offender
	On parole
	Crime in progress (burglary)
	Other suspect present
Gonzales	None
Patterson	Obsessive relationship
	Family member present

In two of the three cases, a family member or other suspect was present during the incident. This is a new trend with this age group.

As mentioned previously, Bowling—as a hard-core offender—is the exception to the rule in this group.

Discussion: Mental Factors

Two of the offenders were involved in the use of drugs and/or alcohol before the encounter with police. These impaired offenders include one shooter who was using alcohol and the prescription antidepressant Prozac. This increase in drug and alcohol use echoes that of younger offenders.

Examining the mental factors, we can see few trends. Let us examine them side by side:

Bowling   Drug use (heroin)
              Alone with officer
Gonzales   Alcohol use
              Drug use (Prozac)
              Affinity for firearms
              Alone with officer
Patterson   Depression
              Suicidal ideation

The top factors are noted in the following chart:

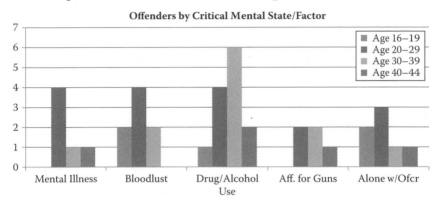

Offenders by Critical Mental State/Factor

Discussion: Motives

All of the offenders in this group were facing imminent arrest.

Bowling   Avoid arrest for crime in progress (burglary)
Gonzales   Avoid arrest for DWI, weapons possession
Patterson   Avoid arrest for domestic violence

Thus, the motive to kill a police officer in order to avoid arrest continues with offenders in every age group thus far:

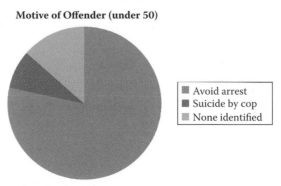

Motive of Offender (under 50)

Seventy-eight percent of offenders under age forty-five were facing imminent arrest when they killed a police officer.

Discussion: Circumstances

What were the circumstances of the encounters with police that led to the deadly outcomes in this group? Let us examine these events side by side:

Bowling	Surveillance operation
	Escaping from crime in progress (burglary)
	Foot pursuit
Gonzales	Initiated by shooter
Patterson	Domestic disturbance call
	Barricaded in garage

No trends are clear with this small group. One offender was under surveillance when he committed a crime in progress. One initiated the contact with police.

Discussion: Outcomes

Although every officer in this study was killed, an examination of the outcome of the incident for offenders provides some interesting data.
    Let us examine the cases side by side:

Bowling	Killed by police
Gonzales	Fled in vehicle; captured
Patterson	Shot by police; captured

We continue to see a shift in the outcome for offenders who are older. A set of clear trends exists for shooters over age thirty-five: They are killed by police less often than their younger counterparts.

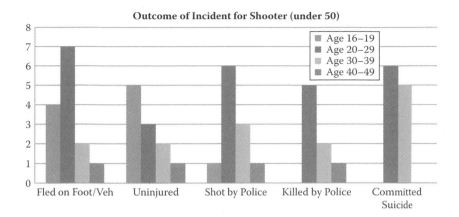

None of the shooters aged thirty-five to forty-four committed suicide.

Conclusion

Among shooters in the forty to forty-four age group:

- All shooters were white males.
- Most offenders used long guns, including shotguns or rifles. Only one offender used a handgun.
- Most offenders had a criminal history including domestic violence or DWI. One had no criminal history.
- Drug and alcohol use was seen more often in this group, similarly to the pattern of younger offenders.
- No shooters were gang members.
- All offenders shared the same motive: to avoid imminent arrest.
- Two of the shooters were shot by police, including one that was killed.

Bibliography

Associated Press. "Texas Deputy Gunned Down at Traffic Light," May 29, 2011, San Antonio, TX: APO.

———. "Texas Sheriff: Deputy's Killer Looked for Lawman," May 31, 2011, San Antonio, TX: APO.

———. "NY Sheriff Deputy Is Shot Dead after Standoff with Domestic Violence Suspect," *Boston Globe*, June 8, 2011, p. 2.

———. "Review of Standoff, NY Deputy's Death under Way," Associated Press, June 15, 2011, Oriskany, NY: APO.

"Bexar County Deputy Killed in Apparent Ambush," *Fort Worth Star-Telegram,* May 29, 2011, p. B.

Brasier, L. "Officer Tells How Burglary Arrest Led to Deaths," *Detroit Free Press,* May 5, 2011, p. A6.

———. "Man Takes Plea Deal in Officer's Shooting Death," *Detroit Free Press,* September 27, 2011, p. A6.

Garcia, G., and Tedesco, J. "Bexar Deputy Is Shot to Death at Traffic Light," *San Antonio Express-News,* May 29, 2011, p. 1A.

Lawrence, E., and Baldas, T. "Brother Faces Charges in Shooting Death of Livonia Officer," *Detroit Free Press,* January 21, 2011, p. A4.

Lawrence, E., Swickard, J., and Anderson, E. "A Stakeout Explodes into Tragedy," *Detroit Free Press,* January 19, 2011, p. A1.

Lawrence, E., and Wisely, J. "Livonia Officer, Suspect Die in Gunfight," *Detroit Free Press,* January 18, 2011, p. A5.

Mariani, J. "Suspect in Killing Expected to Survive," *Post Standard,* June 9, 2011, p. A3.

Martindale, M., and Greenwood, T. "Officer Killed with Gun Just Stolen in Break-In," *Detroit News,* January 19, 2011, p. A1.

Mondo, M. "Suspect Is Arrested in Deputy's Slaying," *San Antonio Express-News,* June 6, 2011, p. 1A.

Moravec, E. "Deputy's Slaying Sparks New Worry," *San Antonio Express-News,* May 30, 2011, p. 1A.

———. "Man Accused in Death of Deputy Was Drinking," *Houston Chronicle,* June 7, 2011, p. 5B.

———. "Suspect Told Friend of Killing," *San Antonio Express-News,* June 7, 2011, p. 1A.

Moses, S. "Man Arraigned in Oneida Deputy's Killing," *Post Standard,* June 24, 2011, p. A9.

Potrikus, A. "Deputy Had No Lethal Weapon Drawn," *Post Standard,* June 16, 2011, p. A3.

States News Service. "Arrest of Mark Anthony Gonzales," June 5, 2011, San Antonio, TX: SNS.

Sweeting, P. "Man Sentenced to 100 Years in Murder of Livonia Cop," CBS Local Detroit, October 26, 2011. Retrieved December 13, 2011, from http://detroit.cbslocal.com/2011/10/26/man-faces-life-in-prison-in-murder-of-livonia-cop/

Targeted News Service. "Deputy Sheriff Kurt Wyman, 24, Shot and Killed in the Line of Duty," June 7, 2011, Utica, NY: TNS, LLC.

Weissert, W. "Drug Ties Ruled Out in Killing of Texas Deputy," Associated Press, June 6, 2011, San Antonio, TX: APO.

Williams, C. "Gun Used to Kill Michigan Officer Stolen from Home," Associated Press Online, January 18, 2011, Detroit, MI: APP.

WKTV News. "Officer Shot 5 Times, Slain by Suspected Burglar," Associated Press Online, January 19, 2011, Detroit, MI: APP.

———. "Christian Patterson Takes Stand Late in Day 5 of His Own Murder Trial," NBC-WKTV News Channel 2, February 9, 2012. Retrieved February 17, 2012, from http://www.wktv.com/news/local/Testimony-resumes-in-Christian-Patterson-trial-138788559.html

———. "Deputy: Weapon Malfunctioned, Failed to Fire at Patterson," NBC-WKTV News Channel 2, February 9, 2012. Retrieved February 17, 2012, from http://www.wktv.com/news/local/Deputy-when-Patterson-reached-for-jacket-authorities-fired

———. "Last Day of Testimony in Patterson Trial," NBC-WKTV News Channel 2, February 9, 2012. Retrieved February 17, 2012, from http://www.wktv.com/news/local/last-day-of-testimony-in-patterson-trial-138930934.html

———. "Patterson: 'I Wasn't Aiming at Anyone,'" NBC-WKTV News Channel 2, February 9, 2012. Retrieved February 17, 2012, from http://www.wktv.com/news/local/Christian-Patterson-trial-day-6-138845714.html

7

HIGH AND LOW:
COP-KILLERS IN THEIR
LATE FORTIES

Overview

In this chapter, we will examine three cases involving cop-killers aged forty-five to forty-nine. The cases include:

- **Wesley Davis,** who murdered an officer who confronted him during a domestic disturbance
- **Victor Bigman,** who killed an officer who tried to arrest one of his sons for domestic violence
- **George Hitcho, Jr.,** who killed an officer investigating a disturbance between neighbors

This group shows a continued increase in the use of drugs and alcohol as a contributing factor that led to the death of police officers involved in confrontation with these subjects. Domestic disturbances were the primary triggers for confrontations with these offenders.

Case 38: Wesley Davis, Forty-Seven

On April 23, 2011, deputies were dispatched to a domestic disturbance involving weapons at an isolated rural home in Texas. Three officers, including Deputy Clifton Taylor, responded to the call. Deputy Taylor arrived to the call first. After knocking on the front door, Deputy Taylor located three people inside the home. They were the sister and wife of suspect Wesley Davis and a third, unidentified person connected with the family.

They told police that Davis had brandished a handgun and threatened the family. Davis had then been locked out of the home by the victims. The victims told Deputy Taylor that the armed Davis had gone into a storage shed on the property. Deputy Taylor waited for backup.

The three officers then approached the shed and found the door was closed. When they knocked on the door, they received no response. They opened the door and saw Davis sitting inside, with his right hand concealed. After ordering Davis to show his hands, the suspect responded:

I can't.

Davis then opened fire with a .380 caliber handgun, striking Deputy Taylor fatally in the neck, side, and back. Davis continued to fire rounds at police. The other deputies returned fire, killing the suspect.

In the years before the incident, Davis had apparently lived quietly for several years with his wife in a remote rural area near Burneyville, Oklahoma. However, Davis had recently become an accidental murderer. He fled the state, seeking refuge at the home of his sister in Texas, where he took the life of a police officer.

At around 9 p.m. on the evening of April 5, Davis was pulling a flat-bed trailer with his truck on a rural road. A local woman, fifty-two-year-old Ginger Bamburg, and her friend had stopped at the crest of a hill on the same road to get cellular phone reception and make a call. While they were stopped, Bamburg's dog jumped out of the car and into the roadway. Bamburg got out of her car to retrieve the dog. She was struck by Davis's truck, which continued without stopping. Bamburg died on impact.

Oklahoma Highway Patrol investigated the accident and determined that a late 1980s Chevrolet pickup truck was involved. The following day, an OHP trooper stopped a truck matching the description near the accident scene. Front-end damage to the truck appeared to have been very recently repaired and OHP impounded the vehicle to examine it further. Davis was known to be a skilled auto body repairman and was viewed as a likely suspect in the hit-and-run accident. Police reported that, just hours after the accident, Davis had replaced the damaged front end in an attempt to escape prosecution

for the crime. A search warrant executed on Davis's home the following week revealed additional evidence of his guilt.

Just one week before the shooting, Davis was arrested in Oklahoma
for the hit-and-run offense. He was arraigned and posted bond.
Several days later, Davis made his way to his sister's home, where he
stayed for only a few days before threatening his family with a handgun. Police who responded faced the distraught and desperate Davis,
who did not survive the incident.

Like Leonard Statler (Case 26), the suspect in this case was in an
alcohol-driven haze and may have been seeking to commit "suicide
by cop" through futile and violent action against police to ensure one
outcome: his death.* The likelihood that Davis was involved in the
abuse of alcohol is almost certain. Davis was involved in a hit-and-
run accident just weeks before as he drove his truck on a rural road
and unexpectedly encountered a pedestrian in the roadway. Far from
being a careless driver, police reported that the pedestrian was most
likely at fault in this incident. One report indicated that, as she chased
her loose dog, Ginger Bamburg stepped directly into the path of the
oncoming truck driven by Davis. However, Bamburg was no typical
innocent victim. She was also a convicted, violent felon who had spent
six years in prison for manslaughter and had a history of substance
abuse and selling drugs. It is certainly possible she was intoxicated
and impaired at the time of her death.

Unfortunately, Davis could not have known any of these facts at
the time of the accident. So, Davis fled the scene because he was
intoxicated and did not want to go to jail for killing a woman while
driving drunk. Davis then quietly repaired his truck in the hours after
the accident. He cleaned off the inevitable blood and debris and had
hoped to escape the notice of police. But he was not able to do so
successfully.

Despite his best efforts to conceal his guilt, he was going to face
serious charges for the accidental death. His worst nightmare came
true when he was arrested for the crime. He ran to his family for
help. And, he continued to drink, lowering his inhibitions and

---

* Statler was heavily intoxicated at the time he shot at police and fled into an alley,
  where he shot and killed Officer Zapata before committing suicide.

predisposing him to violent and self-destructive action that ended his and Officer Taylor's lives.

Davis's case can be summarized as follows:

Name	Davis, W.
Age	47
Race	W
Gang affiliation or criminal HX	Manslaughter
Social factors	Family members present (wife and sister)
Mental factors	Alcohol use
	Bloodlust*
Motive	Avoid arrest for domestic violence
Circumstances	Domestic disturbance call
Outcome	Killed by police

Case 39: Victor Bigman, Forty-Eight

On June 25, 2011, Sgt. Darrell Curley and his partner responded to a domestic disturbance call at a housing complex on a Navajo Indian reservation. Two brothers were reportedly drinking alcohol and fighting. Their mother called police to request help.

Police initially saw three men outside. One brother, Johnson Bigman, was lying on the ground and appeared to be "passed out" or unconscious. The other brother, Tyson, appeared to be stumbling around the front yard intoxicated. Once Sgt. Curley arrived, the officers determined that they had been physically violent toward one another and moved to arrest both brothers.

Both men resisted arrest. As one officer handcuffed Johnson, the suspects' father, Victor, stepped in-between Sgt. Curley and Tyson in an attempt to prevent Tyson's arrest. Tyson and his father then went back inside the house, with Sgt. Curley following behind them. Once inside, Tyson tried to punch Sgt. Curley.

Sgt. Curley used pepper spray to subdue Tyson. The other officer quickly left his handcuffed prisoner Johnson outside and went inside the house to assist Sgt. Curley with Tyson. During the struggle, Sgt. Curley was able to get one handcuff on Tyson's wrist. Officers used a

---

* Recall that "bloodlust" refers to an offender who has recently committed another murder.

second set of handcuffs to shackle Tyson's other wrist, then linked the two sets together, binding Tyson's hands behind his back.

Officers then turned and saw that Johnson had returned inside the house wearing handcuffs. Meanwhile, the father, Victor, had disappeared from view. Sgt. Curley escorted Tyson out the back door while the other officer escorted Johnson out the front door. Victor crept outside and fired a handgun at Sgt. Curley, who was struck fatally as he placed Tyson in the patrol car. Victor was then shot by police.

Victor had no previous criminal history. He was arrested and transported to the hospital, where he remained in critical condition for several weeks. Victor was scheduled to stand trial in January 2012. No additional information was available regarding the outcome. Tyson, a US Marine, was on leave at the time of the shooting. He was released to the custody of the USMC pending an assault charge. In August 2011, the charges against him were dropped.

After the incident, neighbors of the Bigman family reported that the shooting should have never happened, but that drunken brawls were common at the home. The Bigman family was described as having a "mean streak" and easily aroused to anger. Another neighbor gave a more simple explanation:

> When they got firewater in their bodies, that's when they would start [fighting].

The lack of information available in this case reflects the insular nature of the contemporary Navajo community. As one member of the community said:

> We mind our own business. We keep to ourselves around here.

As a nation apart, they are policed by their own tribal organizations sharing concurrent jurisdiction with federal agencies for major crimes like homicides and drug offenses. They are not bound to the same customs and culture as mainstream America and, generally, prefer privacy in community matters.

No direct evidence is available that confirms that the suspect in this case, Victor Bigman, was intoxicated at the time of the offense. However, many Bigman family relatives spoke (under the condition of anonymity) with the local media about this incident after the fact. One fact seems clear: The Bigman family had a history of alcohol-fueled violence. A relative recalled one episode years before in which Bigman and his wife were having a heated argument. They were screaming so loudly at one another that they did not notice when their own infant fell out of their truck and lay on the ground crying. Luckily, the infant was not seriously harmed. A second relative said that drunken arguments between the couple occurred every weekend.

Another relative described the original patriarch of the family—Victor's father—as notoriously violent and unpredictable:

> He was known to break windows and beat people up.

Is it possible that the Bigman family had a genetic predisposition to alcoholism or mental illness? The answer may never be clear. Whatever is the truth about the Bigman family, alcohol certainly played a role in this incident. Both brothers were highly intoxicated and behaving violently. Given the father's history, it was very likely that he was also intoxicated. If this is true, then this incident is reminiscent of three other cases: Leonard Statler (Case 26), Wesley Davis (Case 47), and Mark Gonzales (Case 36).

The ties that bind families together can also work against law enforcement officers at the scene of a domestic disturbance. With mandatory enforcement of domestic violence laws now a widespread practice, police are increasingly called into homes to arrest offenders who are both the heads of households and the aggressors. Victims, especially those with codependent personalities, can become combative—even homicidal—toward police when they realize that their loved ones are actually heading to jail. A large number of law enforcement injuries occur in these circumstances—and not necessarily as a result of injuries inflicted on a police officer by the offender. In a heated domestic disturbance, even the victim should always be perceived as a potential combatant.

Bigman's case can be summarized as follows:

Name	Bigman, V.
Age	48
Race	I (American Indian)
Gang affiliation or criminal HX	None
Social factors	Family members present
Mental factors	Alcohol use
Motive	Prevent arrest of son for domestic violence
Circumstances	Domestic disturbance call
Outcome	Shot by police; captured

Case 40: George Hitcho, Jr., Forty-Six

On August 11, 2011, Officer Robert Lasso responded to a call regarding a disturbance in the alley behind a residence. A man reported that he had confronted the driver of a red truck—his neighbor, George Hitcho, Jr.—who was speeding by his home. The man told the officer that after parking his truck, Hitcho walked down the alley toward him carrying a wooden club, yelling and cursing. Hitcho had finally returned to his home and the man called police.

As Officer Lasso approached Hitcho's property, located across the alley, he radioed for backup. Police Chief George Bruneio responded to the call and found Officer Lasso inside Hitcho's backyard fighting with two dogs. Chief Bruneio stated that a pit bull and a German shepherd were on top of Officer Lasso when he approached the yard. Officer Lasso removed his electricity-conducting weapon (ECW) from the holster with his left hand and pointed it at the dogs. Chief Bruneio stated that he then ordered Officer Lasso:

Shoot the dogs! Shoot them!

Before Officer Lasso could deploy his ECW, the suspect fired a single shotgun blast through the glass window in the side door of the house, striking Officer Lasso fatally in the head. After Officer Lasso was shot, Chief Bruneio ordered Hitcho to drop the weapon. Confused, Hitcho responded:

He's breaking into my house.

After repeated commands to drop the weapon, Hitcho put the shotgun down and was taken into custody without further violence.

Hitcho's past offenses included marijuana possession, drunken driving, harassment, and domestic violence. Hitcho was also described in court filings as diagnosed with bipolar disorder. Yet, Hitcho was a local man who lived most of his life in Freemansburg, Pennsylvania, where he worked intermittently as a master carpenter. Although Hitcho had a long history of criminal conduct, he did not have much of a violent history. When he was fourteen years of age, Hitcho was charged with causing eighty thousand dollars' worth of damage to his junior high school. Along with three other boys, he was sent to a detention center and later sued for restitution.

In 1991, twenty-six-year-old Hitcho married and moved into the house on New Street, where he would live for the next twenty years. After having a child, Hitcho's explosive temper cost him his marriage. His wife left him in 2003, after filing for a protective order against him. The court documents in the divorce case stated that Hitcho was bipolar and abusive to both his wife and young son. The protective order required Hitcho to turn over his guns, which were later returned.

His divorce was made final in 2005. After the divorce, Hitcho began acquiring dogs. At the time of the shooting, he housed at least ten dogs at his home, including seven German shepherds.

After his arrest, Hitcho was read his Miranda rights by police. The suspect refused to waive his rights and then stated:

> The only thing I need to know is what is going on with my dogs.

During the interview, Hitcho defended his actions by saying that he had warned the officer to get off his property and not come over the property line unless he had a warrant. He continued by stating:

> He [Officer Lasso] tried to kill my dogs and pointed a gun in my face. I do not care if you're a cop or not…unbelievable.

Hitcho was generally described as loud, belligerent, and difficult. His neighbors reported that he was often drunk, would not clean up after his ten dogs, and treated other people with rage and contempt. One neighbor said that she had dealt with Hitcho just once, when he threatened to kill her young son for throwing a tennis ball against the side of his house.

Items seized from Hitcho's home after the shooting included a handgun, bulletproof vest, several live marijuana plants, pipes, a bong, three rifles, several homemade weapons including a spiked wooden club, a duffel bag full of ammunition, containers of marijuana seeds, grinders, scales, and a twelve-gauge shotgun.

In October 2011, Hitcho agreed to be interviewed by the local media from jail. Although he refused to talk about the shooting, he reported that he had no history of animosity toward police. He also said that he and Officer Lasso shared a fondness for dogs and that Officer Lasso would sometimes pet his dogs. Official records show that Officer Lasso had a previous contact with Hitcho. He had arrested Hitcho on

December 11, 2006, after finding two bags of marijuana and a glass pipe in his vehicle, probably during a traffic stop.

Since his arrest, Hitcho's legal troubles have continued. In January 2012, a prison inmate informant testified that Hitcho flippantly introduced himself to other inmates with this statement:

Hi. I'm in for homicide. I killed a cop.

Hitcho took the informant into his confidence and stated that his only regret was that he did not kill the neighbor who called police and then himself. Hitcho went on to say that he "had the drop on" Officer Lasso when he shot him in the back of the head and that he would have shot Chief Bruneio if he had seen him sooner. Hitcho received the death penalty.

Like Alexander Haydel (Case 9) and Jayson Eggenberg (Case 17), Hitcho was diagnosed as bipolar and certainly involved in significant abuse (and likely illicit sales) of marijuana. Under the circumstances, the suspect's state of mind and perception at the time of the shooting could very likely be characterized as impaired.

Hitcho's case can be summarized as follows:

Name	Hitcho, G.
Age	46
Race	W
Gang affiliation or criminal HX	Drugs, harassment, domestic violence, DWI
Social factors	None
Mental factors	Drug dealer
	Drug use (marijuana)
	Bipolar
	Affinity for guns
	Alone with officer
Motive	Avoid arrest for assault/threats
Circumstances	Disturbance-between-neighbors call
Outcome	Captured by police

Discussion: Age

Shooters in their forties account for the fewest number of cop-killers in this study.

Age of Shooter (under 50)

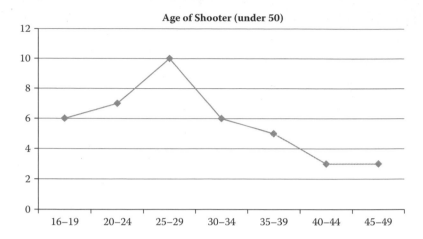

Discussion: Race

Like the other shooters in their forties, none of the offenders in this group were black males. The majority were white, with one Hispanic and one American Indian shooter:

Race of Offender (under 50)

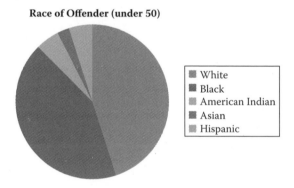

For comparison with offenders, we should also briefly examine the role of the officers' races. This distribution remains relatively unchanged throughout the study:

Race of Officer Killed by
Offenders (under 50)

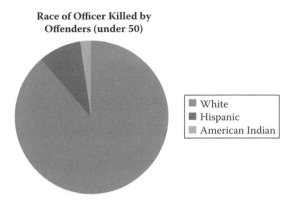

Of the forty-four officers killed by offenders under age fifty, thirty-nine (eighty-eight percent) were white. Four officers were Hispanic. One was American Indian.*

Discussion: Gang Affiliation

Like most of the previous groups, none of the cop-killers in this group were affiliated with a gang.

Discussion: Criminal History

The majority of the shooters in their forties had a minor criminal history, including half who had been convicted of DWI. Generally, the offenders in this age group were less violent than those in other groups.

Criminal History by Number of Offenders (under 50)

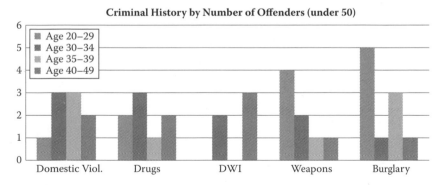

Two offenders had no criminal history.

---

* It is interesting to note that the only American Indian officer in this study was killed on an American Indian reservation by an American Indian shooter.

Discussion: Social Factors

Let us look at the comparisons of offenders in this group:

Davis	Family members present (wife and sister)
Bigman	Family members present
Hitcho	None

In most of the cases triggered by domestic disturbances, a family member or other suspect was present during the incident.

Discussion: Mental Factors

All but one offender in the forties age group (eighty-three percent) were involved in the use of drugs and/or alcohol before the encounter with police. These impaired offenders include one shooter in the last group (Gonzales) who was using alcohol and the prescription antidepressant Prozac. This sharp increase in drug and alcohol use reverses the trend seen in the previous age group.

Examining the mental factors, we can see few trends. Let us examine them side by side:

Davis	Alcohol use
	Bloodlust
Bigman	Alcohol use
Hitcho	Drug dealer
	Drug use (marijuana)
	Bipolar
	Affinity for guns
	Alone with officer

The top factors are noted in the following chart:

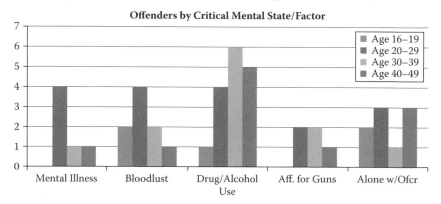

Discussion: Motives

With one exception, all of the offenders in this group were facing imminent arrest*:

Davis	Avoid arrest for domestic violence
Bigman	Prevent arrest of son for domestic violence
Hitcho	Avoid arrest for assault/threats

Involvement in an episode of domestic violence is a theme for many of the offenders in this age group. However, the trend to avoid arrest continues with all offenders under age fifty.

Discussion: Circumstances

What were the circumstances of the encounters with police that led to the deadly outcomes in this group? Let us examine these events side by side:

Davis	Domestic disturbance call
Bigman	Domestic disturbance call
Hitcho	Disturbance-between-neighbors call

All of the offenders were the subjects of calls to police involving domestic disturbances.† Interestingly, this trend echoes the number of offenders aged twenty-five to twenty-nine who were often the subjects of domestic disturbance calls.

Discussion: Outcomes

Although every officer in this study was killed, an examination of the outcome of the incident for offenders provides some interesting data.

---

* Although he was not facing arrest, Bigman was seeking to prevent the arrest of one of his sons for domestic violence.

† Domestic disturbances generally involve partners in an intimate relationship arguing inside a home. Hitcho argued with a neighbor and threatened him with a club. Although not clearly "domestic" in nature, he is included in this group of domestic disturbances.

Let us examine the cases side by side:

Davis	Killed by police
Bigman	Shot by police; captured
Hitcho	Captured

We continue to see a shift in the outcome for offenders who are older. A set of clear trends exists for shooters aged thirty-five to fifty: They are injured or killed less often than their younger counterparts.

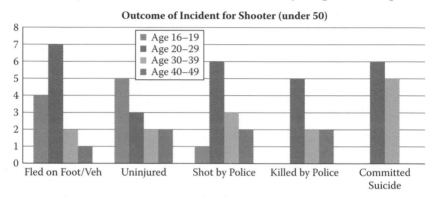

Outcome of Incident for Shooter (under 50)

Suicides peaked with offenders in the twenty to thirty-four age groups. None of the shooters aged thirty-five to forty-nine committed suicide.

Conclusion

Among shooters in the forty-five to forty-nine age group:

- The majority were white males. One American Indian male is included.
- Two of the offenders used handguns. The other shooter used a shotgun.
- Most offenders had a criminal history including domestic violence or DWI. One had no criminal history.
- Drug and alcohol use was seen more often in this group, similar to the pattern of younger offenders.
- All offenders shared the same motive: avoid imminent arrest.
- Most of the shooters (sixty-six percent) were shot by police, including one that was killed.

Bibliography

Associated Press. "Sheriff: Man Threatened Wife before Killing Deputy," April 25, 2011, Venus, TX: APO.

———. "Slain PA Officer Had Pointed Stun Gun at 2 Dogs," August 13, 2011, Freemansburg, PA: APO.

———. "Suspect Talks about Cop Killing," *Eastern Express Times*, October 24, 2011, p. B5.

Baker, S. "Gunman Kills Johnson County Deputy," *Fort Worth Star-Telegram*, April 24, 2011, p. B.

Cassi, S. "Death Sought for Cop Killing," *Eastern Express Times*, November 11, 2011, p. A1.

Drug Enforcement Administration (DEA). Shooting indices, Office of Chief Counsel DEA, CD-ROM, 2009 release.

Eiserer, T. "Deputy Shot by Gunman in Shed," *Dallas Morning News*, April 24, 2011, p. A02.

Esack, S. "'He Was So Loved,'" *Morning Call*, August 13, 2011, p. A1.

Fonseca, F. "Brothers Charged in Navajo Officer Shooting," Associated Press, June 28, 2011, Flagstaff, AZ: APO.

———. "Feds Charge Arizona Man in Navajo Officer Shooting," Associated Press, June 29, 2011, Flagstaff, AZ: APO.

———. "Son Charged in Incident That Killed Tribal Officer," Associated Press, July 2, 2011, Flagstaff, AZ: APO.

Hendricks, L. "Suspect Released to Marines," *Arizona Daily Sun*, July 1, 2011. Retrieved February 21, 2012, from http://azdailysun.com/news/local/crime-and-courts/suspect-released-0to-Marines/article_63c5cdf5-e09e-5a40-0faa-1cf3d4699280.html

"Kaibeto Man Charged in Navajo Nation Police Officer Murder," *U.S. Fed News*, June 28, 2011, Flagstaff, AZ: HT Media, Ltd.

Kendall, P. "Man Who Killed Deputy Was Suspect in Oklahoma Hit-and-Run," *Cleburne Time-Review*, April 26, 2011, Cleburne, TX: McClatchey-Tribune Business News.

KXII-TV Staff. "Woman Killed in Love County Hit & Run Accident," April 7, 2011. Retrieved February 1, 2012, from http://www.kxii.com/home/headlines/119316909.html

Lehman, P. "Weapons, Drugs Taken from Home of Suspect in Police Officer's Killing," *Morning Call*, August 17, 2011, p. A7.

———. "Man Threatened Neighbor after Police Officer Was Shot, Police Say," *Morning Call*, August 24, 2011, p. A2.

———. "Man Held in Cop's Killing: I've Already Been Judged," *Morning Call*, October 23, 2011, p. A8.

———. "Suspect in Police Officer's Killing to Face Trial," *Morning Call*, October 25, 2011, p. A1.

Malone, J. "Officials Say Hitcho Kept Stash of Guns," *Eastern Express Times*, August 16, 2011, p. A1.

———. "Chief Says Officer Shot from Behind," *Eastern Express Times*, October 25, 2011, p. A1.

Matthews, G. "Love County Man Suspected of Repairing Truck after Fatal Hit-and-Run," April 12, 2011. Retrieved February 1, 2012, from http://www.news9.com/story/14426874

McEvoy, C. "Robert Lasso, 31, Was Shot While on Duty," *Eastern Express Times,* August 12, 2011, p. A1.

Miller, R. "George Hitcho Wishes He Killed Neighbor, Police Chief and Himself, Prison Inmate Claims," *Express-Times,* January 27, 2012. Retrieved March 16, 2012, from http://blog.lehighvalleylive.com/bethlehem_impact

Ramirez, D., Jr. "Johnson County Deputy's Killer Had Threatened Wife, Two Others," *Fort Worth Star-Telegram,* April 25, 2011.

Stoddard, E. *United States of America v. Victor Bigman* [criminal complaint], June 28, 2011, United States District Court case 11-04170M-PCT-MEA filed at Flagstaff, AZ.

Yurth, C. "Neighbors: Bigmans Had History of Drunken Fights," *Navajo Times,* August 5, 2011. Retrieved February 21, 2012, from http://navajotimes.com/news/2011/0811/080611bigman.php

8

ULTRAVIOLENCE:
COP-KILLERS IN THEIR
EARLY FIFTIES

Overview

In this chapter, we will examine six cases involving cop-killers aged fifty to fifty-four. The cases include:

- **Charles Smith**, who killed an officer during a warrant service operation at his home
- **Mark Hasty**, who killed an officer during a warrant service operation at his home
- **Randall Newberry**, who set up a sniper's nest in the woods and fired on police who responded to investigate
- **Kevin Randleman**, who murdered an officer who stopped him for riding a bicycle at night without a headlight
- **Jeffrey Krier**, who killed an officer during a delusional episode of mental illness
- **Stephen Bannister**, who killed an officer investigating a domestic disturbance

After a steady decline in the number of offenders aged thirty to forty-nine, the offenders in this group demonstrate a surprising increase in the number of offenders of mature age.

Case 41: Charles Smith, Fifty

On February 16, 2011, a group of law enforcement officers, including three deputy US Marshals, two West Virginia state troopers, and members of a task force, arrived at a home to serve a warrant. The warrant for the suspect, Charles E. Smith, was related to a case nearly five years old, for drug and firearms charges.

After announcing they were there to serve a warrant, the officers breached the door and made entry into the home. The suspect opened fire with a shotgun, hitting three of the officers. Two other marshals were shot in the chest and hand by the suspect. Deputy Marshal Derek Hotsinpiller was struck in the neck, fatally. Other officers immediately returned fire, killing Smith.

Smith's warrant stemmed from a charge of possession of cocaine with intent to distribute three ounces of crack cocaine and unlawful possession of a firearm. He had a history of owning large numbers of firearms and had been a fugitive since 2006. In 2005, Smith was arrested in a nearby county for driving on a revoked license and possession of a controlled substance with intent to deliver. The local charges were dismissed, but in 2006, a federal grand jury indicted Smith for drug and weapons charges. In that case, Federal officers seized eight handguns, $354, a Rolex wristwatch, digital scales, and crack cocaine pipes.

In August 2006, after Smith failed to appear for his trial, a federal judge issued an arrest warrant from an indictment charging Smith with the federal offenses. However, Smith had gone into hiding. A search warrant for the Smith home was issued in March 2010. Marshals made contact with a man at the home who told them that Smith did not live there. The residence was not searched, and marshals returned to their investigation. On March 22, 2010, marshals interviewed Smith's wife, Sherry. She said that the suspect did not live with her, he was living somewhere in Indiana, and she had had no contact with him for six months. The trail then went cold until 2011, when an informant contacted police.

The informant reported that Smith was living in a house in Elkins, West Virginia, and had needed his furnace repaired the month before. According to the informant, the repairman who went to the home was not allowed in certain areas of the home, suggesting perhaps an illicit drug operation or other illegal enterprise might have been in operation. Further investigation revealed that the couple began receiving food stamps from the state in April 2010, at the same residence. A medical card for the suspect was also delivered to the residence; it was being used at the local Wal-Mart pharmacy.

Police set up surveillance on the residence. They noted that a large blanket blocked the view through the front windows. Just days before the shooting, a police sergeant saw a man matching Smith's description outside the rear of the home. He reported this sighting to the US Marshals, who filed for a search warrant that same day.

After the shooting, neighbors of the Smiths generally described them as "quiet" and "a nice family." One neighbor had a different view, describing how both Smith and his wife shouted at people walking by on the street. She suspected they were heavy drinkers and said that they had a lot of people who came and went from the home at all hours. She summarized her observation:

They seemed like very aggressive people.

Smith's case is summarized as follows:

Name	Smith, C.
Age	50
Race	W
Gang affiliation or criminal HX	Drugs, weapons
Social factors	Fugitive
Mental factors	Affinity for guns
	Drug dealer (cocaine)
Motive	Avoid arrest for warrant
Circumstances	Warrant service
Outcome	Killed by police

Case 42: Mark Hasty, Fifty-Two

On March 8, 2011, the US Marshals Service contacted the local sheriff's office near Limon, Colorado, with information that a sex offender, Mark Hasty, was believed to be living in the area and was wanted for failing to register. A computer search indicated that the fugitive's wife, Jackie Hasty, had registered a vehicle at a residence inside the Wagon Wheel Mobile Home Park. The US Marshals warned that Mark Hasty might be armed and had a history of fleeing from police.

Around 6:00 p.m. on the following day, a team of three officers and a deputy assistant district attorney went to the mobile home park to search for Hasty. The officers knocked at the front door and announced their presence. Hasty's wife, Jackie, answered the door and told police that her husband was not home. The officers asked for permission to search the premises for Hasty. Jackie agreed and let the officers enter the home.

The three officers moved down the hallway toward a closed bedroom door. Hasty was inside, waiting for police. As they opened the door, they observed Hasty sitting on the bed with a towel covering his lap. His hands were under the towel and the room was dimly lit. Officers ordered Hasty to raise his hands. Hasty refused and began yelling. Officer Jay Sheridan then told the other officers that he was going to use his ECW and holstered his firearm. As the officers moved in, Hasty pulled out a .25 caliber handgun and shot Officer Sheridan once in the chest, killing him.

After shooting Officer Sheridan, the suspect barricaded himself in the bedroom. The two other officers retreated and took cover in another room of the home, where they remained for a short time. The two officers tried to negotiate for Hasty to surrender. While Hasty was barricaded, he telephoned his cousin in Tennessee. When Hasty did not get an answer, he left a voice mail that suggested his next move:

> I'm in deep shit, man. They busted in the house and I shot a cop by accident. I didn't mean to . . . then they pulled out a gun on me and stuff. It was an accident . . . I gotta go. Tell everybody I said goodbye.

Hasty then shot himself once, fatally. A short time later, a SWAT team tore down one wall of the trailer, finding Hasty dead.

In 1993, Mark Hasty was convicted of incest, stemming from a 1990 offense in Tennessee involving a minor. He was given probation on a suspended sentence. In 1996, he was charged with aggravated rape of an eight-year-old girl; he pleaded guilty to a lesser charge and was sentenced to prison. Once he was released, after failing to register as a sex offender, he was returned to prison again in 2001. The same year, he also met his wife, Jackie.

After his release, he complied with the registration requirements. Hasty and his wife moved to Texas where, in 2007, he registered for the last time as the law required. The couple soon returned home to Tennessee. In January 2008, deputies went to a home in Roane County, Tennessee, where Hasty was staying, to conduct a welfare check. They found Hasty, who ran from police. Inside the home were two runaway teenage girls. In 2009, a warrant for his arrest was issued. He remained on the run for the rest of his life.

By Christmas 2009, Hasty's marriage had become unstable. Jackie called her family to ask if she could return home after she suffered a stroke. When they refused, they did not hear from her again. Jackie's relatives later told the media that Hasty was an abusive husband and that Jackie was afraid of him.

In November 2010, the couple began living at the Wagon Wheel Mobile Home Park. They used an alias last name of "Hasting" to rent the trailer. Hasty told the manager of the mobile home park that he was an ordained minister and made an ominous threat:

> If police try to come into my house, they are going to get shot.

He also told acquaintances that he was never going back to jail. By early 2011, Hasty told an acquaintance he was profoundly troubled and apparently unhappy:

> He told me every day how much he hated life. Every day, he told me he wished he was dead.

This incident represents the seventh death in the line of duty in a single year involving the same kind of enforcement activity—a warrant service at the residence of a fugitive offender. Like six other police officers in a two-month time frame—Officer Sheridan and his team confronted a wanted, convicted felon who was committed to not returning to custody and willing to kill police officers. This fact illustrates how dangerous warrant service operations can be for law enforcement.

Hasty's case can be summarized as follows:

Name	Hasty, M.
Age	52
Race	W
Gang affiliation or criminal HX	Incest, child molestation, failure to register as sex offender
Social factors	Family member (wife) present
	Fugitive
Mental factors	Suicidal ideation
Motive	Avoid arrest for warrant
Circumstances	Warrant service
Outcome	Committed suicide

Case 43: Randall Newberry, Fifty-Two

On March 13, 2011, the owner of a salvage business in rural southwest Virginia received a call from a neighbor who lived across the street from the salvage lot. The caller told the owner, seventy-year-old Roger Daniels, that there was an unknown man on the property in a car.

Daniels told the neighbor to block the car in with his own vehicle and then he called 911 before heading toward the lot. Along with the state police, two deputies from the local sheriff's office were dispatched. When the owner Daniels arrived, he saw an unoccupied, red Pontiac Sunfire parked in the driveway of the business. Deputy Shane Charles was searching the parked car; Deputy Eric Rasnake arrived a few moments later. The officers ran the tags on the vehicle. It came back registered to Randy Newberry, a local man.

The officers walked around the property with Daniels, shouting Newberry's name, but got no response. Then, Daniels saw the silhouette of a man hiding in the woods up on the hillside above the business. Daniels pointed out the suspect to one of the deputies. They started walking toward Newberry, calling for him to come out. In response, Newberry raised his rifle. Daniels crawled under a pickup truck for cover, as Deputy Charles radioed for assistance.

Nearby, an eyewitness heard five shots from the woods. She looked out her window and saw the two deputies fleeing from the shooter toward the door of a nearby house. Both were shot. Although wounded, Deputy Rasnake reached the front door first and crawled inside. Deputy Charles was shot again just before he reached cover and collapsed in the yard.

Within minutes, the Virginia State Police and every Buchanan County deputy on duty responded to the call for assistance and began to set up a perimeter. Another eyewitness watched as a third deputy, responding to the call for assistance, was shot and killed. That officer was Deputy William Stiltner.

The sheriff also responded to the scene, scrambling for cover and flanked by Deputy Cameron Justus. Undeterred by the gunfire, Deputy Justus courageously tried to remove fallen Deputy Stiltner's body from the road. During the rescue attempt, Justus was shot; he died just a few feet away from the sheriff, who said:

I was pinned down. My deputy's laying [*sic*] there and there's nothing I can do. I was so helpless. It was so hard just watching him die and I couldn't get there to help him.

After wounding two police officers and killing Deputies Stiltner and Justus, Newberry picked up his rifle and moved through the woods toward his home. He would never get there.

Two hours later, as police helicopters hovered overhead and deputies combed the woods, Newberry emerged about a quarter mile from the scene. After setting the loaded rifle down beside a telephone pole, he walked into James Conley's front yard and asked if he could use the telephone. Conley had been watching the news and heard that police were searching for an armed man who had killed police officers. Conley's wife, daughter, and grandson were hiding inside the home, in the upstairs bathroom.

Conley told police what happened next:

I asked him [Newberry] if he was the guy they were looking for. He said, "Are they looking for somebody?" And I said, "Don't you hear the helicopters?"

Conley handed Newberry a cell phone from his belt; Newberry used it to call his wife. Conley remained on his front porch, while Newberry stayed in the driveway. Conley listened as Newberry spoke into the phone:

When [Newberry's wife] picked up, he said, "What did the police say I did?" And then he looked at me and said, "What did they say I did?" I didn't respond.

Newberry discussed his car being impounded by the salvage yard with his wife as police closed in through a neighbor's yard. He then told his wife:

They are going to kill me.

Police told Newberry to get down on the ground. He ignored their commands, with his back to the officers. Conley pleaded with Newberry to give up. With his left hand, Newberry set the cell phone down next to Conley's feet. With his right hand, Newberry turned and drew a pistol from his pocket. Officers shot and killed him.

Newberry's motive in the shooting was unclear. The two injured deputies were transported to the hospital in critical condition. They survived the incident.

Newberry was described as a disabled former coal miner. His early history remains a mystery, although he had been licensed as a concealed handgun owner in Virginia since 1999 and had maintained hunting and fishing permits with the state for nearly every season since 1995. He was married and lived a quiet life, sharing a tidy white house with his wife, just a few miles away from the shooting scene.

Clearly, Newberry valued his privacy; his rural home had an eight-foot-tall security fence around the property. His neighbors said he was a nice, friendly man who plowed their driveways in the winter and helped the elderly residents. One neighbor said:

> Ask anyone in this hollow and they'll tell you the same thing. He's a good man. I just can't believe he done this.

Newberry had no criminal history, no digital footprint in social media, or any other legal troubles aside from a civil debt suit for $1,875 brought by the local hospital in 2005. After the shooting, an anonymous source speculated that Newberry had a long history of family instability, writing:

> I knew him...his father killed his mother...this is not the Randy I knew.

Another wrote:

> Randy was a nice guy...but he would tell you he was crazy, he told me he had papers to prove it, and he was on a crazy check...and lots of meds. I hear the doctor changed his meds a few weeks ago and he quit taking them. He has threatened to kill people before and it has been reported to the sheriff's dept.; however, nothing was done about it...nobody does anything till it's too late.

The suspect in this case generally fits the stereotypical profile of the "lone-wolf shooter." In his late middle age, perhaps coping with issues like significant mental illness, depression, and history of trauma and in possession of multiple deadly weapons, Randy Newberry hastily planned and executed a sniper attack on officers from a concealed position in the woods. After a lifetime of quiet compliance with the law, why did Newberry choose this particular time and place to execute his final act of violence? The answer may never be known.

In a chilling display of malevolence, Newberry intentionally targeted those officers who were attempting the rescue and retrieval of the downed officers. Just like Hydra Lacy (Case 30), Newberry observed no gentlemanly rules of warfare for officers trying to tend casualties. Unlike Lacy, reports indicated that Newberry had not taken any rounds or even been fired on. The officers in this case were not killed while firing at the suspect; they were shot while trying to secure the perimeter and rescue other officers.

Newberry's case is summarized as follows:

Name	Newberry, R.
Age	52
Race	W
Gang affiliation or criminal HX	None
Social factors	None
Mental factors	None
Motive	N/A—mental illness
Circumstances	Ambush and execution
Outcome	Suicide by cop

Case 44: Kevin Randleman, Fifty

At around 3:00 a.m. on March 19, 2011, Officer Andrew Dunn observed a man riding a bicycle in the roadway without a headlight. He radioed in a stop:

2083 [Dunn's call sign], at Tyler and Hayes with a subject. Check papers on Kevin Randleman. He's continuing on me.

Clearly, the officer recognized the suspect. Randleman initially refused to stop and was followed by police for a few moments. As dispatch checked the subject for warrants, another officer started toward Officer Dunn's location. Dispatch performed a check and then radioed a response:

Negative papers on Randleman.

The sound of a struggle was transmitted a few moments later. Randleman fired six shots from a .38 caliber revolver at Officer

Dunn, striking him five times. Officer Dunn was shot three times in the back and once in the left forearm; a fifth bullet was deflected by the officer's vest but still penetrated his body. Fatally wounded, Officer Dunn unleashed twelve shots from his .40 caliber Glock at Randleman, striking him twice, as Randleman fled on foot. Clearly in pain, Dunn made one final transmission:

Signal 11! [Officer needs assistance]

Randleman was quickly apprehended near the scene and captured without incident.

Randleman began his criminal activities in 1987, when he was charged with retail theft. In 1990, he was acquitted of aggravated murder and manslaughter. Reports indicated that Randleman got into a bar fight, where he was punched in the stomach by the victim. He left the bar to get a pistol and returned to the bar to shoot the man, fatally. At trial, Randleman claimed he fired in self-defense when a large group of men confronted him outside the bar. Although Randleman was acquitted, he was convicted of a weapons charge and sentenced to two years in prison.

After being released from prison, he continued to be involved in a violent criminal lifestyle. In 1996, Randleman was convicted of aggravated assault and was sentenced to eighteen years in prison. He did not stay behind bars for long. Two years later, he was convicted of trafficking marijuana, for which he received three additional years in prison. All of these offenses occurred in Sandusky, Ohio, where Randleman eventually became a cop-killer.

Randleman's case is summarized as follows:

Name	Randleman, K.
Age	50
Race	B
Gang affiliation or criminal HX	Theft, murder, aggravated assault, drugs
Social factors	Hard-core offender
Mental factors	Bloodlust
	Alone with officer
Motive	Avoid arrest for felon in possession of firearm
Circumstances	Pedestrian stop (bicycle)
Outcome	Shot by police; fled on foot
	Captured

Case 45: Jeffrey Krier, Fifty-Three

On April 4, 2011, Deputy Eric Stein and two other officers returned to the scene of an overnight crime of vandalism at a rural home. Twelve hours before, deputies had responded to a call from a man who reported that when he and his wife returned home from a trip out for ice cream, they discovered that two bullets had been fired through the front windows of their home. The front yard was muddied by tire tracks and their garage door had been rammed by a vehicle.

When the sheriff and deputies returned the next morning, they gathered evidence from the scene, including taking measurements of the tire tracks. Officers examined the paint transfer on the garage door and then told the victim that they were looking for a small blue pickup, the same kind of vehicle driven by their neighbor, Jeffrey Krier.

Krier had already come to the attention of the sheriff's department over the weekend by making multiple telephone calls, acting disturbed, and threatening to harm others. One month before, Krier had been taken into custody by deputies and placed in a mental hospital in Des Moines. One of the officers called Krier to ask if he was willing to talk with officers. He agreed to meet with them, but then abruptly stated:

> Kill the person in the black dually truck.

Krier then hung up. Deputies had already contacted the county attorney over the weekend regarding Krier's possible mental illness and requested information about how to proceed. They had a definitive plan:

> We had to make contact to be able to determine what his mental health status was.

Just before noon, the three deputies went to speak with Krier, who lived about a mile away from the scene on a farm. After arriving, the three officers asked Krier to come out and talk, but received no response. After several minutes, Deputy Stein used a loudspeaker to ask Krier to come out of the house; Krier did not respond.

Deputy Stein then spotted Krier at the window and advised the other officers that Krier had a gun. Krier opened fire, striking both of the police vehicles and disabling them. Stein retrieved his AR-15 semiautomatic rifle and returned fire, as Krier continued to rain bullets from inside the home. Stein's SUV was struck twenty-three times.

Facing tremendous gunfire from the suspect, Deputy Stein radioed in that shots had been fired and requested assistance. At 12:19 p.m., he told the approaching officers to turn off their sirens and remain nearby. He stated that he was low on ammunition but told backup officers repeatedly not to approach the property, saying the situation was too dangerous.

A few minutes later, another deputy spotted the suspect outside the home, armed with a shotgun fifteen yards away. He fired at Krier with his rifle, missing him. Krier returned fire. One of the nine rounds the suspect fired traveled through the window of the battered police SUV, striking Deputy Stein in the head and killing him instantly.

After killing Deputy Stein, Krier returned to the front of his home. As the other officers retreated to a defensible position, Krier mocked them, saying:

Come on back, you sons of bitches!

Krier then barricaded himself inside his home. As the SWAT team assembled, state police negotiators attempted to contact Krier to negotiate his surrender. Police were able to get Krier's brother to speak with him by phone; however, these attempts ended without success, and the suspect eventually stopped answering his phone.

At around 2:50 p.m., the suspect emerged from the house armed with a rifle, handgun, and shotgun. As he walked toward officers, Krier loaded his rifle and ignored repeated orders to drop the weapons. Two teams of concealed police snipers fired on Krier, striking him three times. As Krier fled toward a shed, he was shot several more times, killing him.

Krier had a lengthy criminal history, as well as a history of significant mental illness. At the time of the incident, he was engaged in a series of random criminal acts as a result of a paranoid delusional episode centering on his belief that his wife had been kidnapped. Krier had never been married.

Jeffrey Krier was born and raised in the same town where he would eventually become a cop-killer. After graduating from high school in

1976, Krier studied aircraft mechanics at a local community college. During early adulthood, Krier was apparently diagnosed as bipolar.

His legal troubles began when he was in his late thirties. Krier was stopped while driving a tractor trailer and arrested for carrying a handgun and marijuana possession. He requested and received a competency hearing and was placed as an inpatient in a mental facility. In October 1995, he was judged not guilty by reason of insanity and released into his parents' custody.

In 1996, he was charged with stalking a woman who told police that he called, visited, and wrote letters to her, causing her fear. In the stalking case, the victim told police that she had to disarm Krier, who was reportedly carrying a very large knife and planning to use it. After his arrest, Krier reported to corrections officials that he had a twenty-two-year history of "mixed chemical abuse," identifying alcohol, marijuana, and methamphetamines use dating back to his teen years. He was acquitted of the stalking charge by reason of insanity. He also spent thirty days in jail for an assault charge on a separate incident in 1997.

During this period of his life, Krier was treated several times as an inpatient in a mental health facility and drug treatment program and, in October 1997, the thirty-nine-year-old was again released to the custody of his parents. He would live with his parents at the family home for the rest of his life, unable to achieve any level of independence or work for the next thirteen years.

On December 8, 1999, Krier assaulted two police officers during an incident, possibly as they tried to make Krier return to a mental hospital. Neither assault was serious. There was a delay in the criminal proceedings due to the fact that Krier was in fact committed to a mental facility again in 2000. Krier eventually pled guilty to one count and spent ninety days in jail for this offense. Over the next ten years, Krier remained out of legal trouble.

On March 3, 2011, Krier was taken into custody by deputies and placed in a mental hospital in Des Moines. It is not known what triggered the commitment, but it is likely that it was at the request of his family. While he was in the hospital, the county attorney attempted to obtain an involuntary commitment order to keep Krier in treatment. The order was denied. Krier was released from the hospital after seven days and returned to the family home. Around the time he came home from the hospital, both of Krier's parents moved into a nursing home twenty miles away. Both were in ill health and required access to more skilled medical care.

On the evening of April 1, Krier called the county health center where he had been treated and told a nurse that he was going to kill his treatment provider, Robert Baker. The nurse called Baker on his cell phone and informed him of the threat, which was reported to the sheriff's department. Baker's wife was terrified for her husband when she saw Krier drive by their home at least a dozen times in the following twenty-four hours.

At around 4 a.m. the following day, Krier called the sheriff's office to report that his wife, Melissa Gentry, had been kidnapped and taken to Texas. About an hour later, another man who lived a few miles away from Krier called the sheriff's office to report that Krier had entered and searched his house, shouting that he was looking for Melissa Gentry. Krier was now floridly psychotic.

That night, Krier drove his blue pickup truck into the yard of his elderly neighbors, fired rounds through the front window and rammed their garage door with his truck. After taking a report, the sheriff and deputies went to confront Krier, which would prove to be a fatal encounter for both Deputy Stein and the suspect.

Subsequent investigation revealed that Krier had fired forty-nine rounds during the incident. However, Krier was clearly prepared for a much longer siege. Right inside the front door of the residence, investigators located a large knife, a hatchet, six additional rifles, and another shotgun, along with sufficient ammunition to sustain a prolonged firefight.

Krier's case can be summarized as follows:

Name	Krier, J.
Age	53
Race	W
Gang affiliation or criminal HX	Weapons, drugs, stalking, assault on police
Social factors	None
Mental factors	Bipolar
	Affinity for guns
Motive	Avoid mental hospital commitment
Circumstances	Disturbance call
Outcome	Suicide by cop

Case 46: Stephen Bannister, Fifty-Two

At around 10:30 p.m. on July 8, 2011, Sgt. Steven Kenner and his partner responded to a domestic disturbance at a run-down trailer park. The caller reported that a man at the location was threatening his mother with a knife. When the officers arrived, they spoke with the victim, Myra Flemmer. She reported that the suspect, Stephen Bannister, was her boyfriend and had left the house after her son called police. The caller, Flemmer's nineteen-year-old son, was described as autistic.

The officers searched the trailer to ensure the suspect was not hiding inside. They then asked for a description of the suspect's vehicle. Flemmer then looked out the kitchen window and told police Bannister's white van was still parked across the street. Sgt. Kenner and Officer Jerome then approached the van. A witness reported what happened next:

> They yelled at the . . . van: "Police officers! Show me your hands!" They asked that several times. I walked out of view and I heard about eight shots.

Bannister opened fire on the officers from inside the van, striking Sgt. Kenner fatally. Bannister was immediately shot by the other officer. He survived his injuries and is expected to stand trial for murder.

Bannister's early history is not known. As an adult, he lived for a time in Nebraska, where he was convicted of assault in 2002. After serving a year of probation for that offense, Bannister relocated to North Dakota in 2003. He reported that he was a self-employed flooring installer.

In 2006, he was convicted of a misdemeanor charge of terrorizing and carrying a concealed weapon on the premises of a bar or gaming establishment. He was given probation on a three-year suspended sentence, which he successfully completed in 2008. Over the next few years, Bannister received several traffic citations, but no additional criminal charges. However, in April 2011, just three months before the shooting, Bannister was charged with "actual physical control of a vehicle," a municipal charge for DUI when a driver is in control of vehicle, but not actually in motion. He was acquitted of this charge in June 2011.

On the night of the shooting, Bannister came over to spend the evening with his girlfriend, Myra Flemmer, and her son. He brought a 1.75-liter bottle of vodka with him and began gambling on horse races online after dinner. When a woman came by to visit Flemmer, Bannister became extremely irritated and began calling Flemmer a "whore." He then settled back into his routine on the computer when the woman visitor left.

Over the course of the evening, Flemmer received several phone calls from her children, which angered Bannister. She said:

> He went out to the kitchen and grabbed a knife out of the cupboard. Then he grabbed me by my neck and held the knife to my neck ... [and] my stomach.

In a neighboring room, Flemmer's son heard his mother begging Bannister to put the knife down and called police. Flemmer told Bannister that there was going to be trouble and he should leave. Bannister placed the knife on the table and told her to lock the door because he was leaving.

A few moments later, Flemmer went outside to look for Bannister, but did not see him. When she returned inside, she noticed the knife Bannister had been holding was missing. When police arrived, she told them that Bannister had left, but might have the knife with him. She then noticed his vehicle was still parked outside, sending officers to look for Bannister there. Unfortunately, he was waiting with a gun and killed a police officer.

Bannister's case is summarized as follows:

Name	Bannister, S.
Age	52
Race	W
Gang affiliation or criminal HX	Assault, weapons, DWI
Social factors	None
Mental factors	Alcohol use
Motive	Avoid arrest for domestic violence
Circumstances	Arrest for family violence
Outcome	Shot by police; captured

Discussion: Age

The shooters in this mature age group show a dramatic upsurge in numbers of cop-killers in this study:

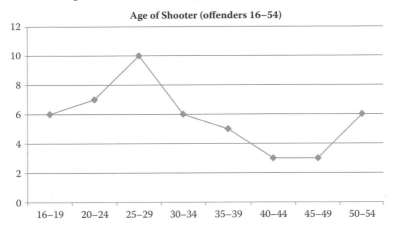

The even downward trend in the number of shooters by age takes a significant turn and peaks, surprisingly, for a final time with the six shooters in this age group. This number matches the number of shooters who were age thirty to thirty-four.

Discussion: Race

All but one of the shooters (eighty-three percent) in this age group were white. One shooter was black; at age fifty, he was also the youngest shooter in this group.

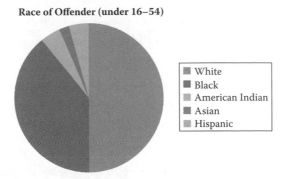

For comparison with offenders, we should also briefly examine the role of the officers' races. This distribution remains relatively unchanged throughout the study:

**Race of Officer Killed by
Offenders (under 50)**

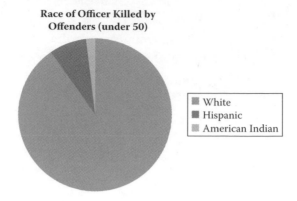

Of the fifty-one officers killed by offenders in this study thus far, forty-six (ninety percent) were white. Four officers were Hispanic. One was American Indian.

Discussion: Gang Affiliation

Like the previous groups, none of the cop-killers in this group were affiliated with a gang.

Discussion: Criminal History

The majority of the shooters in this group had a criminal history, including fifty percent who had been arrested for drugs, weapons, and/or assault. Fewer offenders had been handled for violence against police, DWI, or burglary.

Unlike the other age groups, none in this group had a history of domestic violence. However, they did demonstrate a much higher level of weapons convictions, similar or equal to that of younger offenders in their twenties and thirties.

Criminal History by Number of Offenders (under 16–54)

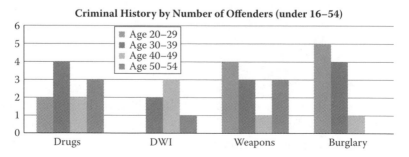

Only one hard-core offender, Kevin Randleman, is included in this group of cop-killers. Interestingly, both of the hard-core offenders over age fifty in the study were black males. This group also includes one of only two sex offenders in the study.*

Discussion: Social Factors

Let us look at the comparisons of offenders in this group:

Smith	Fugitive
Hasty	Family member (wife) present
	Fugitive
Newberry	None
Randleman	Hard-core offender
Krier	None
Bannister	None

This group contains a mixed assortment of offenders, with two fugitives: Smith and Hasty. No clear trends with regard to social factors are present with this age group. In fact, this group is remarkable for its lack of social factors.

Discussion: Mental Factors

This group shows a wide disparity among the mental factors, with two major features: mental illness and affinity for guns. Let us examine them side by side:

Smith	Affinity for guns
	Drug dealer (cocaine)
Hasty	Suicidal ideation
Newberry	None
Randleman	Bloodlust
	Alone with officer
Krier	Bipolar
	Affinity for guns
Bannister	Alcohol use

---

* Hydra Lacy was convicted of sexual assault. Mark Hasty was a child rapist.

Two of the offenders in this age group could be classified as mentally ill. The top three factors trending in this group are noted in the following chart:

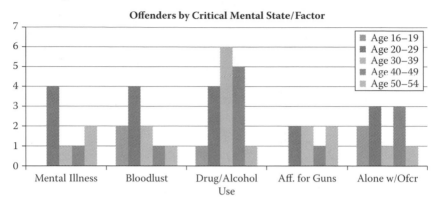

Offenders by Critical Mental State/Factor

Discussion: Motives

Half of the offenders in this group were facing imminent arrest:

Smith	Avoid arrest for drug warrant
Hasty	Avoid arrest for failure to register as sex offender
Newberry	N/A—mental illness
Randleman	Avoid arrest for felon in possession of firearm
Krier	N/A—mental illness
Bannister	Avoid arrest for domestic violence

This group contains two mentally ill shooters. However, the trend toward motive to avoid arrest continues with all offenders in the study:

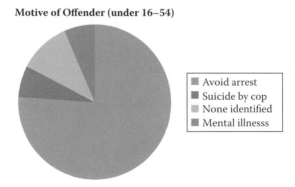

Motive of Offender (under 16–54)

Seventy-five percent of all cop-killers in this study were facing imminent arrest when they killed a police officer.

Discussion: Circumstances

What were the circumstances of the encounters with police that led to the deadly outcomes in this group? Let us examine these events side by side:

Smith	Warrant service
Hasty	Warrant service
Newberry	Ambush and execution of two officers
Randleman	Pedestrian stop (bicycle)
Krier	Disturbance call
Bannister	Domestic disturbance call

Again, no trends based on the circumstances of the encounters with law enforcement can be defined within this group.

Discussion: Outcomes

Although every officer in this study was killed, an examination of the outcome of the incident for offenders provides some interesting data.

Let us examine the cases side by side:

Smith	Killed by police
Hasty	Committed suicide
Newberry	Suicide by cop
Randleman	Shot by police; fled on foot; captured
Krier	Suicide by cop
Bannister	Shot by police; captured

We see an increase in the number of offenders killed by police with this age group.*

---

* This number includes those who committed suicide by cop by emerging from their homes brandishing weapons and ignoring commands to put them down or reaching for a weapon when police were aiming weapons at them.

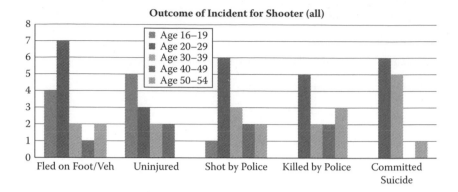

Outcome of Incident for Shooter (all)

Only one offender over thirty-five in the study—Hasty—committed suicide.

Conclusion

Among shooters in the fifty to fifty-four age group:

- Almost all shooters (eighty-three percent) were white.
- Fifty percent of the offenders used handguns. The others used long guns, including shotguns or rifles.
- Half of the offenders had a criminal history including drugs, weapons, or assault. One had no criminal history.
- Fifty percent of the offenders demonstrated an affinity for guns.
- Two of the offenders could be classified as mentally ill.
- Most of the shooters (eighty-three percent) were shot by police, including three (fifty percent) that were killed.

Bibliography

AMM. "Salvage Yard Shootout Leaves 3 Dead," *Metal Bulletin Daily Alerts*, March 15, 2011, Vansant, VA: MBDA.

Associated Press. "Officer, Suspect Killed in Colorado Standoff," March 10, 2011, Limon, CO: AP.

———. "Suspect Killed Was Sex Offender from Tennessee," March 11, 2011, Limon, CO: AP.

———. "Witness Describes Sniper Shootout with Va. Police," March 14, 2011, Vansant, VA: APO.

———. "Va. Mountain Shooter Made Final Phone Call to Wife," March 15, 2011, Vansant, VA: APO.

————. "Police Officer Dies in Ohio Shooting; Suspect Hurt," March 20, 2011, Sandusky, OH: AP.

————. "Man Accused of Shooting Deputy Had a Criminal Record," April 15, 2011, Signourney, IA: AP.

————. "Man Faces Murder Charge in Death of ND Officer," July 11, 2011, Bismarck, ND: APO.

————. "Shooting of Suspect in Cop Killing Ruled Justified," August 18, 2011, Bismarck, ND: APO.

————. "Elkins Woman Pleads Guilty to Lying to Feds before Shootout," West Virginia Gazette [electronic edition], October 20, 2011. Retrieved December 22, 2011, from http://wvgazette.com/news/201110200216

Burnett, S. "Shooting of Officer Detailed; Limon Lawman Jay Sheridan Was Slain Serving a Warrant," *Denver Post*, November 20, 2011, p. B-01.

Clark, B. Letter to Sandusky Police Department from the NAACP [memorandum], December 30, 2011.

CNN. "Suspect in Deputies' Deaths Is Identified," CNN.com, March 14, 2011, Vansant, VA: CNN.

Craig, A. "Sources Led Authorities to Wanted Man in Elkins," *Charleston Daily Mail*, February 18, 2011, p. P7A.

Denver Post "Cop Killer Was Wanted for Sex-Offender Reg. Violation," March 11, 2011. Retrieved December 29, 2011, from www.monster.com/policelink/news/articles/151585

Does anyone know the gunman in yesterday's shooting? March 14, 2011. Retrieved January 5, 2012, from http://www.topix.com/forum/citu/grundy-va/T66UGM5KU8315BHHI/p2

Dungjen, T. "Officer Shot Dead Stopping Bicyclist; Fatality in Line of Duty Is City's 1st," *Toledo Blade*, March 20, 2011, p. A1.

————. "Autopsy Report Shows Sandusky Officer Died Minutes after Being Shot Five Times," *Toledo Blade*, March 22, 2011, Toledo, OH: McClatchey-Tribune Business News.

Farnsworth, M. "Murder Suspect's Girlfriend Describes Night of Shooting," *Great Plains Examiner*, July 12, 2011. Retrieved March 8, 2012, from http://www.greatplainsexaminer.com/2011/07/12/murder-suspects-girlfriend-describes-night-of-shooting/

Fowler, B. "ET Fugitive Kills Colo. Officer, Self in Standoff; Sex Offender Hasty Sought in Roane for Not Registering," *News Sentinel*, March 11, 2011, p. A01.

Garofalo, C. "Conley: 'It Smelled Like It Smelled in Vietnam. It's Like Those Shots Fill the Air and Hang There Forever,'" *Bristol Herald Courier*, March 15, 2011, Vansant, VA: McClatchey-Tribune Business News.

————. "An Emotional 'Welcome Home' for Deputy Eric Rasnake," March 25, 2011. Retrieved January 5, 2012, from http://www2.tricities.comnews/2011/mar/25/emotional-welcome-home-deputy-eric-rasnake-ar-926708/

Harki, G., and Gregory, K. "U.S. Marshal, Suspect Killed; Two Other Marshals Wounded Serving Drug Warrant in Elkins," *Charleston Gazette*, February 17, 2011, p. P1A.

Harold, Z., and Fallon, P. "US Marshal Killed in Elkins; Suspect Opened Fire on Deputies Serving Warrant for Five-Year-Old Drug, Firearms Charges," *Charleston Daily Mail,* February 17, 2011, p. P1A.

Jordan, E. "Krier Had Long History of Mental Illness, Substance Abuse Records State," *Eastern Iowa News,* April 5, 2011. Retrieved January 19, 2012, from http://easterniowanewsnow.com/2011/04/05/144391/

Kincaid, S. "Bismarck Police Officer Killed," *Bismarck Tribune,* July 10, 2011, p. 1A.

"Krier had long history of mental illness, substance abuse, records state," *Gazette,* April 11, 2011. Retrieved January 19, 2012, from http://thegazette.com/tag/jeffrey-krier/

Krogstad, J. "Family Says Man Who Killed Deputy Had History of Mental Illness," *Des Moines Register,* April 6, 2011, Sigourney, IA: Des Moines Register & Tribune Co.

———. "Report: Officers Justified to Shoot," *Des Moines Register,* April 6, 2011, p. A1.

———. "Deputy Dies of Single Gunshot," *Des Moines Register,* April 7, 2011, p. B1.

Krogstad, J., Forgrave, R., and Witosky, T. "Iowa Sheriff's Deputy Fatally Shot near Signourney," *Des Moines Register,* April 5, 2011, p. A1.

MacPherson, J. "ND Officer Killed during Domestic Disturbance Call," Associated Press, July 10, 2011, Bismarck, ND: APO.

Magee, D. "New Details Emerge into Deputy Shooting in Keokuk County," *Waterloo Courier,* April 5, 2011, Sigourney, IA: McClatchy-Tribune Business News.

Michael, J. "Bannister Charged with Murder in Bismarck Officer's Death," *Bismarck Tribune,* July 11, 2011. Retrieved March 8, 2012, from http://bismarcktribune.com/news/crime-and-courts/bannister-charged-with-murder-in-bismarck-officer-s-death/article-6ddb99d2-abe4-11e0-8fcc-001cc4c002e0.html

———. "Bannister Makes First Appearance in Packed Courtroom," *Bismarck Tribune,* July 13, 2011. Retrieved March 8, 2012, from http://bismarcktribune.com/news/crime-and-courts/bannister-makes-first-appearance-in-packed-courtroom/article_8757f2d8-ad98-11e0-9db6-001c4c002e0.html

Newman, M. "Investigation: Lethal Force Justified," *Ottumwa Courier,* April 12, 2011, Sigourney, IA: McClatchy-Tribune Business News.

Nguyen, K. "Dennis Marc Hasty Wanted on Sex Offender Registry Violation," March 10, 2011. Retrieved December 29, 2011, from www.thedenverchannel.com/news/27140922/detail.html

Nicholson, K. "Limon Police Arrest Wife of Gunman Who Killed Officer," *Denver Post,* March 12, 2011, p. B-01.

Novak, D. "Sandusky Ohio Police Officer Andrew Dunn Killed in the Line of Duty," March 29, 2011. Retrieved January 6, 2012, from http://911responsephotography.blogspot.com/2011/03/sandusky-ohio-police-officer-andrew-dunn.html

Payerchin, R. "Officer Down in Ohio," March 20, 2011. Retrieved January 6, 2012, from http:/forums.leoaffairs.com

———. "Trial Set for Man Accused of Killing Sandusky Officer. *Journal Register News Service,* April 23, 2011. Retrieved January 6, 2012, from http:/www.news-herald.com/articles/2011/04/23/news/nh3922892.prt

Raby, J. "Deputy US Marshal, Suspect Killed in WV," Associated Press, February 17, 2011, Charleston, WV: AP

"Randleman Indicted in Killing," *Toledo Blade,* March 24, 2011, Toledo, OH: McClatchey-Tribune Business News.

Shan, J. "Limon Police Officer Jay Sheridan Shot and Killed Serving Warrant, Suspect Dead from Apparent Suicide," *Hinterland Gazette,* March 10, 2011, Limon, CO: Newstex.

"Shootout in Virginia Leaves Two Sheriff's Deputies Dead, Two Officers Wounded," *Boston Globe,* March 15, 2011, p. 2.

Topey, M. "Attorneys, Family Reflect on Previous Randleman Murder Trial, March 25, 2011. Retrieved January 6, 2012, from http://www.sandusky-register.com/news/2011/mar/25/everettfamly032311mtxml

"Virginia State Police Investigate Fatal Shootings in Buchanan County," *Targeted News Service,* March 14, 2011, Richmond, VA: TNS.

Welte, M. "Review: Deadly Force Justified in Deputy Shooting," Associated Press, April 12, 2011, Des Moines, IA: AP.

9
UNPREDICTABLE: ELDERLY COP-KILLERS

Overview

In this final chapter, we will examine five cases involving cop-killers aged fifty-five and over. These cases include:

- **Michael Ferryman**, who killed an officer investigating a shots-fired call
- **Thomas Hardy**, who murdered an officer during a traffic stop
- **Cheryl Kidd**, who killed an officer during a delusional episode of mental illness
- **Eli Myers, III**, who killed an officer during a traffic stop

This group holds a few unusual shooters, including a sixty-year-old cop-killer, a female offender, and a former police officer.

Case 47: Michael Ferryman, Fifty-Seven

In the late morning hours of January 1, 2011, Deputy Suzanne Hopper and her partner responded to a shots-fired call at a run-down mobile home park and seasonal campground close to a major interstate. Michael Ferryman and his girlfriend were living in a 15-foot camper in the park. Ferryman had shouted for an unknown person to come outside and had fired shots at a neighbor's home, shattering a window. Finding no immediate threat, one officer went to interview the caller at the door of his trailer. Deputy Hopper stopped to investigate footprints in the soft ground just outside the suspect's trailer.

As she began to photograph the footprints, Michael Ferryman opened the front door of his trailer, leveled a shotgun at the officer's head, and fired a single shot, striking her in the mouth and severing her spine. The officer was killed instantly. Ferryman had a history of violent behavior toward police and had been diagnosed with bipolar disorder and dementia. He was legally barred from owning firearms, due to his criminal and mental health history. He was killed by police during this incident.

Ferryman was an Ohio native with an unremarkable childhood. He married his high school sweetheart and had two sons before the union ended in divorce. In court records, his wife claimed that Ferryman was abusive and once threatened her with a gun. After his divorce, Ferryman began a nomadic existence, traveling between Georgia, Texas, and Ohio as a self-employed landscaper. Ferryman became a heavy drinker; he was arrested twice for driving while intoxicated in the 1980s.

Ferryman had been involved in a similar incident ten years before. In 2001, Ferryman was involved in an armed standoff with police in Morgan County, Ohio, about a hundred miles away. After firing at police who responded to a shots-fired call, Ferryman remained barricaded inside his trailer for more than 26 hours before surrendering. During the incident, he fired sixteen shots at police. He was taken into custody without injury. No police officers were injured in this incident.

When asked why he had fired at police, Ferryman stated that "it seemed like a good idea" and continued:

> It's just that you're a police officer . . . [That is] no job to have.

In 2002, Ferryman was found not competent to stand trial and was sentenced to a maximum security mental hospital. In 2003, he was diagnosed with bipolar disorder, paranoia, and experiencing delusions. In 2004, in accordance with laws requiring less restrictive environments for those adjudicated not guilty by reason of insanity, Ferryman was first transferred to a minimum security mental facility and then placed on conditional release. Ferryman was viewed by his treatment team as at risk for going off his medications because of his lack of insight into his own diagnoses as lifelong conditions requiring lifelong treatment.

In 2005, he returned to the community to live in the mobile home park where, six years later, he became a cop-killer. Ferryman spent nearly six years living there with his longtime female companion Blessing. One neighbor reported:

> He was a quiet person, but if you made him mad, he wasn't very pleasant.

In 2009, Blessing's son reported to police that Ferryman had threatened him with a knife and was "mental." However, the victim did not want to press charges. The day before the shooting, Ferryman made a complaint to the campground manager about dog waste outside his trailer.

After the shooting, Ferryman's companion returned to their trailer. She reported that she had left the residence about one hour before the incident. When she returned, the area was surrounded by police. She told police that Ferryman had been taking his medication, but had recently become "confused and had been diagnosed with dementia." The shotgun used in the incident had been provided to Ferryman "for hunting" by Blessing's eighty-one-year-old father.

Ferryman's case is summarized as follows:

Name	Ferryman, M.
Age	57
Race	W
Gang affiliation or criminal HX	DWI, attempted murder of police
Social factors	None
Mental factors	Bipolar disorder
	Dementia
Motive	N/A—mental illness
Circumstances	Shots-fired call
Outcome	Killed by police

Case 48: Thomas Hardy, Sixty

On January 23, 2011, Officer David Moore conducted a traffic stop in a residential neighborhood. The car was driven by a single male occupant, Thomas Hardy. Moore entered the vehicle's information into his computer. The officer's computer showed that the car was reported stolen on December 22, but the reason for the stop was not reported by the officer. Officer Moore may not have seen the information regarding the car before he stepped out.

Officer Moore approached the car and, standing near the trunk, asked the driver to step out. Hardy stepped out of the car with a .380 handgun and fired seven shots, fatally wounding the officer. A woman who heard the gunfire looked out the window and saw Officer Moore lying in the street directly in front of his patrol car. She called police. When they arrived, Hardy had already left the scene.

Hardy drove to a friend's house, asked his friend for money, and borrowed a cell phone to call a relative. Next, Hardy drove the stolen car to a local Dollar General and robbed it. The robbery call came in to police at 9:56 a.m. Hardy got away with only $101 in cash and coins.

Around 11:15 a.m., two hours after killing Officer Moore, Hardy called his girlfriend and told her he was in "big trouble" and wanted to meet her one last time before he went back to prison. Hardy then drove the stolen car into a downtown parking garage, abandoned it, and took a taxi back to his friend's house. Hardy was arrested at 5:30 p.m. at that location without incident.

Hardy was a convicted felon in possession of a firearm and driving a stolen vehicle at the time he was stopped by police. He was also on parole for burglary at the time of the offense.

His early history is unknown. His criminal history dates to 1984, when he was sentenced to prison for burglary. After his release, he was rearrested in November 2010, just two months before the shooting, for theft. He posted bond and was released.

A systemic failure in follow-up procedures on active parolees meant that Hardy was not adequately monitored by the Department of Corrections after his release. Hardy should have received a parole violation and been considered for return to prison in November. However, his arrest for theft while on parole went unreported and fell through the bureaucratic cracks. Hardy was also not reported to a law enforcement database as an active parolee in the community. The parole officer in charge of Hardy's case was later suspended.

The night before the incident, Hardy met with an acquaintance named "Boo." Boo had acquired two guns in a drug deal and only needed one. Hardy told Boo he wanted a gun to shoot someone who had cheated him out of one hundred dollars. Boo gave Hardy the gun, but cautioned him not to shoot anyone. Unfortunately, Hardy used the gun to kill a police officer instead.

The gun was found in a search of Hardy's belongings at the time of his arrest. Hardy's fingerprints were also found in and on the suspect vehicle and on evidence at the scene of the Dollar General robbery.

Hardy's friends and family gleaned a lot of details from Hardy before his arrest. After he shot Officer Moore, Hardy told them he acted out of fear of going back to prison. Hardy said he knew he would be arrested and sent back for possessing a handgun. He said that once he loaded the gun and switched off the safety, the situation spiraled out of control.

Hardy's case can be summarized as follows:

Name	Hardy, T.
Age	60
Race	B
Gang affiliation or criminal HX	Burglary, theft
Social factors	Hard-core offender
Mental factors	Driving stolen vehicle
Motive	Avoid arrest for stolen vehicle, firearm possession
Circumstances	Traffic stop
Outcome	Fled in vehicle; captured

Case 49: Cheryl Kidd, Fifty-Six

On April 22, 2011, Officer Chris Kilcullen was operating his police motorcycle eastbound on the highway near Springfield, Oregon. A witness later reported that a 1998 Buick Skylark driven by the suspect Cheryl Kidd began tailgating the officer. Kidd tried to pass Officer Kilcullen on the right side, but then veered back to the left after almost colliding with another vehicle.

As Kidd's vehicle swerved into his lane, Officer Kilcullen narrowly avoided a collision by moving to the left. Kidd then suddenly accelerated toward a highway exit. Officer Kilcullen activated his emergency lights and siren and attempted to stop Kidd and then radioed for assistance as she began to flee.

Kidd's vehicle traveled at speeds of up to eighty miles per hour before it reached an intersection where other vehicles had stopped for a red light. Officer Kilcullen rode up next to the driver's side of the car and put down his kickstand. As the officer then pointed to the driver to pull over, Kidd pulled out a .38 caliber revolver and shot the officer, striking him in the right side of his torso, just above his vest.

After killing the officer, Kidd continued in her vehicle eastbound along the highway, chased by police. The chase continued into a deserted forest service area, where it ended in a dead end logging road. One officer began negotiating with Kidd as others set up a perimeter. Kidd remained in her vehicle for more than two hours before surrendering. She was arrested without further violence.

After her arrest, investigation revealed that Kidd had struggled with developmental disabilities and schizophrenia for over thirty years. During the police interview that followed, it became clear that Kidd was delusional. She reported to police and a psychiatrist that Officer Kilcullen had shot at her car during a previous encounter, shattering the driver's side window. It is uncertain why Kidd believed this; forensic examination revealed the officer did not fire any rounds during the incident.

The interviewing detective said that Kidd also believed the police were always after her:

> When asked why she shot the officer, Kidd told me, "They told me I am a mongrel idiot. They're always after me, you know. [They say] I'm an erratic driver and reckless."

Detectives also assessed Kidd's awareness by asking if she understood that she had shot and killed a man. Her response:

> I didn't shoot a guy. I shot a cop.

Cheryl Kidd was the youngest of four children. Kidd's father died in 1963, when Cheryl was just eight years old. After Kidd graduated from high school in 1972, she attended a community college. She was talented at playing the piano, but struggled socially.

Kidd's sister said:

> She was always kind of a loner.

Kidd was also lonesome; she sometimes stayed with her elderly mother, despite having her own apartment. Kidd's mother also worried about her:

> Cheryl would come with her [mother] to church every once in a while.
> I think she tried to look after her daughter.

Kidd's ninety-three-year-old mother died in December 2008. Kidd was also a mother herself. A provision in the elderly woman's will indicated that Kidd had, at some point, given birth to a child who was adopted outside the family. This incident may have been the reason for her initial psychiatric evaluation in 1977, when she was twenty-two years old. In 1989, she was diagnosed as schizophrenic.

In general, Kidd lived a relatively quiet existence for over twenty years, alone in her apartment in Springfield, and continued to receive counseling and medicine for her conditions through a local health clinic. However, three months before the shooting, Kidd's physician referred her to the emergency room for another mental evaluation. Her caseworker reported:

> [Kidd was] demonstrating out of control behaviors and was not using her psychiatric medications.

At around this time, Kidd presented her landlady with a painting of a clown that had random, handwritten messages on the back that read:

> While playing her golden harp in cloud 9-heaven 1400 AD. Warner, Julio, Judge Judy, T.V.

The week before Kidd killed Officer Kilcullen, she was the subject of a noise complaint at her apartment. The neighbors reported that Kidd was loudly playing an electric guitar with all of her doors and windows open at around 10 p.m. According to the media, the local police spoke to Kidd and discovered she was mentally ill, but took no enforcement action.

One of her elderly neighbors said:

> She was a nice lady. But when she was trying to talk to me, she was not coherent. Nothing made sense.

At Kidd's arraignment a week after the shooting, she mumbled slurred phrases like "it's all good, it's all good" again and again. Kidd, appearing disheveled, interrupted the judge to say, "I had to get to the DMV" and "I'm missing my pills." Her jail-issued top was worn conspicuously backward.

However, Kidd's delusions had begun well before her encounter with Officer Kilcullen. A search of her apartment after her arrest revealed a variety of psychiatric and narcotic medications used in her treatment. A rambling jumble of notations on a desk calendar included the odd phrase:

Bullet-hole inside well of side of Buick.

In an interview with the media conducted after Kidd's arrest, her brother voiced his concern that Kidd did not receive the mental illness care and support that she needed. A subsequent psychiatric evaluation in May 2011 revealed that Kidd was unable to distinguish temporal reality:

She speaks of the present and being in high school in 1972 in the same sentence as if they are contemporary events.

In June 2011, Kidd was remanded to the custody of the Oregon State Hospital for treatment until she is deemed fit to proceed in her trial. She will have up to three years to achieve a level of sanity that is needed for her to assist in her own defense. Her ultimate fate will depend on the success of her treatment to prepare her adequately for trial.

As the only female offender in this study, Kidd's case is summarized as follows:

Name	Kidd, C.
Age	56
Race	W
Gang affiliation or criminal HX	None
Social factors	Isolated
Mental factors	Schizophrenia
	Developmentally disabled
Motive	N/A—mental illness
Circumstances	Traffic stop
Outcome	Fled in vehicle; captured

Case 50: Eli Myers III, Fifty-Eight

On December 18, 2011, Officer David Dryer conducted a traffic stop on a van driven by the suspect, Eli Myers III. Myers did not immediately stop when signaled to do so; instead, he entered the expressway before pulling over. After making contact with Myers, Officer Dryer issued two citations for expired registration and no insurance and handed them to Myers.

When Myers became belligerent, Officer Dryer called for backup. Officer Robert Caldwell, a former state trooper, responded as cover. The officers then called for a tow truck to impound the suspect's vehicle. A short time later, the officers approached the vehicle and Officer Dryer told Myers his vehicle would be impounded. Officer Dryer asked Myers if there were any weapons inside the van. When Myers said yes, Officer Dryer ordered him to step out. As he got out, Myers opened fire with a large-caliber handgun, striking Dryer once in the groin. Myers turned the gun on Officer Caldwell and fired once, striking him in the right hand.

Seeking cover, Officer Caldwell switched the gun to his left hand and returned fire. Myers then turned back to Officer Dryer, lying on the ground. Standing over him, Myers fired a second and fatal shot into the officer's head, executing him.

At 11:12 p.m., Officer Caldwell radioed in for emergency assistance. Seconds later, tow truck driver Leroy Marker arrived at the scene, unaware of the dangerous, unfolding situation. After noticing Officer Dryer on the ground, Marker heard the suspect say:

I got to get out of here.

Seeing Myers climbing back into his van, Marker replied:

No, you're not!

Marker tried to restrain the suspect. As Myers drove off, Marker punched out the side window of the van with his fist. However, Myers escaped and returned to his home, about thirty miles away. Local police spotted his minivan, described as wanted in a police shooting, as it returned to the city limits. They followed Myers, but he ran from his vehicle and barricaded himself inside the home. He called his girlfriend just after midnight to tell her he was in trouble. He admitted:

I shot a couple of cops.

Converging on Myers's home around 1 a.m., police fired multiple rounds of tear gas through the windows. SWAT made entry and then quickly retreated when Myers began firing on them. Using loudspeakers throughout the night, police told Myers to surrender:

> Don't shoot us . . . leave the gun in the house. It's for your own safety.

At around 9:30 a.m., Myers emerged from the back door of the home carrying a large caliber handgun. A police sniper shot and killed Myers. Inside the suspect's trash-filled home, investigators found discarded food and dirty dishes strewn about, holes gouged in the walls, and carpets torn to shreds. Myers had apparently become unable to maintain his own living areas and ended his life in squalor.

Myers was an avid gun collector. He had no criminal history and was, in fact, a former police officer. The oldest of several children, Myers grew up in nearby Monesson, Pennsylvania, where he graduated from high school in 1970. The same year, he and his family moved to Webster, into the home where Myers would make his final stand against police more than thirty years later.

In the late 1970s, Myers became a police officer in West Newton. A fellow officer recalled Myers as a discriminating gun advocate:

> He loved guns. He was one hell of a shot. [Eli] had 357s, 40-calibers, 9-mms, AK-47s, Uzis. He always bought good guns.

Myers told fellow officers that he planned to build an underground bunker at his home. They believed he was joking. He left police work in 1980.

Neighbors described Myers as an "odd duck," a loner, and a recluse. An avid collector, Myers had scratched out a living buying and selling firearms, knives, and antiques. A fellow collector and retired police officer who knew him said:

> We never talked about militias or conspiracy stuff. [Eli] always looked like he needed a shave, his hair was always a touch long and he wore cargo shorts. If anything, you'd think he was a hippie.

Through the years, he grew increasingly ill, eventually becoming an obsessive hoarder of junk. Myers also had financial difficulties. In 2001, Myers was sued by Citibank for loan default on a commercial building he had purchased.

In 2009, Myers's mother and father died within months of one another. It is not clear in the media reports, but Myers may have lived with his parents at the time of their deaths. He had never married. In 2010, Myers's longtime girlfriend also died. After her death, Myers's level of functioning began to deteriorate rapidly, but he had even more troubles on the horizon. The state of Indiana filed against Myers for more than one hundred thousand dollars in taxes owed on firearms sales. Westmoreland County, Pennsylvania, had filed a tax lien for more than ten thousand dollars in unpaid property taxes.

In June 2011, a two-story brick building Myers owned was sold for back taxes. Another storefront building Myers owned was seized after the roof began to cave in and it became unsafe. Both dilapidated structures were filled with broken furniture, old newspapers, and other trash. One of the buildings was razed to the ground.

On September 3, 2011, Myers was cited for driving without insurance and no registration. In mid-November, he was ordered to pay $467 in fines and court costs. These were the *same exact citations* Officer Dryer would write just before he was shot and killed by the suspect a month later.

Just weeks before the shooting, Myers fell at home and injured both legs. In significant pain, he began using a walker to steady himself and had to rely on others to drive him around. In November, a new girlfriend, Lynn Deicas, drove him to a gun collector meeting in a nearby city.

Just five days before the shooting, Deicas drove him to another meeting, where collectors noticed Myers looked gaunt and had great difficulty getting in and out of his car. However, on the night of the shooting, Myers was driving alone. Facing a situation just like the previous encounter with police, he was angry to have been stopped again. When he faced the loss of his van, in addition to all of his other troubles, he snapped and committed an unthinkable crime.

The end of this incident has parallels with Jeffrey Krier (Case 45). Both men were mentally ill, isolated in the community, and well armed, and they exited their homes with firearms in their hands after being barricaded for several hours after the shootings. Both men were also seeking a suicide-by-cop solution. Both men were killed by police.

Myers's case is summarized as follows:

Name	Myers, E.
Age	58
Race	W
Gang affiliation or criminal HX	None
Social factors	Isolated
Mental factors	Hoarder
	Former police officer
	Affinity for guns
Motive	Avoid impound of vehicle
Circumstances	Traffic stop
Outcome	Fled in vehicle; suicide by cop

Discussion: Age

As the final age group in our study, shooters in the age group of fifty-five and older return to a steady decline in number of offenders:

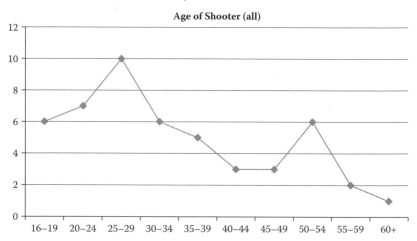

The graph shows that cop-killers over forty are less common in this study, with the exception of offenders aged fifty to fifty-four.

Discussion: Race

The majority of shooters (seventy-five percent) in this age group were white, including one white female. This brings the final analysis to a clear majority. Fifty-two percent of shooters in the study were white, including the only female shooter in the study.

However, cop-killers vary significantly when both race and age are considered:

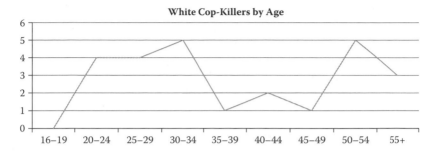

White cop-killers have dramatic numbers in the twenty to thirty-four age range, followed by another peak in the fifty and over age group.

Thirty-eight percent of shooters in the study were black. In contrast with white shooters, black cop-killers over the age of forty are quite rare, accounting for only three shooters (six percent). Black cop-killers demonstrate peak activity in the teen, late twenties, and late thirties age groups:

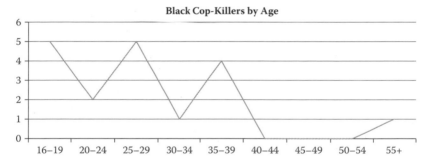

In the final analysis, white shooters outnumber other shooters of other races by a slim margin:

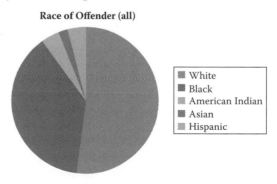

For comparison with offenders, we should also briefly examine the role of the officers' races. This distribution remains relatively unchanged throughout the study. Of the fifty-five officers killed by offenders in this study, fifty (ninety percent) were white. Four officers were Hispanic. One was American Indian. None of the officers killed in this study were black.*

Discussion: Gang Affiliation

Like the previous groups, none of the cop-killers in this group were affiliated with a gang. Gang membership peaks with the sixteen to nineteen age group and is a rare feature of older cop-killers. No offender over thirty in this study was characterized as a gang member.

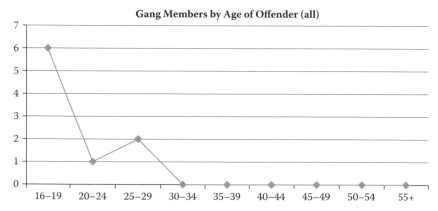

Gang Members by Age of Offender (all)

Discussion: Criminal History

Only two of the shooters in this group had a criminal history.

Discussion: Social Factors

Let us look at the comparisons of offenders in this group:

---

* Recall that the three black officers initially included in the study were killed by black shooters while off-duty (two cases) or by friendly fire (one case). Thus, their shootings were not included in the examination of cop-killers, which looked at the murders of uniformed and on-duty police only. Three white officers were also excluded on the same basis.

Ferryman	None
Hardy	Hard-core offender
Kidd	Isolated
Myers	Isolated

This group contains three mentally ill shooters, including two who were significantly isolated in the community. Interestingly, Hardy can be classified as the only hard-core offender in this group. Like Randleman in the last group, black shooters over fifty are seen as much more likely to be hard-core offenders.

Discussion: Mental Factors

This group shows a wide disparity among the mental factors, with one major feature: mental illness. Let us examine them side by side:

Ferryman	Bipolar
	Dementia
Hardy	Driving stolen vehicle
Kidd	Schizophrenia
	Developmentally disabled
Myers	Hoarder
	Former police officer
	Affinity for guns

Most of the offenders in this age group could be classified as mentally ill. Like three others in the over fifty category, Myers demonstrated an affinity for guns. However, drug and alcohol use is significantly less in this age group, affecting only ten percent of offenders.

The top factors trending in this group are noted in the following chart:

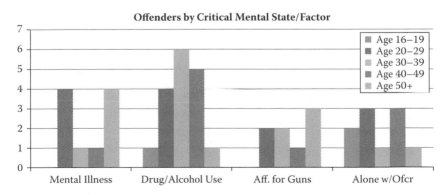

Discussion: Motives

Half of the offenders in this group were facing imminent arrest:

Ferryman	N/A—mental illness
Hardy	Avoid arrest for stolen vehicle, felon in possession of firearm
Kidd	N/A—mental illness
Myers	Avoid impound of vehicle

The over-age-fifty group contains the largest number of mentally ill shooters in this study. Forty percent of shooters aged over fifty were mentally ill. However, the trend to avoid arrest continues with all offenders in the study:

Motive of Offender (all)

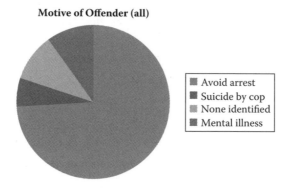

Avoid arrest
Suicide by cop
None identified
Mental illness

Seventy-five percent of all cop-killers in this study were facing imminent arrest when they killed a police officer.

Discussion: Circumstances

What were the circumstances of the encounters with police that led to the deadly outcomes in this group? Let us examine these events side by side:

Ferryman	Shots-fired call
Hardy	Traffic stop
Kidd	Traffic stop
Myers	Traffic stop

Traffic stops were the precipitating factor in all but one case in this chapter.

Discussion: Outcomes

Although every officer in this study was killed, an examination of the outcome of the incident for offenders provides some interesting data.

Let us examine the cases side by side:

Ferryman	Killed by police
Hardy	Fled in vehicle; captured
Kidd	Fled in vehicle; captured
Myers	Fled in vehicle; suicide by cop

We see a new increase in the number of offenders who fled the scene of the murder they committed.

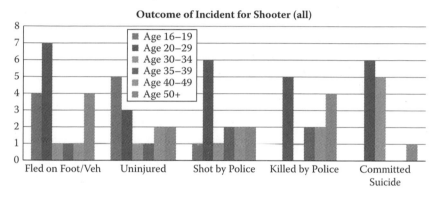

Outcome of Incident for Shooter (all)

No offenders in this group committed suicide.[*]

Conclusion

Among shooters in the over-fifty age group:

- The majority (seventy-five percent) were white, including one white female shooter.
- Most of the offenders used handguns.
- Two had no criminal history.
- Most of the offenders (seventy-five percent) could be classified as mentally ill.
- Most of the shooters (seventy-five percent) were stopped on a traffic stop, committed the murder and fled in a vehicle, but were later captured or killed.

---

[*] "Suicide by cop" incidents in this chapter are counted as "killed by police" statistics.

Bibliography

Associated Press. "Recordings Detail Events in Ohio Deputy's Killing," January 5, 2011, Springfield, OH: AP.

———. "Indianapolis Police Officer Wounded in Shooting," January 24, 2011, Indianapolis: AP.

———. "OR Detective Says Woman Admitted Shooting Officer," April 26, 2011, Eugene, OR: AP.

———. "Witness Says Suspect Tailgated Slain OR Officer," April 26, 2011, Eugene, OR: AP.

———. "Ohio Pair Indicted on Charges Linked to Shootout," April 30, 2011, Springfield, OH: AP.

———. "Lawyers: Suspect in Officer Shooting Delusional," May 2, 2011, Eugene, OR: AP.

Begos, K. "Suspect Wanted in Penn Officer's Death Is Killed," Associated Press, December 19, 2011, Webster, PA: APO.

Bogue, E. "Honoring the Fallen: Pain of Losing a Fellow Officer Still Fresh for Some on C.O.P.S. Memorial Ride," *News-Sentinel*, July 28, 2011, Fort Wayne, IN: McClatchey-Tribune Business News.

Callahan, R. "Convicted Felon Accused of Killing Indiana Officer," Associated Press Online, January 28, 2011, Indianapolis: AP.

"Dramatic Shoot-Out at Caravan Park Is Captured on Camera," *Daily Telegraph*, January 3, 2011, p. 13.

Ferenchik, M., and Price, R. "Gunman Kills Deputy; Female Veteran Dies, Township Officer Wounded in Gun Battle with Suspect at Campground in Clark County; Police Kill Shooter," *Columbus Dispatch*, January 2, 2011, p. 1B.

Flam, L. "Slain Ohio Sheriff's Deputy Was Dedicated to Duty," *AOL News*, January 3, 2011. Retrieved November 18, 2011, from http://www.aolnews.com/2011/01/03/slain-ohio-sheriffs-deputy-suzanne-hopper-was-dedicated-to-duty/

Gazarik, R. "Police Kill Suspect in Shooting of Officers," *Tribune-Review*, December 19, 2011, Greensburg, PA: McClatchy-Tribune Business News.

———. "Two Officers Shot, 1 Fatally in Washington County," *Tribune-Review*, December 19, 2011, Greensburg, PA: TRPC.

Gazarik, R., and Peirce, P. "Friends Say 'Odd Duck' Came to Unlikely End," *Tribune-Review*, December 21, 2011, Greensburg, PA: TRPC.

Gildow, M., Sweigart, J., and Lough, V. "Career Callings Led to Collision with Violence," *Dayton Daily News*, January 9, 2011, p. A13.

"IMPD Officer David Moore Dies from Injuries Suffered in Shooting during Traffic Stop, Convicted Felon Thomas Hardy Arrested," *Hinterland Gazette*, January 26, 2011, Indianapolis: Newstex.

Johnson, K. "Mix of Societal Ills Increases Risk for Police; Cuts, Disputes, Mental Illness All Play a Part," *USA Today*, August 26, 2011, p. 8A.

"Judge: Kidd Unfit for Trial," *Register-Guard*, June 8, 2011, p. A1.

Ko, S. "Neighbors Give Insight into Alleged Officer Killer's Mind," April 23, 2011. Retrieved January 30, 2012, from http://kezi.com/page/210556

Leibowitz, B. "Suspected Killer of Ohio Sheriff's Deputy Suzanne Hopper Was Previously Committed for Insanity, Released," CBS News, January 4, 2011. Retrieved November 18, 2011, from http://www.cbsnews.com/8301-504083_162-20027085-504083.html

Lough, V., and Gildow, M. "Suspect in Deputy's Death Reportedly Threatened Man with Knife in 2009," *Springfield News Sun*, January 3, 2011. Retrieved November 18, 2011, from http://www.springfieldnewssun.com/news/crime/suspect-in-deputys-death-reportedly-threatened-man-with-knife-in-2009-1044111.html

McCowan, K. "Police: Suspect Confessed," *Register-Guard*, April 26, 2011, p. A1.

———. "Defense Lawyer Says Kidd Is Delusional, Unfit to Stand Trial," *Register-Guard*, May 3, 2011, p. A1.

Miller, E. "Ex-Cop Opens Fire on JPD Officers," *Juneau Empire*, April 8, 2012. Retrieved May 17, 2012, from http://juneauempire.com/local/2012-04-08/ex-cop-opens-fire-jpd-officers#

Moran, J. "Officer Shot Dead during Car Chase," *Register-Guard*, April 23, 2011, p. A1.

———. "Witness Details Pursuit," *Register-Guard*, April 23, 2011, p. A1.

Peirce, P. "Washington County Officer Killed after Making Routine Traffic Stop," *Pittsburgh Tribune-Review*, December 20, 2011, Pittsburgh, PA: TRPC.

Penner, D. "Answers Sought in Cop's Shooting," *Indianapolis Star*, January 24, 2011, p. A1.

Ritchie, C. "Suspect Appears in Court," *Indianapolis Star*, January 30, 2011, p. B1.

Ritchie, C., and Tuohy, J. Parole Officer Suspended in Release of Alleged Shooter," *Indianapolis Star*, January 26, 2011, p. A7.

Schmitz, J. "Policeman Killed after Routine Stop," *Pittsburgh Post-Gazette*, December 20, 2011, p. A1.

Schmitz, J., Gurman, S., and Balingit, M. "Suspect in Officer Killing Shot to Death," *Pittsburgh Post-Gazette*, December 19, 2011, p. A1.

"Standoff in Morgan County Ends; 2 Charged," *Zanesville Times-Recorder*, September 7, 2001, Zanesville, OH: ZT-R.

"Suspect Calm before Deputy's Shooting, Friend Says," *Morning Journal*, January 4, 2011. Retrieved November 18, 2011, from http://www.morningjournal.com/articles/2011/01/04/news/doc4d23162eba540166653121.txt

"Suspect Talks about Oregon Officer's Slaying," May 1, 2011, Eugene, OR: Tribune Publishing Co.

Tuohy, J. "Officer Moore, a 'True Warrior,'" *Indianapolis Star*, January 26, 2011, p. A1.

———. "Being an Officer Just Came Naturally," *Indianapolis Star*, January 27, 2011, p. A1.

———. "'One Thing Led to Another,'" *Indianapolis Star*, January 28, 2011, p. A1.

Wasu, S. "Ferryman Was Not Allowed to Have Guns," WDTN News, January 4, 2011. Retrieved November 18, 2011, from http://www.wdtn.com/dpp/news/local/clark/how-did-cop-shooter-get-a-gun

Welsh-Huggins, A. "Deputy, Suspect Dead in Ohio Trailer Park Standoff," Associated Press Online, January 2, 2011, Springfield, OH: AP.

"Woman Held in Slaying of Oregon Police Officer," *Lewiston Morning Tribune,* April 24, 2011, Eugene, OR: Tribune Publishing Co.

Wright, J. "Possible Murder Weapon Found," *Register-Guard,* April 25, 2011, p. A1.

10
CONCLUSION AND RECOMMENDATIONS

Overview

Like all true narratives, the stories of cop-killers are varied and complex. Reducing any human being's history and motivation to a series of short paragraphs, as has been done in this work, will always present a risk of poor portrayal. The aim of this book is not to provide a complete history of each offender, but rather to present a snapshot of the circumstances, identity, and factors that may have led to each offender's decision to kill a police officer on a given day, within a given encounter. This approach presupposes that the truth of these incidents can become known and that the focus can be narrowed to each offender and then broadened again to encompass groups of offenders by certain characteristics. It is for the reader to decide if this is an accurate-enough accounting of these incidents.

This chapter is designed to offer a comparative analysis of the trends across groups by overarching factors such as age, race, and criminal history. When these events are viewed with a broader examination by phase of life, cultural identity, or historical label, previously unseen data that may be germane to the discussion of cop-killers become apparent.

Trends by Age: Adolescence

Renowned psychologist Erik Erikson spent a lifetime studying the concepts of social development by phase of life. He classified human existence into a series of development stages, each with its own unique struggles and victories. Erikson's model established the possibility that people, despite their chronological age, might become "stuck" in an earlier developmental stage.* Let us examine Erikson's stages with the group of offenders in this book.

For adolescents, Erikson defined the struggle of youth ages twelve to eighteen as one of identity and role confusion. Teens try on different personas, grappling with morality, ethical dilemmas, and social interactions—both positive and negative—and examining the results. The task of adolescence is to determine who we wish to become. Thus, when examining teenage cop-killers, we should recognize that the identity of these offenders was in no way fixed at the time of their acts. They were still experimenting with their self-concepts at the time they killed a police officer.

Like the experience of all people, part of the process of identity formation for these young men was the result of their family experience. However, much of the remainder was being imparted by the street gangs these shooters were associated with, emphasizing values such as the need for self-reliance, "juice," and violence as a response to provocation. One gang expert tells us:

> Did you tell your kids you loved them today? If you don't, the street gang will.

Children seek a place where they can feel loved and accepted. Adolescents also want to become a part of something revolutionary, exciting, and personally rewarding. They want prestige, recognition, and respect from others. For some, it takes the form of athletic performance or art, music, or academic accomplishments. For others, the gang becomes their vehicle for acceptance.

This observation also relates directly to the work of criminologist Lonnie Athens, whose process of "violentization" is chronicled in author Richard Rhodes's work *Why They Kill*. Athens interviewed hundreds of offenders in prison for violent crimes. He discovered that many, if not all, had been conditioned to violence and a certain mindset, having been "coached" into becoming predators, usually by the end of adolescence. Ironically, the same process is used on those who enlist in military service and police work. These two sides of the same

---

* Freud certainly felt this was possible, with his focus on unintegrated sexuality in the form of oral and anal fixations arising from early childhood experiences.

coin—one representing societal justice, the other glorifying criminal acts—often set the stage for the violent encounters in this book.

The violentization process requires subjugation, horrification, and the subsequent inculcation of values related to physical, brutish action in response to certain triggers, such as disrespect, by another person who acts as a "violence coach." The likelihood that many, if not all, of the teen offenders in this book were subjected to violentization is highly probable and would partially explain their actions. Moving to the study of older offenders, it is often apparent that their overt criminality, characterized by violent acts such as armed robbery, aggravated assault, and even past murders, confirms that this process occurred for them, as well. Put simply, ordinary people do not carjack, rape, or threaten people with firearms; yet, many of the men in this study did. What differentiates these violent offenders from us is a certain confluence of life events, choices made, and successful initiation into aggressive acts as a part of their identity.

Teen cop-killers tend to have no pattern of injury and flee on foot after the shooting. They are taken into custody quickly, often with the involvement of their families. They are often spared the death penalty because of their youthful ages.

Trends by Age: Young Adulthood

Erikson's next category, young adulthood, is applied to adults under age thirty-five. According to Erikson's life cycles, the struggle of young adulthood centers on the desire for intimacy and affiliation with others. Victory culminates in the building of a successful relationship such as a partnership or marriage and, for many, a family life. Erikson describes that failure to master this struggle leads to isolation.

Only one offender under age twenty-five was involved in what might be described as a successful relationship: Alexander Haydel (Case 9), who killed his wife's ex-husband during a family reunion at a downtown hotel. However, seven additional offenders under age thirty-five were involved in relationship turmoil at the time they became cop-killers, including:

- Lee Welch, who killed his estranged wife in front of their young daughter

- Jayson Eggenberg, who ran his wife off the road to confront her
- Christopher Hodges, who fought with his girlfriend on the roadside
- Alan Sylte, who went to his ex-girlfriend's home with a gun
- James Cruckson, who raped his girlfriend when she returned from spring break
- Charles Post, who attempted to kill his boss because he was upset about his relationship with his girlfriend
- Martin Poynter, who went to his estranged wife's home with a gun

If we continue past Erikson's defined age of thirty-five, we will find even more offenders who share this history of relationship problems, including:

- Hydra Lacy, Jr., who stabbed his wife in the face
- Bennie Brown, who killed his girlfriend at her workplace
- Christian Patterson, who was fighting with his girlfriend when he became suicidal
- Wesley Davis, who threatened his wife and sister with a gun
- Charles Smith, who had beaten his wife in the past
- Mark Hasty, who held a gun to his wife's head when police came to serve a warrant
- Stephen Bannister, who held a knife to his girlfriend's throat

Erikson may have a point on the issue of forming successful relationships as the pivotal challenge of adult life, although the time line seems to extend to those even in their fifties, at least within this study. The imminent failure and implosion of their primary relationships was a key factor in the decision of many suspects in this study to kill a police officer. As a result, this very personal turmoil also resulted in the deaths of twelve of the fifteen shooters (eighty percent) listed.

Trends by Age: Middle Adulthood

Erikson's next stage is middle adulthood, defined as ages thirty-five to fifty-five. This stage is associated with productivity, especially in work pursuits. Few offenders in this study could be characterized as very productive with regard to work, unless criminal activity could be considered successful work. Exceptions include:

- Hydra Lacy, Jr., who had been a successful real estate investor after getting out of prison
- George Hitcho, Jr., self-described as a "master carpenter"
- Eli Myers III, who was a former police officer, junk trader, and arms dealer

According to Erikson, lack of success in this phase leads to stagnation and self-absorption. Some observers might say that criminals are, in all likelihood, the most self-absorbed people in society. Because of their lack of respect for the property of others and their use of violence and disregard for others, criminals are among those who are least likely to master the challenge of productivity in midlife.

Trends by Age: Late Adulthood

Erikson's final stage is late adulthood. The challenge of late adulthood is to look back upon life and form a sense of contribution and meaning. Erikson calls this quality "integrity." Adults who struggle in this phase may come to a different conclusion: that life has no purpose or redeeming value. Failure in this phase equates to a sense of despondency and emptiness.

Several offenders of advanced age seemed to have fallen into despair, including:

- Charles Smith, who was a fugitive from justice for years after being arrested for drug distribution
- Mark Hasty, who was a convicted sex offender on the run who told an acquaintance how much he hated life and wished he were dead
- Randall Newberry, who was a disabled former coal miner who constructed a sniper's nest in the woods
- Jeffrey Krier, who was left behind by his family to cope with bipolar disorder on his own
- Michael Ferryman, who was isolated in the community and deteriorating into dementia

- Eli Myers III, a recluse who lost his parents and girlfriend within a short period of time and then suffered an injurious fall, crippling his legs

Whether these offenders were motivated by despair in their acts against law enforcement is not certain. However, all of these offenders committed suicide or were killed by police.

Issues of Race

It is not possible for police officers to anticipate when they will encounter a violent cop-killer in the making. Thus, police officers must use caution with all people they encounter, whatever their race. Yet, in times of political correctness, they face tremendous criticism for using harsh language, arrests, and use-of-force incidents, especially in ethnically diverse communities. However, when we consider judging those who wear the badge, we should consider the cases in this book. They are but one year's worth of incidents involving the clearly violent murders of police officers at the hands of all types of offenders.

Every major racial group is represented in this book, including minorities such as Asians and American Indians. In this particular study, white shooters are the majority. However, black shooters are overrepresented in the numbers of cop-killers. The reasons for this disparity are deeper than this work can explore. White offenders tend to kill white officers, as do black offenders. The only American Indian officer in the study was killed by an American Indian shooter.*

A lay observer of police who consumes one of many biased media reports on law enforcement actions may ask: Why are white police officers involved in so many use-of-force incidents, including shootings? The answer is simple: because most police officers in the United States are white. More white officers are involved in the arrests, fights, traffic stops, and calls for service on any given day. Thus, they are also committing excessive force, saving lives of innocent people, shooting people, driving fast to get to emergency calls, getting shot by criminals, wrecking police cars, serving warrants, acting as backup officers, and, within this book, the victims of cop-killers more often

---

* One of the two Hispanic offenders in this study killed a white officer; the other killed a Hispanic officer. No Asian officers were represented in this study.

than minority officers. It is sheer numbers, not racism, that drive this statistic.

Do not imagine that black officers are not also targets of murder and assault in the line of duty. They are not insulated from the violence by virtue of their race. Although they were not discussed in this study, two black officers were murdered in 2011 by firearms: Officers Daryl Hall and Clifton Lewis. Both were off duty, acting to stop an armed man. Both were killed by black male shooters. Another, Officer William Torbit, Jr., was killed in plainclothes on duty in a friendly fire incident after he was attacked by a group of black males in the parking lot of a club. Other officers mistook him for a suspect when Officer Torbit fired on his attackers in self-defense.

Yet another black officer, Officer Tony Howard, was shot in the face while attempting to conduct a traffic stop on Jamie Hood (Case 25). He survived multiple gunshot wounds. Jamie Hood went on to kill a white police officer in the same incident. Black, white, and Hispanic officers all face the same risks of death at the hands of violent offenders. Viciousness knows no racial boundaries.

Perhaps the best conclusion regarding race that can be drawn from the offenders in this study is that blacks are overrepresented among cop-killers because they are more often established as hard-core offenders and gang members at the time of their final encounters with police. Hard-core offenders and gang members are more conditioned to take violent action as a form of civil disobedience, to enhance their reputation, or to defend their violent self-image. Police tend to challenge these kinds of offenders—whatever their race—when they encounter them in the community, usually during a call for service.

The reaction of the hard-core offender or gang member is often to escalate the encounter to violent resistance, including homicidal action. This does not imply a more criminal nature of any race. This conclusion is a reflection on the higher likelihood of black offenders to live in high-crime neighborhoods, have higher arrest rates, and have higher incarceration rates than other groups. Exceptions do exist within the cases of this study, including:

- Jonathan Bun, an Asian gang member
- Ryan Heisler, a white gang member
- Jesse Mathews, a white hard-core offender

The prevalence of gang membership and hard-core offender labeling is not the only area in which black and white offenders differ. Black offenders almost always use handguns, as opposed to the long guns, rifles, and shotguns preferred by white offenders. Black offenders also commit suicide far less often than white offenders.

White offenders in this study were also far more likely to be diagnosed or perceived as mentally ill. Does this finding indicate a cultural bias to criminalize and incarcerate black offenders while steering white offenders into the mental health system? The answer is not clear. It may be that white offenders who kill police officers simply suffer more underlying mental illness.

Ten out of twenty-six white shooters (thirty-eight percent) committed suicide, outnumbering black offenders who committed suicide by more than a two-to-one margin. Just three black shooters (fifteen percent) were killed by police, compared with six white shooters (twenty-six percent). Thus, white cop-killers are less likely to survive deadly encounters, perhaps because of their overt decisions to die rather than be taken alive.

The issues of race also permeate the discussion of policing. Not every police officer enters the career of law enforcement without racist ideas. Police officers are human beings with varied experiences, histories, and backgrounds. For those who do subscribe to stereotypes or other faulty ideas about race, police officers learn early in their careers that employing racist ideas will be of no help to them, either with their minority co-workers or with the diverse citizens they serve. Exceptions do exist, but racism within law enforcement is less real than most people might believe.

There is a universal saying among police:

The only race in police is blue.

Indeed, one of the white officers chronicled in this study (Tim Warren) wrote this very sentence in response to a black officer's death in his district. In modern times, racism is not tolerated in law enforcement or by citizens. This was not always the case.

Civilians should recognize that few professions in the United States present the risk of being feloniously murdered in the course of day-to-day operations. In terms of the risks of assault or murder, a recent study called policing the second most dangerous profession.* Because police officers bear the responsibility of taking another person's freedom—temporarily—they are targeted for violent resistance and execution by those who do not wish to be confined or subject to the laws of the land. Offenders generally perceive the police as the final authority on freedom, although this is not the case. Police do "lock up" offenders, who are then offered the "innocent until proven guilty" treatment by the court system.

The problem is that, whatever their race, many offenders are guilty of their crimes. The courts, not the police, are responsible for determining what punishment offenders will suffer. Often, police are merely the unwelcome messengers of the judicial system. Offenders do not see it that way. Police are the targets of insurrection, assassination, and rage because they are viewed as the oppressors of freedom. It is for the reader and the selected juries of their peers to decide between reality and an attempt at feigned innocence or a wolf-in-sheep's-clothing defense by a violent offender.

A more germane question on race might be: Why are so many people of color involved in violence against the police? The answer is also beyond the scope of this work. Because the demographics of the United States are changing, the typography of offenders who kill police officers will continue to shift with them. **One conclusion about race is clear: Most murders of police officers are committed by those who share the victim's race.**

Trends in Criminal Histories

The idea of a criminal history pattern has been examined in depth during the chapters on each offender group. Out of the fifty shooters in this study, eight (sixteen percent) had no criminal history. Burglary, robbery, weapons violations, and domestic violence were often found within the histories of cop-killers. However, the most common type of criminal history associated with cop-killers was drug sales or pos-

---

* The most dangerous profession is taxicab driver. Taxi drivers are seen as targets of opportunity—often alone with those who might harm them, in possession of cash, and at work during hours of darkness.

session. More than twenty-five percent of them had a history of drug use or sales.

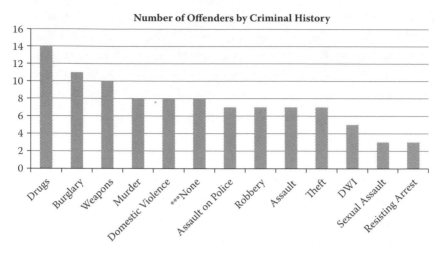

Although offenders in this study used all kinds of drugs, ranging from prescription medicines to cocaine and methamphetamine, the drug of choice is, most often, marijuana.

The current trend in the United States toward legalization of drugs such as marijuana is not likely to reduce the rates of substance abuse. In fact, the opposite is true. With greater availability and less stigma, more people will turn to illicit drug use as an option for recreation, coping with stress, and fuel for violent behavior. The results will not be good for law enforcement. With more impaired people on the roadways, in public places, inside their homes, and the subjects of calls to police, we will be less equipped to protect civilians and other police officers from the consequences of a population of legal drug users.

Those who use marijuana today are not the laid-back, free-loving "hippies" of the past. This generation's higher potency marijuana is not the "ditch weed" of the 1960s. According to the Drug Enforcement Administration (DEA), today's high-THC marijuana is more psychedelic than ever, with up to ten times the concentration of the hallucinogenic properties. Proponents say this drug is no more harmful than alcohol and is a good option for treating stress, pain, and other conditions in the general population. However, this study indicates that, among cop-killers, criminal histories associated with drug use are three times higher than alcohol use. Why? The answer is because drug use is an inherently deviant activity, motivated by hedonism and lack of responsibility or self-respect.

According to its detractors, this so-called "all-natural" drug often leads to psychosis in young and inexperienced users. Marijuana use is also suspected in triggering the development of underlying mental illness. Thus, a user who might be at risk for developing bipolar disorder or schizophrenia is moved from a possible onset to full onset, requiring a lifetime of management with medication and lifestyle changes. Most of the time, these kinds of offenders are instead unable to function in a meaningful way because, as for all addicts, the drug becomes the focus of their lives. They become stoned, demotivated, and delusional—focusing their energy on the opportunity to "get high."

Harmless substance, indeed—not for those who must face reality, including police officers who must contend with these offenders. An increase in the acceptance of marijuana use will lead to more—not fewer—violent encounters with police. Marijuana users become delusional and delusional suspects are always high risk. Those facing arrest while high, in the split second before an arrest, will ask themselves:

What is happening here?

The drug-induced state provides paranoid and deceptive answers, such as:

The police are monitoring me using microchip technology.
The officers are here to kill me.
These cops look like monsters.

This profound experience of fear and terror by the drug-affected offender triggers extreme resistance, led by the fight-or-flight state in the offender, which drives their belief that their lives are at risk. Police officers, the sober and rational opponents of drug users, will continue to become the casualties of this cycle of drug abuse, legal or not.

Social Histories

The largest single indicator within the social histories of cop-killers is the use of drugs and alcohol. Thirty percent of cop-killers had a history of drug and alcohol use and/or were high at the time of the offense. Thus, substance abuse is the key predictor of violence against police within both the criminal histories and social histories of offenders.

The top ten factors are listed in the following chart:

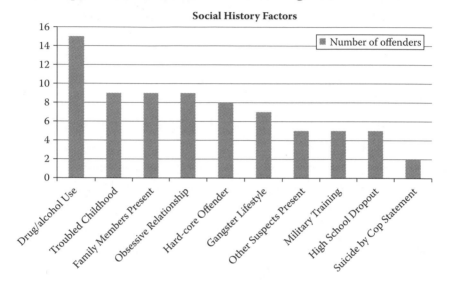

Recognizing the role of alcohol and drugs in the decision to use violence may still offer some insight into the lives of those who killed police officers, especially for professionals who treat alcoholics and drug addicts.

The social histories of cop-killers are not simple portraits to draw. Gathering information on the presence of others, childhood events, military training history, and more is no small undertaking. Much of what can be known about the individuals in this study was learned from media and official police reports. Given the sources, the information cannot be seen as complete. The best sources of information about the offenders' use of drugs and alcohol would be the offenders themselves; this access was beyond the scope of this study.

Mental Factors

Aside from the fact that thirty-percent of cop-killers were high on drugs or alcohol at the time of the shooting, other trends can be noted among the mental factors of the offenders. Many of the offenders were alone with the officer, in a state of bloodlust from committing a recent murder, or had expressed suicidal ideation, such as a suicide-by-cop outcome.

The top factors are noted in the following chart:

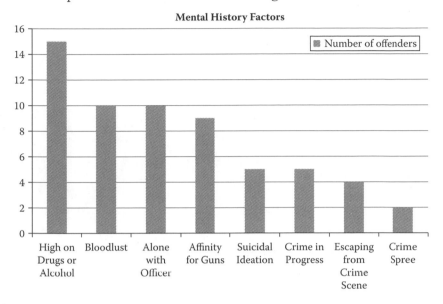

In contrast to the drunk and high offenders, fewer offenders were involved in a crime spree, escaped from a crime scene, or engaged in a crime in progress. Interestingly, most cop-killers make the decision to kill based on their hazy, impaired experience while in a drug-induced state. It is no surprise that these are poorly made, permanently life-altering decisions.

Motives of Cop-Killers

Seventy-five percent of all cop-killers in this study were facing imminent arrest when they killed a police officer. Thus, it seems clear that employing the powers of arrest is the highest area of on-duty risk that police face. However, this is a fallacy. More police officers die each year in on-duty automobile accidents than are shot and killed in the line of duty. Yet, if we do focus on cop-killers who use firearms, as we have in this study, we find that, most of the time, police are murdered by those who do not want to go to jail. Most cop-killers have experience being handled by police and are facing arrest at the time of the offense, but exceptions do exist.

In addition to those who were facing imminent arrest, smaller pockets of offenders were diagnosed as mentally ill. Often, these subjects do not have a clear motive. The known mentally ill offenders in this study include:

- Jeffrey Krier, bipolar
- Michael Ferryman, bipolar
- Jayson Eggenberg, bipolar
- George Hitcho, Jr., bipolar
- Martin Poynter, schizoaffective
- Matthew Connor, schizophrenic
- Cheryl Kidd, schizophrenic

Another group of offenders are relative unknowns. They have no reported history of mental illness, but seem to have no real motive for homicidal rage directed at the police. Were they undiagnosed or simply motivated by hidden factors, such as revenge or animosity for police? These offenders include:

- Ross Ashley, who executed a police officer on the Virginia Tech campus
- Skyler Barbee, who executed an officer across the street from his grandparents' home
- Dejon White, who pulled alongside an officer in his car and executed him
- Randall Newberry, who set up a sniper's nest in the woods and killed two officers
- Mark Gonzales, who executed an officer at a stoplight
- Leonard Statler, who killed an officer in an alley after firing a handgun into the air

Of this group, only two were known to have been drinking alcohol. None of these offenders was facing imminent arrest or wanted by police. Five of the six offenders in this category initiated contact with police. These shooters approached police on foot (Ashley and Barbee) or in a vehicle (White and Gonzales) or acted with specific intent to lure police (Statler).[*]

Circumstances of Encounters with Cop-Killers

The confluence of events that brings together police officers and those who will become cop-killers is quite varied. Often, a call to police triggers the encounter that leads to the fatal confrontation. However, this is not the only method that leads to these encounters. Some offenders initiate the encounter with police, some encounters are motiveless, and some circumstances are more dangerous for police than others.

Within this study of fifty offenders, sixteen separate dimensions were noted. The most dangerous activity in this study for police officers was the serving of arrest warrants. Nearly twenty percent of the officers were killed serving a warrant at the home of the cop-killer. Domestic disturbances and traffic stops are also risky activities for police.

The top trends are noted in this chart:

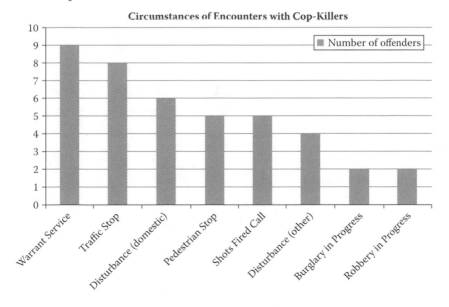

Circumstances of Encounters with Cop-Killers

---

[*] Statler and his brother fired weapons into the air from their front porch and joked that it would bring the police. When police arrived, Statler fired at them.

Many people believe that police officers are killed while chasing criminals involved in crimes in progress; this is often a myth. Crimes in progress leading to officer murders—such as burglaries or robberies—were rare when compared with more "routine" activities of warrant service operations and traffic stops.

The trends in violent encounters with police are never completely static over time. In 2011, the majority of police officers who were killed by firearms were involved in warrant service. Yet, in 2012, more police officers were killed during vehicle enforcement actions such as traffic stops.

Outcomes for Cop-Killers

About half of cop-killers in this study did not survive their encounter with police. However, this is not because police officers routinely use overkill during violent encounters. Surprisingly, police showed significant restraint in the takedowns of cop-killers. Thirteen cop-killers (twenty-six percent) sustained no injury during their arrest, despite being the targets of law enforcement for the most violent of crimes: murder of one of their colleagues.

One-quarter of cop-killers (twenty-six percent) were killed by police, often in the moments immediately after the murder of a police officer by officers who returned fire. Slightly fewer (twenty-two percent) committed suicide before they could be arrested.

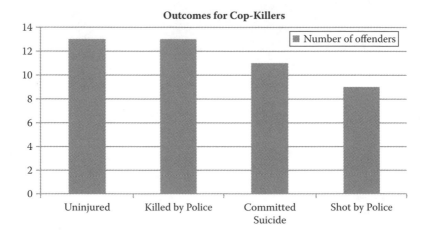

Outcomes for Cop-Killers

More than one-quarter of the cop-killers in this study (twenty-eight percent) engaged in a prolonged standoff with police as a feature of the incident.

Examples of barricaded offenders, along with their outcomes, include:

- Carlos Boles, who was killed by a SWAT team
- Hydra Lacy, Jr., who was killed by a SWAT team
- Christian Patterson, who was shot by police and survived
- Kion Dail, who was captured without injury
- Alan Sylte, who committed suicide
- James Cruckson, who committed suicide
- Jamie Hood, who took hostages and was captured without injury
- Shaun Seeley, who committed suicide
- Bennie Brown, who barricaded himself after being shot by police, but eventually surrendered
- Wesley Davis, who was killed by police
- Mark Hasty, who committed suicide
- Jeffrey Krier, who committed suicide by cop
- Michael Ferryman, who was killed by police
- Eli Myers III, who committed suicide by cop

These standoffs do not always end violently. Most of the standoffs in this study (seventy-one percent) ended in the deaths of the offenders. These events end most often in "killed by police" (including suicide by cop) outcomes:

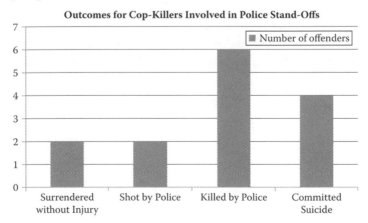

Outcomes for Cop-Killers Involved in Police Stand-Offs

Police officers coping with barricaded offenders require the assistance of expert police negotiators and/or hostage negotiators when other suspects or innocent civilians are present. Negotiators may be helped by the involvement of psychologists or other mental health treatment providers, especially those who know the offender personally. Family members can also be instrumental in the surrender process, but are not always helpful with all offenders.* No certain method has been found to prevent a barricaded person from committing suicide.

Standard communication attempts by police with a barricaded offender are often unsuccessful. Standoffs involving cop-killers usually end in the violent death of the offender.

Conclusions

Policing is a dangerous profession with unpredictable encounters. Offenders who kill police officers are often experienced criminals, mentally ill, or youthful offenders adrift in a world of gang activity, drug use, and sharing a history of violentization. Yet, the journeys of cop-killers can be understood more clearly when viewed with objectivity and tempered with humanity and common sense.

There are essentially three types of cop-killers in this study: the criminal, the ill, and the unknown. The criminal cop-killer has a history of arrests and incarcerations. He views the police officer merely as the obstacle to his continued freedom. The ill cop-killer has a history of mental illness or psychiatric commitment. He sees the police officer as a potential adversary who is trying to kill him. The unknown cop-killer has little or no known motive to kill. He experiences the killing of a police officer as a final, violent performance for his own reasons.

Most cop-killers murder law enforcement officers to escape apprehension and avoid the consequences of their criminal acts. Most of the offenders in this book had been in custody before. Once they had been caged for less serious offenses, they never wished to return to that dark, confined place. Over time, they became more deviant and less controlled. Confronted in a range of circumstances by better men and women in uniform, they chose revenge, death, and mayhem rather than compliance with the law.

---

* Several offenders in this study, including James Cruckson and Jeffrey Krier, refused to surrender even after family members spoke with them during the standoff. They considered death the only alternative.

A less common cop-killer is tormented by his involvement in an obsessive relationship, usually one that is in critical failure or has already failed. This kind of cop-killer is filled with rage and desire for revenge. He is motivated by the fantasy of rebuilding what once was and does not wish to be interfered with in his final acts of vengeance or control. He may not begin his experience with homicidal tendencies toward the object of his affection, but he often brings a firearm to the encounter anyway. These cop-killers are usually suicidal, but may become homicidal when the fantasy of reconciliation begins to slip away. When confronted by law enforcement, they generally choose overkill and self-annihilation.

Teen cop-killers are not usually seen as real threats by the police officers who face them. These young men are seen as "kids," probably just violating curfew or cutting class, smoking dope, or involved in a petty theft. Our culture in modern times overtly encourages the infantilization of young people well into their midtwenties. Developmental psychologist Erik Erikson speculated on this trend:

> Long childhood makes a technical and mental virtuoso out of man, but it also leaves a lifelong residue of emotional immaturity in him.

These youthful killers were immature in their violent acts. Police officers and their families pay the price for this immaturity.

As a society, we must begin to return to the idea of personal responsibility for one's actions. Although only a small number of police officers in this study were killed by offenders under eighteen, it serves as a reminder that youthful subjects encountered under criminal circumstances do not guarantee safety. Their lack of understanding of the gravity of their crimes reduces their ability to make good decisions when confronted by police.

Suspects in their twenties tend to die during or immediately after the encounter with law enforcement, whether by suicide or use of deadly force by police. These offenders are dissatisfied with their lives, failing to master the challenges before them. The cop-killers in this age group are marginalized outliers, unsuccessful in their attempts to move into society from their families of origin. They become consumed with rage and channel that violence against police, who seek to impose control upon their acts. Suicidal endings peak with offenders in their late twenties.

Suspects over age thirty-five are less likely to commit suicide, but more likely to be involved in substance abuse. Having lived a marginal existence, often characterized by failure in occupational, academic, and romantic endeavors, these offenders turn to drugs and alcohol to mitigate their miserable day-to-day lives. They come to the attention of police, who interfere in the outcomes of their criminal lifestyles or destructive relationship exploits. Driven by hedonistic desires to feel better at any cost, they act with extraordinary violence when confronted.

Suspects over age forty are more likely to be mentally ill. By this time, most people have begun to settle down into a stable midlife pattern. For cop-killers, this becomes a time of despair at their lack of success in life through poor decision making, substance use, and episodes of criminality or mental illness. Families of cop-killers of this age have begun to burn out in their capacity to rescue or help their difficult sons. Wives divorce their violent husbands, taking their children and leaving them alone to cope with the consequences. These offenders continue in their cycles of abuse of drugs and alcohol, leading to chronic physical ailments, disease, and further despair.

However distorted or degraded the lives of cop-killers become, they are still human beings. Not every cop-killer can be stopped, but there are warning signs that should be considered. Properly identified and counteracted, these would-be cop-killers might be pulled back from the edge of the precipice before they commit their final acts.

Recommendations

1. Train mental health providers to recognize the top ten risk factors for the identification of potential cop-killers. These factors are:
   a. History of experiencing violentization cycle (as a victim and perpetrator)
   b. Significant criminal history, especially drugs, weapons, burglary, and/or domestic violence
   c. Drug or alcohol use/abuse
   d. History of diagnosed mental illness, especially bipolar disorder and schizophrenia
   e. Verbalization of aggression toward/dislike of law enforcement as a whole

  f. Experiencing current relationship turmoil

  g. History of standoffs with police

  h. Ownership of or affinity for firearms, especially multiple firearms

  i. Military training, deployment, or discharge

  j. Past statements of suicide by cop or cop-killing ideation

   Offenders who are identified in the community with these risk factors should become known to the police and managed with a partnership approach between law enforcement and community supervision. Mental health services should become a right—not a privilege. Stigmatizing populations in treatment for mental illness should not be the norm.

2. Educate police officers and the general public about the dangers of barricaded persons.

 Offenders who barricade themselves inside a building, shed, vehicle, or other closed space are high-risk subjects. Standoffs usually end in the death of the offender, but often lead to the death of police officers who attempt to end these encounters quickly.

 The most dangerous activity in this study was the serving of a warrant at the offender's home, which can quickly devolve into the takedown of a barricaded subject. Police should use good tactics when they are involved in these dangerous operations and recognize that some offenders are willing to die rather than be arrested.

3. Challenge the popular trend to embrace alcohol and illicit drug use—particularly marijuana—as an easy solution to emotional or physical suffering.

 Excessive alcohol use leads to a host of additional health problems and more interpersonal violence, depression, and suicides. Marijuana use leads to the development of a criminal lifestyle characterized by lack of work ethic, demotivation, and hopelessness. This is true for most of the cop-killers in this study. The widespread efforts currently underway to legalize marijuana will drive more—not fewer—offenders into violent conflict with law enforcement.

The same evidence is apparent in the use of cocaine, methamphetamine, and other drugs. Illicit drug use does not lead
to better living, and changing the level of social acceptance for hard drugs does not change the outcome. Drug
abuse colors the entire world of the addict, making the
experience of real life unbearable. It destroys the potential
of unique human beings and leads them to acts born out
of desperate futility, including murder.

4. Become empathetic to the struggles of youth as a strategy to
counteract gang activity in schools and in the community.
Seek new solutions to the age-old problems rife in public
school systems.

The initial battleground for the young takes place in public
schools that, in many cases, currently serve only as a dump-
ing ground and daycare for youth. The wholesale destruction of family-based identity begins in elementary school.
As schools serve as the primary caretakers of children and
teens, they are the foundational venue for improvement.

Teachers should be selected from the best, not the lowest,
performers. Recruiting top college students into a two-
year assignment as a public school teacher after college in
exchange for repayment of student loans would change the
equation for what education could become. Make teaching a public service profession like police work or the military and embrace the contributions of innovative thinkers
who are fresh from the educational experience, are savvy
in technology, and can be real role models for youth.

Alternately, it may be time to abolish traditional school systems
and invest in technology-based education instead. This
approach would transition teaching from a postindustrial
revolution, one-size-fits-all approach to a mentor–student relationship fueled by the Internet and well-designed
web- or CD-based training. Equip each child with a laptop computer at a developmentally appropriate age. Each
teacher/mentor would have responsibility for no more than
five students who work at their own pace, built around the
interests of the child, with the outcome of developing self-

sufficiency in technology and smooth transitions into the workplace as young adults.

5. Develop better communication systems between police departments, mental health professionals, and community supervision providers.

One of the great tragedies of learning about the encounters in this book is the realization that someone—a family member, friend, parole officer, or social worker—knew the offender was at high risk for committing a violent act or seeking a suicide-by-cop encounter before it happened. Families need greater access to mental health services for their loved ones. Mental health professionals need more resources to secure in-patient arrangements for clients who are at risk or in crisis. Criminals in community settings need more careful supervision and immediate rearrests when they do not comply with the requirements of their parole or probation.

Police officers should not serve as the "caretakers of last resort" when all other societal services break down. Law enforcement should be able to call upon teams of trained professionals to mitigate the outcomes for mentally ill populations in community settings.

Although these ideas may be revolutionary, disconnecting from society occurred early in the lives of almost all of the offenders in this study. It will take nothing less than revolutionary ideas to change the future through better risk-identification systems, better training, and better educational opportunities that reflect twenty-first-century ideas.

Police officers' lives depend on our efforts. Until we make progressive improvement in the identification, incarceration, and treatment of offenders who might become cop-killers, we will continue to mourn the deaths of the innocent and guilty alike, both casualties of society's inaction and ignorance.

References

Drug Enforcement Administration. 2012. *Drug Identification: Marijuana.* Quantico, VA: DEA Office of Training.

Rhodes, Richard (1999). *Why They Kill: The Discoveries of a Maverick Criminologist.* New York: Vintage Books.

Index

A

Accident scenes, 58

Age of cop-killers

early fifties, 173, 189, 194, *See also* Cop-killers, early fifties

early forties, 141, 148–149, 153, *See also* Cop-killers, early forties

early thirties, 89, 107–108, 113–114, *See also* Cop-killers, early thirties

early twenties, 21, 37–38, 46, *See also* Cop-killers, early twenties

fifty-five and older, 199, 210, 215, *See also* Cop-killers, fifty-five and older

late forties, 157, 165, 170, *See also* Cop-killers, late forties

late thirties, 119, 132, 137–138, *See also* Cop-killers, late thirties

late twenties, 51–52, 75–76, 84, *See also* Cop-killers, late twenties

teens, 1, 10, 16–17, *See also* Cop-killers, teens

trends and developmental considerations, 237–238

adolescence, 219–221

late adulthood, 223–224

middle adulthood, 222–223

young adulthood, 221–222

Alcohol, 65, 150–151, *See also* Substance use

DWI history, 95, 102–103, 142, 144, 149, 167, 169, 200

involvement in incident, 28–29, 65, 95–97, 144–145, 159, 160–162, 168, 188

recommendations, 239

American Indian cop-killers, 11, 28–30, 160–162, 167n, 224, *See also* Race of cop-killers